The
Scandinavian
Adventure

D1739179

The Scandinavian Adventure

Arland O. Fiske

North American Heritage Press

THE SCANDINAVIAN ADVENTURE

International Standard Book Number: 0-942323-11-4

Cover design by
Sheldon Larson of Creative Media, Minot, ND.

Cover photo by
Reimann Photography, Minot, North Dakota.

The young children on the cover are
Richard Fiske and Crystal Fiske.

Published by
North American Heritage Press
A DIVISION OF
CREATIVE MEDIA, INC.
P.O. Box 1
Minot, North Dakota 58702
701/852-5552

Printed in the United States of America

Dedication

To
Peter Joseph
David Jon
Robert Thomas
Daniel Luke
Crystal Rose
Richard Paul
Cyrus Paul
Anne Marie (Gaylor)
Lara Marie (Gaylor)
Stephanie Grace
Plus any other possible future grandchildren.

"Children are a heritage from the Lord" — Psalm 127:3
Grandchildren too!

CONTENTS

Foreword
Preface

FOREWORD

BEFORE THE PRINTING PRESS and general literacy revolutionized the telling of history, civilizations depended on storytellers to keep their heritage alive. These stories were full of color, personality and passion. The advent of the printed word has enabled us to construct narratives with both contextual breadth and objective, verifiable detail. But while the perpetuation of heritage is indebted to both approaches, in contemporary times storytelling and storytellers have been in short supply. Perhaps it is the capacity of stories to clothe history with flesh and blood that explains the value of, and growing interest in, volumes such as this one.

Arland O. Fiske makes a good deal of history accessible through this collection of stories. He does so in a readable style, with breadth of content and through a variety of subjects. In keeping with the author's intention, the stories entertain, inform and inspire. It is informative to learn about early Norwegian settlements in Chicago and Texas, the Icelandic legends, the Danish ethos and the geopolitical background of modern Finland; it is entertaining to learn about the ways in which pioneers broke the tedium of their daily lives; and it is inspiring to read stories of courage, endurance and faithfulness. These are stories of the famous and the not so famous, stories from the Middle Ages to the contemporary era, stories about high culture and folk life.

The author brings to this task a deep-rootedness in the heritage about which he is writing. His North Dakota origins, his vocational calling and his natural inquisitiveness have shaped this work. The result is a book available to a wide audience, written in love and with deep purpose.

> —Dr. Paul J. Dovre
> President, Concordia College
> Moorhead, Minnesota

THE SCANDINAVIAN ADVENTURE

PREFACE

WHEN I BEGAN WRITING STORIES on Scandinavian themes a few years ago, it turned out to be a publishing adventure that went much farther than either the publisher or I had envisioned. This volume joins *The Scandinavian Heritage* (1987), *The Scandinavian World* (1988), and *The Scandinavian Spirit* (1989) as an attempt to interpret what it means to be Scandinavian.

The people who come from the Scandinavian lands of the North Sea area are a very small minority of the world's population, probably only about one percent of the world's population when those of us who live in diaspora throughout the rest of the world are counted. Because of the low birthrate in Scandinavia, we could soon become an endangered species.

We have never been a large part of the world's population, even though in certain parts of America one might be led to think so. When more than fifty thousand people are counted going through the turnstiles at the Norsk Høstfest on the North Dakota State Fairgrounds for a week each October, one might get the impression that we're soon about to take over the world. Similar celebrations throughout the country may tempt one to believe that this is the case all over.

The Scandinavians were first known to the world as "adventurers," as people on the move who weren't satisfied with things the way they were. If we are going to be remembered by future generations, it will have to be through the legacy we leave. Many races and nations have gone the way of dinosaur. We know that they once existed, but they are not remembered for having left anything of value to the rest of the world.

Some of the record left behind by our forebears we might wish to forget. But the stories in this book and its companion volumes have been written to recall the good that our people have done. Some of them have excelled in noble deeds. They are worthy of remembrance by us and future generations. The challenge for Scandinavians today is to carry on the "adventure" of making the world a safe and better place for children yet unborn.

There are adventures yet to come which will provide us the opportunity to be inventive in technologies, and persistent in sharing the love of freedom and being willing to accept the responsibilities that go with it. It is my hope that these writings might have some part to encourage Scandinavians to remember their heritage and to continue the adventure.

I'm greatly indebted to many people for their interest in these writings and for their help in making them available to the public. My wife, Gerda, assists me with suggestions and with proofreading, as well as patiently enduring my many hours at the word processor. The interest and encouragement of my children and grandchildren has been unfailing. Deep appreciation is expressed to Allen O. Larson and to the North American Heritage Press for publishing this fourth volume. Thanks to Tammy Wolf for her preparation of the manuscript and to Sheldon Larson for designing the cover. Thanks also to my grandchildren, Crystal and Richard Fiske (cousins), for posing for the cover.

I owe special thanks to Dr. E. Theodore Bachmann, Princeton Jct., New Jersey; Bishop L. David Brown, Waverly, Iowa; Dr. Kenneth Christopherson, Pacific Lutheran University, Tacoma, Washington; and to Dr. Paul Dovre, President of Concordia College, Moorhead, Minnesota, for their critical reading of the manuscript and suggestions, as well as their commendations. Their work has been invaluable. The shortcomings of the volume, however, are the author's. You are now invited to join the "adventure."

> —Arland O. Fiske
> Minot, North Dakota
> June 5, 1990 — Denmark's Constitution Day (1849)

CHAPTER 1

America At The
'End Of The Frontier'

I JUST HAVE FAINT RECOLLECTIONS of my grandfathers, both having died before my fourth birthday. There are many things I'd like to have asked them. My maternal great-grandparents, Ole and Kari Bakken, who emigrated from Hallingdal died long before my birth.

I'd like to have known more about the America that they encountered. How did they get along without knowing English? Did they experience prejudice and racism? What were people talking about? My great-grandparents Bakker arrived just after the Civil War in 1867. Grandpa Hellick Thompson arrived from Numedal in 1877 and Grandpa Ole Fiske from Surnadal in 1892. Grandma Beret Eggen Fiske arrived from Storen the following year. All my progenitors emigrated from Norway to America in just a twenty-six year span. 1890 is regarded by historians as the "end of the frontier." There are plenty of statistics and bare facts about the times, but the real issue is how did America look through their eyes?

America was well established by the time my family arrived. Not all the issues of the new republic had been solved, but the issues for the twentieth century were coming into focus.

The years after the Civil War (1861-65), called the "Reconstruction," were turbulent. The rise of the Ku Klux Klan in the South to frustrate the Civil Rights Act of 1866 for Negroes was probably the most extreme form of racism in our country's history, but it wasn't limited to the South. In the western states, the Indian wars were heating up. There was resentment against the Chinese, especially in California. The purchase of Alaska in 1867 brought better times to the Eskimos, but this did not protect them from exploitation.

The immigrants from Europe were in demand for their skills but were not welcomed into the power structures of the New World. Signs in Chicago shop windows saying "Irish Need Not Apply," were common. Epithets such as "dumb Norwegians," and "dumb Swedes," as well as "Kikes," "Dagos," "Pollocks," "Wops," etc. were part of Yankee vocabulary.

But what were people talking about? In the western lands called the "Great American Desert," there was a movement to plant trees. Carl Schurz, an immigrant from Germany who was Secretary of the Interior from 1877-1881, called for a national forest policy. It finally resulted in the planting of shelter belts under Franklin D. Roosevelt's administration in the 1930s. In 1939, our farm near Colfax, North Dakota, was the second one in Richland Country to get a shelter belt. Tree planting is still a long way from completion in the state.

Water distribution, as it is today, was an issue. John Wesley Powell wrote an article in *Century* magazine in May 1890 stating that "the waters must be divided among the states, and, as yet, there is no law for it, and the states are now in conflict." He wrote that "the waters are to be divided among the people so that each man may have the amount necessary to fertilize his farm, each hamlet, town, and city the amount necessary for domestic purposes." This is still not resolved.

Farmers were in trouble. The Grange was established to organize farmers and the Populist movement was on the rise. Theodore Roosevelt wrote in 1888 about the need to "Americanize" the immigrants. He returned vigorously to that theme in 1915.

"Barbed wire" brought struggle to the plains between the cattlemen who wanted open range and the farmers who wanted to do selective breeding of livestock and to grow wheat. This meant the end of the cattle drives and dependence on railroads. The "fence cutters" were ready to murder to keep the open range.

Religion was an issue. President Grant gave a speech in Des Moines in 1876 pleading for the continuation of the separation of church and state. Robert G. Ingersoll, Attorney General of Illinois (1867-69) and an avowed agnostic, militantly campaigned against the churches of the land.

Public schools were an issue in some states, such as Illinois, where it was feared that Catholics and Lutherans threatened the existence of the public school system. Archbishop John Ireland addressed the National Educational Association in St. Paul in 1890, to "declare unbounded loyalty to the Constitution of my country." He further stated "I am a friend and an advocate of the state school. In the circumstances of the present time, I uphold the parish school. I sincerely wish that the need for it did not exist. I would have all schools for the children of the people to be state schools." Ireland, who had been a chaplain in the Union Army and was a founder of Catholic University of America in Washington, DC, was seeking public funds for parochial education.

Red Cloud, chief of the largest tribe of the Teton Sioux Nation, gave an eloquent speech in New York City in 1870 to appeal for reason and justice in the relations of the red and white races. Though a critic of government policies and Indian agents, he opposed war. He said, "We do not want riches, we do not ask for riches, but we want our children properly trained and brought up." Carl Schurz called for justice in the nation's Indian policies in an article published in 1881. He laid the blame on the inability of the government to control "the restless and unscrupulous greed of frontiersmen who pushed their settlements and ventures into the Indian country, provoked conflicts with the Indians, and then called for the protection of the government against the resisting and retaliating Indians." By contrast, Gen. Philip Sheridan said "the only good Indian is a dead Indian."

In California there were anti-Chinese demonstrations. By 1882 about 375,000 Chinese had immigrated to America, with San Francisco being the heart of the settlement. This resulted in Congress passing the Chinese Exclusion Act in 1882. A fine of up to $500 per person was imposed on any vessel which brought Chinese to America.

It was also a time of Anti-Trust legislation. The financial success of the Standard Oil Trust resulted in the Sherman Antitrust Act of 1890. But because the law did not define "trusts," it was ineffective. The laws passed regulating child labor and compulsory attendance at school, however, gained support.

It was the time of new technology. The reaper revolutionized harvesting and the telegraph wire did the same for communications. Medicine was beginning to making great strides.

The purchase of Alaska from Russia in 1867 for $7,200,000 was laughed at as "Seward's Folly." But the Secretary of State was undaunted. Two years later, he went to Sitka and delivered a speech in which he looked forward to Alaska becoming a state in the Union.

3

THE SCANDINAVIAN ADVENTURE

I find the music of the times interesting. The Negro spirituals, revival hymns and cowboy songs were the people's music. They sang "O Bury Me Not On The Lone Prairie!" "The Old Chisholm Trail," and "Good-Bye, Old Paint." But during the "Gay Nineties" in New York's Bowery they sang of the fallen maiden, "She Is More To Be Pitied Than Censured."

What about the Scandinavian immigrants? What kind of a reputation did they establish for themselves? After the war, the South needed people to rebuild its economy. A. J. McWhirter, President of the Southern Immigration Association, encouraged Southerners to cooperate in drawing immigrants to the South. In an address at Vicksburg, Tennessee, in 1883, he said, "The Scandinavian peasantry are born farmers — farmers from instinct — and for industry, sobriety, economy, and general intelligence are not surpassed by any class or nationality seeking homes in free America." Concerning the situation in Texas, he said: "A thousand educated Germans or Scandinavians thrown into the state of Texas would do more for its development and bring it more actual wealth out of its resources than could ever be hoped for from the native Texan."

For the most part, Scandinavians stayed north of the Mason-Dixon line and settled in communities of their own people, where they have preserved much of their culture. The amazing thing to me is how they retained their love of the homeland with a determination to be patriotic Americans. Even though my grandparents spoke English with a foreign accent, they were clear on this point. America was the land of their choice and the place where a new adventure would begin.

4

CHAPTER 2

Alvin N. Rogness —
'Mentor' For Pastors

I HAVE KNOWN QUITE A FEW people of the cloth in many denominations and have learned a great deal from them. But I know of no one in the clergy profession who has been so respected and highly regarded as a mentor and role model for pastors as Alvin N. Rogness.

When I was in the Graduate School of Concordia Seminary in St. Louis, Dr. Richard Caemmerer Sr., from whom I took every course in homiletics which he taught, said to me one day: "I suppose, that pound for pound, Al Rogness is the best preacher that Lutherans have in America."

I first heard Dr. Rogness speak at an Ashram for the Lutheran Students Association of America at the National Music Camp at Interlochen, Michigan, in August 1948. I had just graduated from Concordia College with a degree in philosophy. I was fascinated by every word that he spoke. I thought: "Here is a preacher with a profound intellect, but who speaks so simply that even little children could understand him." When I returned to Luther Theological Seminary in St. Paul in 1955-56 to complete an advanced degree, Rogness had become president.

About twenty years later, I was studying a map of Trondelag in Norway, looking for a farmstead named "Eggen" where my paternal grandmother was born. I recognized a number of place-names by which people of my home community in Richland County were named. Among these were Folstad, Forness, Gylland, Sokness and Wollan. Then I spotted "Rognes," less than ten miles east of Eggen. I checked the "Bygdebog," the regional history for Støren. My hunch was correct. It was Rogness' ancestral home.

I asked Al about his family. His grandfather had left Støren in 1868 for America, settling first near Lanesboro, MN. Because land was already getting scarce, they moved on to Astoria, South Dakota, about

1870. Astoria is about eighty miles north of Sioux Falls and twenty-five miles east of Brookings. Al's grandfather was a farmer, but his father started a general merchandise store in 1903. The railroad had come to Astoria in 1900. Al said that there were about three hundred people in the village, two hundred of them children.

Besides salt blocks, overhauls, groceries, dry goods, and such things, the store also had books. With no public library, Al would borrow books from the store and bring them home to read. Then he'd return them to the store to be sold. Born in 1906, Al went on to Augustana College in Sioux Falls, graduating in 1927, then teaching speech and English for a year before entering Luther Seminary in St. Paul, MN. Returning in the summers to work in the alumni office, he met Nora Preus whose father, O. J. H. Preus, had become president of the college. Graduating from the seminary in 1932, he enrolled at the University of Minnesota in philosophy and history for two years.

In his Ph. D. program, Al discovered Prof. David Swenson, a professor who pioneered the study of Soren Kierkegaard's writings in America. Swenson, a Swedish-American, taught math, logic and philosophy of religion. Al has many good things to say about Swenson. So have many others of his students. The story is told that when Swenson died, his wife learned Danish so she could continue his work of translating Kierkegaard's writings into English.

Al and Nora Preus were married in 1934, the year he was ordained. For the next twenty years he was a pastor in Duluth, Ames, Mason City and Sioux Falls. I attended the convention of the former Evangelical Lutheran Church in 1954 which was annually held at Central Lutheran Church in Minneapolis. At the convention of 1954, Rev. Fredrik Schiotz was elected president of the church and Rogness president of the seminary. George Aus, the other candidate for the seminary, was initially declared the winner, until some late ballots came in to reverse the decison. Meanwhile, not knowing of the final outcome, Rogness had telephoned his children to tell them that they would not need to move from Sioux Falls, and then telephoned his congratulations to Aus. It was Aus who told Rogness that he was named president of the seminary. In 1950, Rogness had been elected president of Concordia College, but declined in favor of remaining at First Lutheran Church in Sioux Falls.

For the next 20 years, the seminary progressed under Rogness' leadership. First, the campus of nearby Breck Military Academy (Episcopalian) was purchased. This allowed for major development of the campus in future years. Second, Northwestern Lutheran Seminary of the Lutheran Church in America (LCA) was invited to relocate its campus from Minneapolis to the former Breck property. This eventually led to a merger of the schools under the presidency of Dr. Lloyd Svendsbye, who has since become president of Augustana College. The school was renamed Luther Northwestern Theological Seminary (LNTS). Today it's the largest Lutheran Seminary in the world.

Not only has Rogness been known as an outstanding preacher, scholar and pastor, but he has excelled as a writer. He's written over twenty books, all of them produced by Augsburg Publishing House. I asked him what he thought were some of his best books. He mentioned three. *Forgiveness and Confession,* a book on spirituality, was published in 1970. Unlike most study documents written with profound meaning, it is written in non-technical language that a high school student would have no difficulty understanding.

Living in the Kingdom is an easy-to-understand explanation of Luther's Catechism which is used by thousands of congregations. I have used it for the instruction of more than five hundred people.

The other book that Rogness cited was the *Book of Comfort.* It was selected by the Academy of Parish Clergy as its "Book of the Year" in 1980, chosen as the best book written for a pastor's use in 1979. The selection was suggested by Fr. Joseph Dooley of Indianapolis, a parish priest who had been a professor at St. Meinrad's seminary in Indiana. I have shared this book with dozens of people who were in need of comfort.

Another of Rogness' books that I've enjoyed is *The Word For Every Day.* It contains 365 readings which reflect his wide range of reading and deep understanding of the human situation. I have read this aloud to my family for after-dinner devotions. No one fell asleep during the readings. He has a knack of making difficult things easy and often draws out meaningful insights from overlooked events. While browsing in a shop in Old Jerusalem, I ran across another of his books, *The Land of Jesus.* It's one of the best books to read on the "Holy Land."

For many years amidst his busy schedule, Rogness travelled to Europe and Asia to conduct retreats and missions for the U.S. Armed forces. Today, Al and Nora live a more quiet life in their home near the seminary in St. Paul during the winter, and at Kabekona Lake near Walker, Minnesota, during the summer.

The Rogness children have followed in their parents' footsteps as workers in the church. Their oldest son, Michael, after twenty-one years as a parish pastor, is a seminary professor in St. Paul. Peter is a bishop in Milwaukee. Andrew is a pastor in Madison, WI. Martha is married to Pastor Wayne Vetter of Cloquet, Minnesota. Steve, the only one not in the ministry, is president of the Minnesota Hospital Association. Tragedy struck the Rogness family in the summer of 1960. Their son Paul, returning from two years in England as a Rhodes scholar, was struck by a truck and killed instantly just a few miles from his home.

There are many of us who have received inspiration from Al Rogness. My impression is that he has never been bored with life. Instead he has opened up windows of hope to people all over the world.

Alvin N. Rogness

CHAPTER 3

Arley Bjella —
'The Man From The Plains'

A MAN FROM THE PLAINS," they called him. That's the best description for Arley Bjella, an attorney from Williston, North Dakota, who was chief executive officer for Lutheran Brotherhood from 1970 to 1982, and chairman of the board from 1970 to 1987.

I first met Arley in July 1948 in Fairview, Montana. The Men's Club of Zion Lutheran Church held a steak fry and invited him to speak about his experiences as a War Crimes Trial lawyer, involving the concentration camps at Dachau-Nuremberg at the end of World War II. He held the rank of captain in the Judge Advocate Division in Europe after receiving his law degree at UND in 1941.

The Bjella story, however, starts in Aal, Hallingdal, a valley in Buskerud, to the northwest of Oslo. Arley's grandfather, Asle Olsen Bjella, immigrated to Gary, Minnesota, in 1896. Arley's father, Asle Asleson Bjella, was the eleventh of fifteen children. He came to America in 1889, the year of North Dakota's statehood, and settled in Epping to become a blacksmith. Arley's great-grandfather had also been a blacksmith. Born in 1916, Arley was the youngest in a family of five. His brother Lloyd of Williston still maintains the blacksmith shop in Epping.

One of the sad events for the family was when Arley's mother died during the flu epidemic of 1918. Arley was just a year and a half old. Every year on May 13, his father took the children to her grave to pray, as they remembered the day of her death. The people of Epping extended their helpfulness to Asle in the rearing of his family, a kindness which Arley never forgot. It affirmed his belief in human dignity.

But Arley was not destined to be a blacksmith. In high school he was a regular on the basketball team. He also played trombone in Epping's first band, one that Lloyd organized in the blacksmith shop. It became a popular band in the community. To show that he had not forgotten his musical touch, Arley played in a reunion band in 1960 which commemorated Lloyd's twenty-five years as band director. According to Lloyd, he still played the trombone well. That was thirty years after graduating from high school.

The trials of Nuremberg, with their disclosures of inhumanity, left an indelible mark on his soul. These deepened his compassion for the suffering. After returning from the war in Europe, Arley married Beverly Heen, his college sweetheart. They have three children: Lance, Brian and Bryn.

Continuing in the law practice, he formed a partnership in Williston with Frank Jestrab. It was a booming time for western North Dakota. Rain had returned to the prairies in the 1940s. There were bumper crops and machinery dealers were busy. Then oil was struck in 1951 on the Clarence Iverson farm near Tioga. Williston became the center of North Dakota's new industry. This brought added business to their law office. His firm had much to do with the state's conservation-minded oil and gas laws.

Arley, however, didn't confine himself just to his law practice. He had some personal values that found expression in the community, serving on boards of hospitals and banks. Active in politics like his father and brother Lloyd who had been state representatives, he ran for Lt. Governor in 1950. Arley served four years as state chairman of the Republican Party. He also served as president of the North Dakota State Bar Association. He is a fellow of the American College of Trial Lawyers and of the American College of Probate Counsel. The University of Norh Dakota's Centennial Program chose him as their chairman. In 1948, he was named the Jaycees "Outstanding Young Man of North Dakota."

The church has also been served well by Arley Bjella. While a student at UND, he was active in the Lutheran Student Association and arranged for Dr. Alvin N. Rogness, then in Ames, Iowa, to speak at the University. In Williston, he was president of First Lutheran Church and taught the *Bethel Bible Series*. He was also a member of Concordia College's Board of Regents and served on the Board of Social Services of the American Lutheran Church.

Without doubt, Arley could have stayed in Williston and had an enjoyable career among the people that were close to his heart. But other currents of history were moving. The Lutheran Brotherhood Insurance Company was going through internal struggles. While he was a student at UND, representatives of the company had tried to recruit him to be an agent. In 1967, he was persuaded to be a candidate for the board of directors. He was elected together with a new majority that changed the operational procedures of the company.

In 1970, when the president of Lutheran Brotherhood died, Bjella was elected its chairman and chief executive officer. For the next two years he commuted between Williston and his office in Minneapolis on the Empire Builder. Long train rides give a person time to think, and I suspect that a lot of the restructuring of Lutheran Brotherhood took place over the Great Northern tracks.

Lutheran Brotherhood began as a fraternal on June 11, 1917, at the close of a church merger convention. Three Norwegian Lutheran groups united in Minneapolis. Jacob Aal Otteson Preus, Minnesota Insurance Commissioner, was one of the leaders. His grandfather, Rev. Herman Amberg Preus, had come from Norway in 1850 to Spring Prairie, Wisconsin, as a pioneer pastor and a founder of the Norwegian Synod, one of the uniting bodies. Preus was concerned that so many Norwegian Lutherans felt it was sinful to have insurance. However, if insurance had the endorsement of church leaders (not the denomination itself), then perhaps people would feel it was not wrong to buy insurance from any company.

Bjella and many others believed that the time had come for improvements in the organization of the company. When Bjella took over the leadership in 1970, the first thing he did was to depoliticize the company. He wanted to make sure the company lived up to its mission. Board meetings which typically lasted only an hour with limited discussion, now became open and democratic. He was known as a "peacemaker," having the ability to reconcile factions and unite them to work together.

The relationship between the insurance company and Lutheran congregations had not always been friendly. There were those who felt that the company was improperly using its name to sell their product, and that the scholarships it awarded were done for publicity rather than with a sincere interest in the work it was to be promoting. Bjella was

11

determined that this was going to change. He did away with the congregational branch system and organized the branches on a geographical basis.

When the Nixon administration devalued the dollar by ten percent in 1973, the world mission programs of the church were in jeopardy. Under Bjella's leadership, Lutheran Brotherhood responded by giving grants totalling $375,000 to sustain the mission budgets. They've also been active in helping start new congregations and developing programs that benefit the church. Bjella retired in 1987, but still has an office in the corporate headquarters in Minneapolis. He remains active in the corporate structure.

As in North Dakota, Arley Bjella did not confine his energies just to his job. He plunged himself into a leadership role in the Minneapolis community. He is a past president of the Downtown Council of Minneapolis and has served on the board of Fairview Hospital and Healthcare Services in Minneapolis. He is also a member of the Norwegian American Chamber of Commerce and was named "Boss of the Year" by the Minneapolis Jaycees.

Bjella has been honored by his alma mater, the University of North Dakota, on several occasions, including the "Sioux Award." He has received the Knight's Cross, First Class from the Royal Norwegian Order of St. Olav. The University of North Dakota, Concordia and Gettysburg Colleges have given him Honorary Doctor of Law degrees. In 1986, the Norsk Høstfest inducted him into the Norwegian-American Hall of Fame. He is also a founder of the America-Norway Heritage Fund which promotes greater understanding by the Norwegian people of the many contributions Norwegian immigrants and their descendants have made to American life.

Despite his highly successful career, Arley has not forgotten his hometown, Williston. He still stays in touch with his family and friends there.

Arley Bjella was one of the most sought after lawyers in Williston, by farmers, housewives and businessmen. Some are secretly hoping that he'll move back there some day. At Epping, they often stop by Lloyd's blacksmith shop and say they wish Arley were back in Williston. To them he is still the "man from the plains." That's quite a tribute. He represents the best in the Scandinavian heritage.

CHAPTER 4

The Burning
Of Njal

NJAL (PRONOUNCED "nee-ALL") Thorgeirsson was an influential farmer in Iceland who was born about A.D. 930 and died about 1011. Magnus Magnusson, who wrote the book *Vikings!* on which public television based a series of movies, has called "Njal's Saga" "the mightiest of all the classical Icelandic sagas." It's the story of people who lived in Iceland between A.D. 930 and 1016, and written about 1280.

Sagas are not exactly history but the oral tradition or folk tales which re-tell the stories of the past, especially about their heroes which they idealized. Njal was such a hero. He had the reputation of always speaking the truth. His counsel was sought by many and respected by all. Njal is Icelandic for the Celtic name "Neil." It's quite possible that he had Irish as well as Norwegian ancestry. The name also sounds suspiciously like Nils or Nels.

Iceland never was a Viking colony, even though it was settled by Norwegians during the Viking period. The leaders among the setters were an aristocratic class of Norwegians that fled Norway during the tyrannical reign of King Harald Haarfagre about 870. They were joined by more immigrants from the Norse colonies in Ireland and the Hebrides. A number of Irish slaves, constituting 7% or more of the population, also became a part of the Icelandic nation. In a short time, all the agriculturally productive land of Iceland was claimed. It's estimated that the population numbered about 60,000. Unlike the lands from which they came, the Icelanders set up a parliamentary government in 930, unique in its time. It was the purest form of democracy known in the Middle Ages.

Njal represented what was noblest among the Icelanders. His saga was written just a few years after Iceland lost its political independence to Norway in 1262. It's my guess that the tragedy of this just man and his family prefigured the fall of the nation in the mind of the saga writer.

His death was a blow to stable government. The Icelanders did not have much culture in the way of music and art, but they were far ahead of the rest of the world in constitutional law. Even in North Dakota, though the Icelanders are a tiny minority they have distinguished themselves in many professions, but especially as lawyers and supreme court justices.

Beginning with a society based on paganism, the legal system of Iceland made full allowance for revenge. If a man who killed someone escaped death through vengeance before the annual Althing (parliament) convened each June, the worst that could happen to him was a three year exile, likely in Norway. In Leif Erikson's case, he went to Greenland for the years of his outlawry and returned afterwards to establish a new colony. Fate and luck were the powers believed to determine success or disaster.

Njal was a farmer who lived about five miles from the ocean at Bergthorsknoll in southwest Iceland. His troubles started when he helped his friend Gunnar in a dispute. Gunnar's kinswoman, Unn, had a financial claim against another Icelander. The attempt to reclaim this money led to a series of vengeful acts leading to the deaths of many, and eventually to that of Njal and his family.

The role of women in the sagas is notably prominent. In Njal's saga, they are the master conspirators who goad men to bloody deeds. This caused a chieftain to say to his kinswoman, who wanted assistance for revenge, "cold are the counsels of women." The women are strong people in this saga and they do not shrink from the sight of blood. In fact, they drive their men to use the sword knowing that it might mean their deaths. One woman got revenge on her husband for having slapped her in an argument by refusing him some of her long hair to restring his bow when he was fighting for his life. It meant his death. Icelandic women could also be intensely loyal. Njal's wife has gained immortality in the saga literature for refusing asylum when Njal's house had been surrounded by enemies and set on fire. She replied: "I was given to Njal in marriage when young, and I have promised him that we would share the same fate."

Among the wealthy, marriages were arranged by families after the financial settlements were made. One wonders if there was much love in marriage. Frances and Joseph Gies in their book *Marriage and Family in the Middle Ages* make the claim that this was normal for those times. Through strong mindedness, scheming and charisma, women often got their way, but their lot in society was not a happy one and their opportunity for self development was limited.

Though Njal was respected throughout the land for his wise counsel and sterling character, he was inevitably drawn into the blood feuds through his relatives and finally through his sons. The only fault which people found with Njal was that he was beardless. Hallgerd, Gunnar's wife, and Bergthora, Njal's wife, were the main instigators of the feud that led to their husbands' deaths. Despite the animosity between their wives, Gunnar and Njal never broke their friendship. Many of their servants were murdered as the acts of revenge increased. In each case they cheerfully paid the amount of silver prescribed by the law. But as always happens when there is no forgiveness and reconciliation between the families, death was destined to destroy them despite their personal loyalty to each other.

The Althing convened at Thingvellir in southwest Iceland, a place called the "Law Rock." People came to settle grievances once a year before judges and jury. They also brought their weapons. And it happened more than once that if they didn't like the verdict, a pitched battle followed which determined the settlement.

The most memorable Althing was held in 1000. Thorgeir, a pagan priest, was called upon to decide whether Iceland would remain faithful to Thor or follow the White Christ. There already were many Christians among the people through the missionary efforts of Norway's King Olaf Tryggvason. His evangelist, Thangbrand, was attacked by a farmer named Thorkel. Instead of using a shield, he defended himself with a crucifix and killed his adversary. He did not hesitate using a spear in conflict. Knowing that the power of the new religion was great in the world outside Iceland, Thorgeir went into his shelter and crawled under his cloak for a whole day and meditated. After "sleeping" on the matter, he emerged and gained their consent that they would accept one religion, whichever he decided. Then he ruled that everyone should be baptized and become Christians. Njal and his family were converts before the ruling. They were joined by many more Icelanders. This did not, however, turn this hot-blooded people into cool-headed pacifists.

The pay-off was when Flosi, a powerful chieftain, was goaded by his niece Hildigunn to get revenge on the sons of Njal for murdering her husband, Hoskuld. It had been a stupid act which showed they didn't possess the good judgment of their father. Flosi led a hundred men to attack Njal's home. Njal played into the hands of fate by telling his defenders to retreat into the large farm house. One of his sons predicted that this would be a fatal mistake for "these people will not hesitate to use fire if they cannot overcome us in any other way." Kari, Njal's son-in-law, escaped the holocaust and reported the fiery massacre.

Flosi had told his followers, "There are only two courses open to us, neither of them good: we must either abandon the attack, which would cost us our own lives, or we must set fire to the house and burn them to death, which is a grave responsibility before God, since we are Christian men ourselves. But that is what we must do." Fear and the desire for revenge controlled their behavior.

In the end, Kari, a mighty warrior, followed Flosi's outlawed followers when they fled Iceland. He inflicted vengeance on all except Flosi, whom he spared because he had set out to avenge Hoskuld's murder. At the end of the story Flosi and Kari are reconciled. And so they lived happily, at least for a time.

CHAPTER 5

The Norwegians
In Texas

TEXAS IS A BIG STATE. You'd hardly expect that a handful of Norwegian immigrants would even be noticed. But they were. The first Norwegian settler in the Lone Star state was Johan Nordboe from Ringebo in Gudbrandsdal. Deeply in debt at age sixty-four, and with four children, he went to America as his only hope. Nordboe was also one of the founders of the Fox River settlement of Norwegians in northern Illinois. He bought land in Dallas County in 1838.

The first Norwegian community in the state was in Brownsboro in Henderson County in 1845. The leader was Johan Reinert Reiersen who is considered to be the "Father of Norwegian Immigration to Texas." Reierson spent two years in Texas before meeting his family in New Orleans and bringing them to Kaufman County. He represented a liberal political view which was common to Norwegian immigrants (the conservatives stayed in the Old Country). Reierson became a personal acquaintance of General Sam Houston, the president of the Republic of Texas.

The best known writer among early Norwegians in Texas was Elise Waerenskjold who arrived at Brownsboro in 1847. She was the daughter of a Lutheran pastor in Norway and she, at age nineteen, became a schoolteacher. This was unusual for a woman in those days. Elise and her husband, Wilhelm, were skilled writers and became staunch defenders of their new home. She wrote: "I believe Texas is the best of the States to migrate to, partly because the climate is milder and more pleasant than in the Northern States and partly because the land is cheaper."

The first real Texan that I ever met was a classmate at seminary, Bernt I. Dahl, Jr. We all called him "B. I." After graduation, he became a pastor in Vashon Island, Washington. Today he lives in Spokane.

At the 1987 Norsk Høstfest, I became acquainted with Wayne A. Rohne, an attorney in Arlington, home of the Texas Rangers baseball team. He had purchased my book, *The Scandinavian Heritage,* and read it on a trip to China. The chapter about the Norsk Høstfest attracted him to Minot. Returning to America, he received a letter from Vester-heim, the prestigious Norwegian-American museum in Decorah, Iowa, announcing that its 1987 Annual Meeting was to be held in conjunc-tion with the Høstfest. That's how we first met. We visited again at the 1988 Nordic Fest in Decorah. In the meantime, he'd sent me a large packet of information about the Norwegians in Texas.

Included in the packet was the Centennial Gathering booklet of the Dahl family which left Romedal, Hedemarken, Norway in 1850 for Bosque County in eastern Texas. Rohne's deceased wife's great-grand-parents were prominent among the Norwegian in Texas. Their picture appears on the cover of "The Norwegian Texans," a pamphlet published by the Institute of Texan Cultures, The University of Texas at San An-tonio (1985).

The name "Dahl" shows a Danish influence on the spelling of the Norwegian "Dal," which means a valley. Since Norway has so many valleys, it's not an uncommon name, but it frequently suggests a family which had lived on better than average farm land. Travelling through the port of New Orleans, the Dahls settled down to become loyal Tex-ans. The oldest son of Hendrik Dahl, Ole, served in the Texas Cavalry in the Civil War. He returned safely after the conflict ended.

There's an interesting story about Indians coming to the Dahl home and wanting a swordlike knife that was placed between the ceiling and the shingles. Mrs. Dahl stomped her foot so forcefully and told them they could not have it that they left peacefully. The Dahls lived in fron-tier country where the Kiowas and Commanches were still raiding set-tlements. Sentries had to be posted to keep a lookout for raiding par-ties. It was not unusual for farm houses to be looted and children to be kidnapped for a ransom of groceries and other merchandise.

Later when Henrik returned to Norway to visit his aged mother, forty new immigrants joined him on the return to America. Crossing the Atlantic, they encountered a fierce winter storm. Dahl became ill on the return trip and died shortly after arriving home. His reputation as a horse trader is still remembered.

Mrs. Dahl took up the responsibility of rearing nine children. With their help, she became an expert farmer and continued to increase the land holdings, the cattle and horses. She also took time to help the church, even attending all the business meetings. Because of her strong interest, she was given the right to speak and vote at the meetings, a rare courtesy extended to women in those days. She was also one of the boosters of Clifton Lutheran College, which later merged with Texas Lutheran College in Seguin. The Dahl farm has never been sold out of the original family. In 1954, their descendants held a centennial celebration with about 240 people at the homestead. B. I. Dahl, Sr., was named President of the family association to plan the next gathering.

The most famous of the Texas settlers was Cleng Peerson (1782-1865) who sailed from Stavanger in a converted herring boat called the "Restauration" in 1825. His biographies by Alfred Hauge give an interesting account of this famous Norsemen who is credited with starting the Norwegian immigration to America. Even though Peerson was sixty-seven years old when he moved to Texas in 1850, he was influential in bringing many new settlers. The Texas legislature created Bosque County in 1854 and offered 320 acres of free land to anyone who would settle there. In recognition of his services to Texas, Peerson also received an allotment. Peerson made his home wih Ovee Colwick, a cousin of Mrs. Rohne on her father's side. The southwest part of the county is the most thoroughly Norwegian community in Texas. It is the only place in the state where the Old Country customs still are observed.

As the Civil War clouds overshadowed Texas, Elise Waerenskjold expressed the sentiments of Norwegians in the state when she wrote: "I believe that slavery is absolutely contrary to the law of God . . . People have asked me if I would tolerate having a Negro woman as a daughter-in-law. I must admit that it would not please me very much, to have grandchildren who are slaves . . . We immigrants, to be sure, can do nothing to abolish slavery; we are too few to accomplish anything for this cause and would merely bring on ourselves hatred and persecution. All we can do is to keep ourselves free of the whole slavery system." About fifty Norwegian-Texans, however, did serve in the Confederate armies. Distasteful as slavery had been, the Reconstuction period was not kind to the former slaves either. Extreme poverty was to be their lot for many years.

19

THE SCANDINAVIAN ADVENTURE

The first pastor to become a resident in Texas was Ole Olsen Estrem (1869-1877). He was followed at Norse, Texas, by John Knudsen Rystad who served Our Savior's Lutheran Church for 58 years. He also served as the first president of Clifton Academy in 1896 which was later to become a college.

Norwegians kept coming to Texas, but not in such large numbers as came to the Middle West or Far West. By 1880 there were 880 Norwegians who were born citizens in the state. By 1900 the number had reached 1356.

One of the best known Norwegian-Texans was Mildred Didriksen (Babe Zaharias). She became one of the greatest women athletes of all time, dominating the 1932 women's events at the Olympics and named Woman Athlete of the First Half of the Twentieth Century in 1950. She is usually pictured swinging a golf club.

These folks are exciting people. They have an enthusiastic dancing group that performs in colorful "Texas bunads" which blends rosemaling and original Texas motifs. Those wishing to learn more about the Norwegians in Texas should write to the Norwegian Sociey of Texas, c/o Dr. Alfhild Akselsen, Rt. 2, Box J-13, Beaumont, Texas 77705.

CHAPTER 6

Agriculture
In Denmark

MOST PEOPLE LIKE to eat well, and none eat better than the Danes. About 75% of Denmark's land surface is agriculturally productive, of which 62% is under cultivation. That's considerably higher than their Scandinavian neighbors. Only about 3% of Norway's land is agriculturally productive, while Sweden has 9% and Finland 8%. Iceland has 23% of its land in meadows and pastures, but only .01 of its land under cultivation. The United States has 21% of its land under cultivation, plus 26% in meadows and pastures.

That makes agriculture an important part of Denmark's economy. Not only do the Danes produce enough barley, sugar beets, wheat, potatoes, cattle and hogs for their own use, but they are the world's largest exporter of pork products. They've scientifically bred the Landrace hog into a high quality of bacon, and now they are about to market an "organic hog" which will be low in cholesterol. The Danes prize their Landrace strain so highly that there is a law against exporting them. They also feed these hogs with special care for quality.

But for all their fame in agriculture, farm products make up only 5% of Denmark's gross national product. Small manufacturing makes up the bulk of the economy. Fifteen percent of the nation's 5,250,000 people live on 75 percent of the land. The number of farms is getting smaller, while the size of the farms is growing larger. There are about 140,000 farms today, averaging about 60 acres. That seems pretty small when compared to Midwestern United States where farms are often a thousand or more acres.

The difference is in the intensive farming methods used in Denmark. No land is wasted along the roadsides as we have in America. Farm buildings are often joined together to conserve space and for convenience to the operator. In Denmark you don't see abandoned automobiles stacked on a lot along the roads or at the edge of towns. The Danes are proud of their country and keep it beautiful ("dejlig").

21

Denmark is a land of farmer-owned cooperatives. As a small nation among much larger neighbors, they've got to be pretty careful about managing their industries, especially agriculture. Since the price on the world market is subject to sudden changes, the cooperatives have a stabilizing effect on their agricultural production and marketing. The Danes established the first dairy cooperative in the world on June 10, 1882. This enabled the small farmers to compete with the larger ones. By 1888 there were 350 dairy cooperatives in Denmark.

The cooperative experiment was an idea of Stilling Andersen, a young farmer who had attended the agricultural school in Ladelund. He proposed that all the farmers should send the milk from their dairy herds to a central creamery. An association of farmers, each having one vote, had control of the business. A bacon cooperative was established in 1887 by Lars Peter Bojsen, a schoolteacher who also farmed near Horsens. As a result of these well managed cooperatives, the quality of bacon and butter improved and won prizes in competition. It also brought a better price for the producer. Today 90% of pork and dairy products are marketed through the cooperatives and about 50% of the eggs in Denmark are marketed by cooperatives. Every egg is tested and stamped so that if there are bad ones they can be traced to the farm which produced them.

Denmark's first cooperatives were also credit unions. The farmers organized associations so that they could help their neighbors buy cattle, machinery and land at low-interest rates. The first marketing cooperative was organized by Dean Hans Christian Sonne in 1851 at Thisted, in northern Jutland, not far from my wife's family origins.

The farmers of Denmark take great pride in their principle of self-government in the cooperatives. They practice economic democracy without regard to a person's political persuasions or economic status. No one is excluded who is qualified to join. Profits are distributed according to the member's production. I was surprised to learn that there are over six hundred kinds of cooperative societies in Denmark. Even the fisheries have formed coops, as well as banks, insurance companies, colleges, bakeries, fuel companies, housing associations and many other businesses. It is not correct, however, to call Denmark's economy socialism, as businesses and manufacturing plants are all privately owned.

They've also begun specializing so that chicken producers, for example, are consolidating and modernizing their operations to increase their efficiency. This reduces the number of people employed in agriculture while realizing greater production. The Danes produce enough food to feed three times their own population.

It's a good thing that the Danes have done such a good job with their agriculture because they are short of natural resources. They're heavily dependent on trade for raw materials for their manufacturing. Besides iron and steel, shipbuilding, furniture making, electronics, diesel engines, and other manufactured products, 17% of their labor force is employed in food processing. Recently, Denmark has entered into the North Sea oil exploration, but no major production has begun yet. The quality of the petroleum is high.

Agriculture was introduced into Denmark about five thousand years ago by migrations from the south. Prior to that time, people lived by hunting, fishing and eating cereal grains which grew wild. With the tilling of soil and reclamation of forests, domestic animals became a part of their life. Cattle produced milk, meat and hides for clothes. The flintstone ax was introduced for clearing land. The ax also became a religious symbol, sometimes being buried in the floor of home and laid alongside of corpses in the graves. Thousands of them have been found in fields and peat bogs. It's interesting that the excavated ax handles are similar in shape to ours today. The two hundredth anniversary celebration of a royal proclamation that liberated Denmark's peasant farmers to take charge of their own affairs took place in 1988.

Niels Hansen and his wife Aase (pronounced OS-eh) operate a seventy acre farm on the island of Fynn near Odense, the home of Hans Christian Andersen. When Robert Cross, a reporter for the *Chicago Tribune* visited their farm home, together with a group from America, he was entertained with "an impeccably set and candlelit dining room table." When one of the guests asked if most Danish farm families ate like that on Saturday evenings, Mrs. Hansen winked and replied, "Sometimes I like to show off." But if you've ever eaten a meal at a Danish home, you'd know that this kind of "showing off" is not unusual. Denmark is a land of delicious food. It's fairly expensive, but eating well is part of the national way of life.

The Hansen's don't only milk cows (they do have thirty-two Holsteins and Danish red cows), but are also active in community life. Aase operates a successful catering business from her modern kitchen, sings in the church choir, is the head of an Amnesty International chapter and plays bridge. Niels is the head of a chess club, competes in tennis and rides bicycle in cross-country races. During the summer vacation months, many farmers are off on a vacation (up to five weeks). Hired help is paid for by the government.

Evidence that food is on their minds a great deal is that the Danish Dairy Board, a cooperative owned by the farmers and headquartered in Aarhus, publishes a national cookbook every three years. They send it free of charge to every home in Denmark. It's called *Karoline's Kitchen*.

The food industry of Denmark actively promotes sound health. They're starting to use less butter in their cooking these days since we've all become cholesterol conscious. Heart disease accounts for one-third of all deaths in Denmark, compared to about half in the United States. To lower it further, they're introducing new recipes with less fat. The life expectancy in Denmark is identical to that in the United States, seventy-two years for men and seventy-seven for women.

Their new "organic pork" production feeds the hogs on organically produced cereals. Any pig which requires medical care is not called "organic." This is part of their program for better health.

Despite all their interest in health, the Danes are not nearly so fanatical as Americans in promoting physical fitness and health foods. Still, the Danes that I have met looked to be in pretty good shape. I think it's probably because they walk a lot and ride bicycles everywhere. Maybe we can learn from them how to enjoy life more while being healthier.

CHAPTER 7

The 'Vikings'
In Benson County

I N THE SUMMER OF 1886, six young North Dakota Norwegian farmers walked from their new land south of Maddock to Devils Lake to file their homestead claims. August Aanderud, Abraham Faleide, Andrew Gilbertson, Timan Quarve, Rasmus Wisness and Tosten Lommen were the vanguard of settlers from Spring Grove, Minnesota, who settled in Viking Township of Benson County. In the early days, there was a post office named Viking in their community as well as a country store.

It was a hardy bunch of people who went out in search for land that took them as far west as Burlington. Their records indicate that they also spent a little time in Villard, east of Minot. They stayed with Johannes Kopperdahl, the "Skole Laerer" (parochial schoolteacher) who had come from Norway. They travelled in prairie schooners and brought their oxen with them for the trip.

Before the 1880s were over, a sizeable migration had taken place to the Maddock community west of New Rockford and southwest of Minnewaukan. The Northern Pacific and Great Northern railroads came through in those same years, bringing new Norwegian settlers to this land of promise. At that time, Benson County bore the name of De Smet, named after the famed Belgian Jesuit missionary from St. Louis who travelled vast areas of the trackless prairie.

The 1880s were known as the Great Dakota Boom period. Lumberyards, hotels, banks, general stores, medical doctors, and lawyers, plus lots of shysters appeared in this land that had once been the home of buffalos and Indians. Free land was the reason they risked this adventure with the unknown. The United States law entitled any man over twenty-one to file on two quarter sections of land. One quarter could be a pre-emption and the other either a tree claim or homestead. After proving that he had lived on it for fourteen months and paid the government $1.25 an acre, he could take a third quarter of land. It's no wonder

25

that the Norwegian communities from Minnesota, Wisconsin and Iowa began moving westward. The land further east had all been taken.

The first thing the homesteader had to do was build a shack, usually with a minimum of lumber, covered with tar paper and built up around with sod. The six young settlers from Spring Grove completed their first shack on July 6, 1886. The record states that July 4 that year fell on Sunday so they rested from their work. Then they averaged a shack a day until completed. Lumber was transported from New Rockford and cost $6.24 per 10 X 12 shelter, including windows, and sash. They had to move swiftly in filing their claims and getting some evidence of occupancy or their claims might be "jumped" by other land seekers.

One of the farm implements which they carried with them while travelling was a sod busting plow. That was tough soil to break with their kind of equipment. I got in on breaking up some sod for a farmer north of Lindsey, Montana, in the 1940s and it really made his tractor grind. I can imagine what it would have been like for horses or oxen. Patience was the rule for success.

It often happened that while these folks were travelling to their destinations their horses ran away while loose for grazing. In one such case they searched for many days until the horses were found. They'd occasionally meet a stray, but well armed, traveller coming across the prairie on horseback. This happened to Timan Quarve while looking for horses. There was always some danger in this, but fortunately the one he met was a Norwegian named Ole Berg. Ole had been roaming the prairies for several years, hunting, trapping and travelling between army posts. He had three outfits gathering up buffalo bones which could be sold for up to $10 a ton. The buffalo had been slaughtered for their hides and the carcasses were left for birds and animals. By the 1880s they were practically extinct.

One of the unusual things to see for the newcomers was the "Minnie H.," a big side-wheeler steamboat that travelled between Devils Lake and Minnewaukan. It made regular trips from spring to fall. In the late 80s the lake began to dry up and the excursions were limited to Fort Totten and the Chatauqua grounds six miles south of Devils Lake. By 1905 the lake had shrunk so much that the famous old steamboat was abandoned and left to fall apart.

After a number of country post offices and general stores closed, Maddock became the chief trading center and remains so today for people of southern Benson County. It was named after an Irish settler from St. Croix, Minnesota, named Michael Maddock (1861-1904), well known for his pioneer success and generosity. An earlier settler named Peter Anderson might have given his name for the city if he had stuck around when he first visited there in 1881. The Maddock family still lives on a farm in the community.

Benson and Bottineau counties have the two largest concentrations of Norwegians in north central North Dakota, according to Fr. William C. Sherman in his book, *Prairie Mosaic: An Ethnic Atlas of Rural North Dakota*. In the Maddock area, two townships carry a Norse preference, North Viking and South Viking. The six settlers from Spring Grove built their farmsteads in South Viking, and the community center was the Viking Lutheran Church. They date their history to November 6, 1887, on the Timan Quarve farm. For their centennial in 1887 they published a handsomely bound volume of 414 pages. The history of the church and community are bound together.

The nearest Lutheran pastor to the Viking community was in Devils Lake, more than fifty miles away over some rough road. Rev. T. L. Aaberg conducted the first service in July 1887. The second service was not held until October. Worship services were first held in the Aanerud School until a building was constructed in 1903. In June 1909, the Viking Church was host to the national convention of the Norwegian Lutheran Synod, at which time the building was dedicated. The cornerstone was opened in 1962.

I've come to know a lot of people from the two Viking townships and they have a deep pride in their community. They are also well represented at the Norsk Høstfest in Minot each year. I first became acquainted with the Norwegians from Maddock when I was a student at Concordia College. Later when I lived in New Rockford I came to meet many more. I had family living in the Maddock community from 1961 to 1981 who still maintain close ties to the people there. My father was living there at the time of his death in 1969. If you meet people from Maddock, it's a pretty safe bet to ask if they are Norwegians. And those that are, are proud to admit it.

CHAPTER 8

Hrafnkel — An Early
Icelandic Chieftain

ICELAND HAS HAD A UNIQUE ROLE in the preservation of the Scandinavian heritage. Like Scandinavians in America today, they have been deeply interested in their roots. Had it not been for the Icelandic scholars, we would know very little about the Norse kings and the relationship of Iceland to Norway, its parent country, in the early days.

Many historians have downplayed the accuracy of the saga writers. Not so with Lee M. Hollander, a grandson of German-Jewish immigrants to America and a highly regarded saga scholar. He is a major translator of the sagas. He has compared Snorri Sturluson, the writer of *Heimskringla (The Sagas of the Norse Kings)*, to Thucydides, a great historian of ancient Greece.

The thirteenth century was the "Golden Age" of saga writing, even though the stories have some historical lapses where events may be misplaced by a generation or two. We're fortunate that the scholars often had earlier manuscripts and always phenomenal memories. When you get hooked on the sagas, it's easy to understand how they served as entertainment during the long and dark winter nights.

Old Iceland had no cities, only farms made up of many buildings to house the owner and his family, the servants and domestic animals. Much of the soil covers peat bogs called moors. This often made travel slow and difficult.

The story about a chieftain named Hrafnkel (pronounced RAH-fin-kell) gives us a good insight into Icelandic life shortly before A.D. 1000, when Christianity became the religion of the island. Even though the story was written a couple of hundred years after Hrafnkel lived, it loses none of its charm to the modern reader.

Hrafnkel was a temperamental fellow. His father left Norway during the reign of Harald Haarfagre when Hrafnkel was just 15 years old. He was described as a "handsome and promising youngster." During the summers, he went riding over the moors and became intimately acquainted with the best and safest routes to travel. When he married, he built a temple on his farm to the gods. He devoted half of his treasure to the Viking god Frey (pronounced "fry"), after whom Friday is named.

Being a man of wealth, Hrafnkel became both a priest and a chieftain (godi). According to the *Landnamabok* (*Book of Settlements*), he was one of the leading chieftains of eastern Iceland at the time that the parliament (Althing) was established in 930. Originally there were thirty-six priest-chieftains in Iceland. By 1005 there were forty-eight. After Christianity became the religion of the land, they lost their religious functions and were just "law-makers." They also nominated the judges who presided at the Althing, the annual law court held in June. Since Hrafnkel was the first to take possession of his valley, he had control over who else would be allowed to live there. The new settlers all owed him loyalty and support in case of a feud with a neighbor.

Trouble started for Hrafnkel when he hired a young man named Einar to work as a shepherd. Einar needed the work badly and was willing to do this even though it was not a highly regarded occupation. Hrafnkel gave his new workers complete freedom except that they must not ever ride his prize horse Freyfaxi (Frey's black-maned stallion). He had sworn an oath to kill anyone who did.

As fate would have it (and they were fatalists), Einar got into a situation when it seemed necessary to ride the prized stallion in search of lost sheep. When Hrafnkel discovered it, he killed him without delay. And according to custom, he promptly reported it. This gave him legal protection from immediate revenge.

This murder was the beginning of a blood feud that lasted through the whole story. According to Icelandic custom, Einar's father asked Hrafnkel for compensation in silver for the death. Hrafnkel, as a proud chieftain, had never been forced to pay compensation for his murders and no one had dared to challenge him at the Althing. He did, however, offer compensation in food because they had been good friends up to that time. Einar's father insisted on silver and stated that he'd bring charges the following June. Hrafnkel didn't take the threat seriously.

Reluctantly, a relative named Sam took the job of bringing charges against Hrafnkel. It was a kinsman's duty when asked. A household

29

skill among the Icelanders was to know the laws and the technicalities in presenting their arguments before a jury. Like now, the slightest deviation from accepted procedure could lose an air-tight case. The Icelanders have brought this intense interest and ability in law with them to the New World.

The following June, Sam presented the law suit against Hrafnkel at the Althing before the law-rock at Thingvellir. Legal briefs were not always enough, so both sides would line up the support of armed relatives, neighbors and friends. The air was tense. The one thing that they all felt, however, was a sense of duty to justice, especially in the case of a homicide. Unrequited justice haunted Icelanders until a settlement was made. Through careful procedures, Sam won the case against Hrafnkel and had him declared an outlaw to be banished.

Hrafnkel, humiliated but not crushed, returned to his farm but did not leave Iceland. With eighty armed men, Sam secretly attacked Hrafnkel at his farmstead. It was early morning and they found Hrafnkel still in bed, unable to put up a defense. Together with his eight hired men, he was seized and led up to the beam of the house to be hung. The women and children were herded into a separate room. Hrafnkel pleaded for the lives of his men. Their punishment turned out to be more painful than instant death. They had their heels cut behind the tendons and were strung up from the beam. Then the attackers confiscated all Hrafnkel's wealth that could be carried away. This was the reward for winning the law suit. It could be a profitable business.

Hrafnkel was given a choice of execution or banishment with his household. When Sam let his prisoner go, Thorkel, his ally in the raid said, "You'll have good reason to regret you've spared Hrafnkel's life." And it was so. Hrafnkel relocated, became a great chieftain again and got his revenge against Sam with an early morning raid when Sam was still in bed. It was Sam's turn to be humiliated.

Pride was a major factor among the Icelanders. Sam's brothers offered to help him out, but his pride was so hurt that he couldn't accept charity. So he spent the rest of his life in obscurity without being able to avenge his loss. Hrafnkel, on the other hand, reclaimed his farm and rebuilt his wealth and prestige so that when he died his sons inherited a goodly estate. However, he had rejected the gods and no longer sacrificed to them.

Iceland is not a heavily populated land. In the Middle Ages it is calculated that there were never more than 80,000 people. They counted population according to the tax-paying farmers. That was the purpose of census taking. These records have been amazingly preserved so that we know that there were 3,812 such farmers in 1312. Even today there are only about a quarter of a million people on the island.

The saga of Hrafnkel gives us a good understanding of life in those early times among the Norwegians who fled the tyranny of King Harald Haarfagre to that lonely outpost island, once called Ultima Thule. The Icelanders have done a remarkable job in building a modern republic. The immigrants from Iceland in the New World are justly proud of the land of their origins.

Einar riding Hrafnkel's prize stallion.

CHAPTER 9

Mike Royko
On Norway

I LIKE MIKE ROYKO'S COLUMN in the *Chicago Tribune* for many reasons, but now he has put me and thousands of other Norwegian-Americans in his debt. He wrote some pretty good things about us on September 26, 1988. We Scandinavians aren't used to getting much attention from big name writers unless it's when the Nobel prizes are given out, or when a Russian submarine "mistakenly" loses its directions and ends up in Swedish waters.

For those readers who may not be acquainted with Royko, he is one of the best known columnists in America and has (in my opinion) the most facile pen in the business. I began reading his column when I lived in Chicago from 1967 to 1973. At that time he wrote for the *Chicago Daily News*, made famous in the 1870s by Victor F. Lawson, son of Ivar Larson Boe, who had emigrated from Voss, Norway. During the 1970s, the *Daily News* ceased publication even though it had the backing of the Marshall Field family who own one of the largest department stores in the city. Royko then went over to the *Sun-Times*. But when Rupert Murdoch, the wealthy British entrepreneur bought the paper, Royko switched to the *Tribune*, long associated with the McCormick family.

Royko grew up on the northwest side of the city, around Armitage Avenue some place between California and Western Avenues. I knew that area well in 1950-51 when I had my internship at Bethel Lutheran Church on the north edge of Humboldt Park. Once a classy neighborhood, it's no place to get lost today. This is the neighborhood where Knute Rockne lived his early years. Carsten Ronning, Comptroller of Continental National Bank, who retired to the Minot in the 1960s, also began life there in the Norwegian community. It's been the spawning area for a lot of outstanding people. The one thing I learned there is that it doesn't take long to become "street-wise" and how to handle a car like the stock car drivers at Soldier's Field racing for the big money on a Sunday night.

32

Royko is a controversial writer and doesn't hesitate to take some good swipes at Chicago politicians, including the few token Norwegians in City Hall. His book, *Boss*, on Mayor Daley caused quite a stir a few years ago. But his article on September 26 was all praise for Norway. Well, almost.

He told about a hefty argument with his wife that erupted when he said to her: "I really think we should move to Norway." He'd been reading the newspaper about a woman who was ravished on a downtown subway platform during rush hour in front of a lot of amused bystanders. To make it more threatening, the same paper told of a law-abiding man being shot dead on an elevated train (I used to ride them a lot) and a youth being killed on a bus. That wasn't an unusual day.

I remember the last time I lived there. Many of the crimes and serious accidents were never even reported in the newspapers. I heard about them at the emergency room at Lutheran General Hospital where I was employed. The worst I saw was in the spring of 1968 when Martin Luther King was assassinated. Several miles of city businesses were looted and burned out west of the Loop (the major downtown area) while the police were holed up in their precinct station shooting out the windows at the rioters. Mayor Daley proclaimed a curfew, while the smoke rose for days into the skies and could be seen for miles away. There were also the scarey days that same year when the Democratic convention met to nominate Humbert Humphrey for president. My friend Lloyd Sveen, then Editor of the *Fargo Forum*, told me what it was like to be herded down the streets by the police and walk into tear gas without a protective mask.

I can easily understand why Royko would fantasize about leaving Chicago. I finally did in 1973, though I am still fascinated by the city. But why did Royko choose Norway for his place of refuge? After his wife bugged him for the umpteenth time for a reason to move to Norway, he finally told her, "because Norwegians are nice." That should endear Royko to every Norwegian-American who has any sense of ethnic pride. And Royko isn't Norwegian! But, the tenderness of his heart came out in a syndicated article on April 13, 1989. He has two sons that are half-Norwegian. His ancestry is Polish, Ukrainian and Hungarian. You can tell he's a good judge of ethnic character.

Royko's wife protested that there are also nice people in America. He told her that the nice ones are becoming outnumbered by "hooligans, barbarians, thieves, crooks and plain jerks." If you ever lived in Chicago, you'd understand what he was talking about; though I have a lot of good friends in Chicago who are just as nice as some very fine people who don't live in Chicago.

Finally, he said, "when have you read about Norwegians running amok in the streets with guns?" For good measure, he added, "when was the last time Norway started a war?" When his wife challenged the historical accuracy of some of his statements, he said, "the point is that Norwegians are peaceful and sensible. Their idea of a whoopee time is to drink a cup of glogg and sit around in a sauna discussing the price of herring." Royko is right. When a plane was hi-jacked in Norway a few years ago, the gunman didn't ask for a trip to Cuba, didn't hold hostages or demand money. All he asked for was some beer.

Mrs. Royko then came up with her most powerful argument against moving to Norway, "but how can you live in Norway? You can't speak Norwegian." He answered, "I don't have to. Almost every Norwegian speaks excellent English because they learn it in school. A bigger percentage of Norwegians speak English than Americans do."

In desperation, she said, "but could you adjust to a different culture?" Now Royko showed the genius which makes him a famous writer, coming up with his most noble reply: "Could I adjust to little crime, politicians who talk straight and a society that educates its young, takes care of its aged and tends to its sick? It might be tough, but I could learn."

She had one more argument. "They don't have baseball." "So," he replied, "we don't have it in Chicago, either. Why don't we start packing?"

Mrs. Royko finally conceded the argument and was ready to move to Norway. Then she accidently said the wrong thing. "Okay. At least the Norwegians have rock and roll music." To be sure he heard correctly, he said, "They do?" "Of course," she replied.

I had looked forward to reading Royko's column datelined from the clean air and serene valleys of my ancestral land, just as I had been excited about Garrison Keillor moving to Denmark, my wife's family homeland. But that did it. The last words in the column were, "Say, I wonder what housing costs are like at the South Pole."

But then, Keillor didn't stay in Copenhagen either, and now he's living someplace in the Big Apple. Royko's column, however, will continue to tell us about the interesting sameness of life in the "Windy City." I look forward to every story.

Mike Royko

CHAPTER 10

Early Norwegians
In Chicago

W E CALL MINOT, founded in 1887, the "Magic City" because of its rapid growth. What then shall we call Chicago, founded just forty years earlier, on a swampy river mouth at the southwestern tip of Lake Michigan? First seen by the French explorers Louis Joliet and Jacques Marquette in 1673, it began as a minor trading post with the building of Ft. Dearborn in 1803. The fort, destroyed in 1812 by an Indian raid as a part of the war with England that same year, was rebuilt in 1816, but was still unnoticed when Illinois became a state in 1818.

Before the Civil War was over, Chicago had emerged as the leading city of the Midwest, even exceeding St. Louis. Its population increased seventeen times between 1850 and 1870. Immigrants from northern Europe came in droves to work in construction, in the meat packing plants and factories. Carl Sandburg (1878-1967) characterized the city well in his poem, "Chicago," in 1914. Then came the fire of October 8-10, 1871, which virtually destroyed it. Today it's the hub of travel and business for all mid-America. It continues to grow and nothing seems to stop it.

This is the city which became the Norwegian center of the New World from 1840 to the early 1900s. Only then was it replaced by Minneapolis as the center of "New Norway." The opening of the Erie Canal in 1825 coincided with the beginning of the Norse migration to America prodded by Cleng Peerson and the arrival of the "Restauration" into the New York harbor. Soon newcomers to America were ferried across the Great Lakes to the unoccupied lands of the West.

But Norwegians had arrived ahead of Cleng Peerson's "refugees" from Stavanger. Fredrik Peterson was among the soldiers killed during the massacre of 1812. There were others too who travelled without fanfare to America. After the defeat of Chief Black Hawk in 1832, Illinois was considered safe for settling. The first Norwegian to take up permanent residence in the city was a sailor named David Johnson from Voss in 1834. Having been trained in operating a printing press, he quickly found work and influenced other Norwegians to join him. By 1844, Norwegians were the third largest ethnic group in this new city after the Germans and the Irish. It's interesting that early census records counted the Germans and the Norwegians together as one ethnic group called "Dutch."

The "Vossings" were the most numerous of the Norwegians in Chicago. I've met many people in the "Windy City" who claim their heritage from Voss. That's what attracted Knute Rockne's family to Chicago. The most prominent of these early immigrants was Iver Lawson, whose name had originally been Ivar Larson Boe, who arrived in 1844. Trained in Norway as a tailor, he worked as a day laborer in the beginning and ended up as the publisher of the *Chicago Daily News*. He was also a member of the city council and was appointed marshall of the city. As marshall, he was in command of the police force when Abraham Lincoln was nominated for president in 1860.

Lawson was active in organizing the first Norwegian Lutheran Church in 1848. Today it's known as "Lake View Lutheran Church" near Wrigley Field, the home of the Chicago Cubs. My son Mark attended this church when studying at DeVry Institute of Technology in the early 1980s.

Many of the Norwegians preferred to move on to Wisconsin. The triangle between Chicago, LaCrosse and Milwaukee became the early center of Norwegians in those days. The early Norse settlers preferred the Democratic party. They switched to the Republicans, however, during the heat of the slavery issue which preceded the Civil War. The Norwegians became active in the "Underground Railroad" and were ardent supporters of Lincoln and the Union during that fratricidal war. The Fifteenth Wisconsin Regiment with 890 men was made up of mostly Norwegians under the command of Col. Hans Heg, who was killed at the Battle of Chickamauga in Georgia. When they travelled through Chicago, they were given a rousing patriotic welcome by the Norwegians living there. This demonstrated proof of their patriotism to America.

Health conditions of the new metropolis were deplorable, as they were in most large cities of the time. The streets were filthy, drinking water was polluted, drainage was inadequate and the wet swamps were breeding grounds for mosquitoes. Malaria and cholera combined to bring a plague on the people. Nutrition was also poor. The new settlers rarely took baths or kept themselves clean. In the epidemic of 1850, 45 of the 332 Norwegians living in one area died. When speaking about the plague, it was commented by the Yankees that it was fortunate that the deaths happened mainly "among our foreign citizens."

As the flood of immigrants from Norway swelled, the Norwegian government became alarmed. The clergy were the spokesmen to warn people away from America. The Vossings in Chicago took up the challenge to defend their new land and organized the Vossing Correspondence Society to enlighten their friends back home about the virtues of America. The Norwegian Debating Society was organized to stimulate awareness of life in America, especially slavery. Annual social events were also sponsored by the society. The Vossing Emigration Society, founded in 1856, gave assistance to Norwegian immigrants that needed financial assistance.

Except for the "free-thinkers," the Norwegians adopted Yankee "puritanism" in their opposition to liquor and were advocates of sabbath observance. Their clergy also opposed dancing and theatre. There were a few dissenters among them, especially Dr. Gerhard Paoli from Trondheim, a physician who became president of the Chicago Medical Society. Another noted free-thinker was Marcus Thrane, a socialist reformer. Both of these men, like Bjornstierne Bjornson, opposed the Norwegian clergy and the conservative theology of most immigrants.

The Lutherans weren't alone in doing soul care among the Scandinavians. The Baptists, Episcopalians and Methodists were also active to evangelize the immigrants. Gustaf Unonius, an Episcopalian, is quoted extensively in Page Smith's volumes of American history. Revivalism hit Chicago in the 1860s. Dwight L. Moody, one of the leaders, helped organize the Chicago YMCA in 1858.

An early Swedish Lutheran pastor from Sweden was Erland Carlsson who arrived in 1853 and built a strong congregation. They did much to assist immigrants, meeting them at the train station, finding places for them to live, buying money orders, helping them with language and finding jobs. One Norwegian congregation, Our Savior's Lutheran (named after the cathedral in Oslo), built a brick church that seated 1,200 people.

The new settlement attracted celebrities too. Ole Bull, the famous Norwegian violinist, came to Chicago in March 1854 and gave concerts. He was highly praised by the *Chicago Tribune's* critics. Early ethnic organizations for the Scandinavians included the Swedish Svea Society in 1857, the Norwegian Nora Society in 1860, and the Danish Dania Society in 1862. These secular organizations were often in conflict with the immigrant church on social issues.

The Great Fire of 1871 destroyed almost four square miles of the new frontier city. The wooden sidewalks and dry weather moved the flames along swiftly. Both Swedes and Norwegians suffered heavily from the fire.

By the turn of the century, Humboldt Park and Logan Square to the northwest of the original city had become the center of the Norwegian community. I came to know that area after World War II when quite a few Scandinavians still lived there. Today it has become mainly an Hispanic community. English is again a foreign language there, as it is in many parts of the city. The Norwegians have moved mainly to the northwest suburbs of the city. But they are still there, as I learned when living in Chicago a second time from 1967 to 1973. And they still love their ethnic foods served at Sons of Norway lodges and at their Constitution Day celebrations on May 17.

An excellent resource for learning the story of these early Norwegians in Chicago is *A Century of Urban Life: The Norwegians in Chicago before 1930* by Prof. Odd S. Lovoll. Dr. Lovoll spent two years' leave of absence from St. Olaf College to write his findings. The book was published by the Norwegian-American Historical Association (1988) headquartered at St. Olaf College in Northfield, Minnesota.

CHAPTER 11

Why The Holocaust
Failed In Denmark

EVERY CENTURY IS REMEMBERED for catastrophic as well as happy events. The twentieth century will be remembered as a time of unprecedented progress, especially in medicine, communications and travel. It will also be noted as a century of horror and shame. Many of us have lived through the evil days, some of us at a comfortable distance.

The "holocaust" (destruction by fire), by which an estimated six million Jews perished in Hitler's concentration camps, is one of these tragedies. The Jewish population of Denmark was quite small, less than 8,000. When the Nazis launched their Operation "Weseruebung" on April 9, 1940, the invasion of Denmark and Norway, a veil of gloom descended on those lands.

The world had heard Hitler's rantings against the Jews during the 1930s and many of them fled Germany for America. The Nazi pogrom (systematic destruction) of the Jewish people during the early 1940s was covered up in the beginning. Those who learned of it, didn't want to believe it.

Victor Borge, the great musical comedian, was fortunate to be in Sweden when the invasion took place, since Hitler had been the object of much of his humor. The Nazis never did have a sense of humor. Borge came to America. Another famous Dane, Nils Bohr, whose mother was Jewish and who was a world reknowned scientist in atomic structure was also in possible danger. But Bohr and most Danish Jews felt no personal alarm and weren't worried about their futures. They'd had full citizenship since March 29, 1814, and full political equality since the constitution of June 5, 1849. Denmark was considered a safe place, despite the propaganda of the Danish National-Socialist Workers Party against them. In Denmark, everyone was considered a Dane, regardless of ethnic background.

40

For three years, Hitler tried to pacify the Danes and get them to like him. There was resistance, but not on a large scale. In 1943, the Allies advised the Danish Underground to increase their resistance and blow up factories and railways, or their bombers would do the job and that would result in Danish casualties. By the middle of the summer, resistance was so active that the German military forces attacked the Danish Navy and Army on August 29. The Danes scuttled most of their warships, but a few escaped to Sweden. The military, which up to this point acted as a home guard, was now replaced by the Occupation Force.

Dr. Werner Best, the SS-Obergruppenfuhrer (Civilian Commander), went to Berlin to save his job. He proposed rounding up the Jews and bringing them to prison camps in Germany. G. F. Duckwith, a German shipping expert in Denmark, tried to stop the plan. But since he did not belong to the Nazi party, his opinions were ignored. He did, however, get word to Jewish leaders who sounded the alarm. Many of the Jews didn't believe that such a thing could happen to them.

Fortunately, the information came the day before Rosh Hashannah, the Jewish New Year, so a warning was given at the synagogue services. They were advised to take refuge with their non-Jewish neighbors. Werner Best issued a scurrilous attack on the Jews. This, however, strengthened resistance against the Nazis.

Bishop H. Fuglsang Damgaard issued a statement to be read in the Lutheran churches of Denmark the following Sunday. It began: "Wherever persecution is undertaken against the Jews as such, on racial or religious grounds, it is the duty of the Christian Church to protest against it." Bishop Damgaard's letter powerfully aroused the nation and united the people to help the Jews. (Bishop Damgaard visited the Danish community in Sidney, Montana, in the late 1940s.)

Response to the Bishop's message was immediate. Jews were hidden by friends in homes, hospitals, churches, warehouses and nursing homes. Fishermen offered their boats for transportation to Sweden. Boats of all kinds were used. I saw one at the entrance to the Yad Vashem in Jerusalem which remembers the holocaust victims. Trees have been planted on the Avenue of the "Righteous Gentiles," to commemorate those who assisted the escape. Among those remembered are Raoul

Wallenberg, the Swedish diplomat arrested by the Soviets when he went to negotiate with them on behalf of the Jews in Hungary.

A cargo boat loaded with ice for Bornholm fishermen, also carrying refugees in its hold, was boarded by German Military Police. Rubbish and old boxes covered the hatch. The police demanded, "are there any Jews here?" The captain answered in a mixture of Danish and German, "You bet, I've got a boat full of them." Then he offered the police some aquavit to drink while acting the part of a lunatic. They laughed loudly at him and left the boat after a few minutes. The people hiding below deck couldn't understand what was going on and became terrified. Later, however, they realized that this was his way of diverting the police from searching the boat. Then the captain fed them some hot soup and kept cracking jokes. This was his way of relaxing them until they reached Sweden. The customs officer greeted them, "Welcome to Sweden."

Up to this point the Swedes had been criticized severely by Norwegians in America for their apparent collaboration with Hitler. It's true that Sweden profited from trade with the Nazis, but they had little choice. The alternative was occupation by the German army. Then they couldn't have helped people fleeing either from Norway and Denmark, nor assisted their flight to England and America. This convinced the Allied governments that Sweden was not as neutral as some claimed.

The Gestapo put on a relentless search for Jews and had a network of informers that betrayed some, but in most cases the escapees were successful. The Allies were deeply concerned about Dr. Nils Bohr, a 1922 Nobel physics prize winner. He was reluctant to leave his research laboratory and go to Sweden. It took a direct appeal from King Christian X. Bohr went to America where he worked on the "Manhattan Project" at the University of Chicago with Enrico Fermi. It was their work which did the scientific experimentation necessary to produce the atomic bomb.

Today we look back at the bomb with horror. But forty years ago, people thought differently. I can't remember any public criticism of the bombs dropped on Japan. Terrible as we now know that it was, it ended a war that had aroused the anger and determination of the nation. The Allies feared that if the Nazis had arrested Bohr, he would have been forced to do nuclear research for them.

There were also failures in the rescue attempts. One Danish skipper was shot by the Gestapo together with the twenty Jews on board his boat. In another place, refugees hiding in a church were discovered and deported to Germany. Many of the Danes lost their lives attempting to protect their Jewish neighbors. Some of my wife's family suffered torture and death during those days. Bribery was also used to get German officers to look the other way. Sometimes stormy weather threatened the little boats used in the rescue attempts. They even used hats and shoes to bail water from boats.

The Gestapo succeeded in arresting only 474 Jews, many of whom hadn't gotten the warning or didn't believe they were in danger. They were shipped to Theresienstadt in Bohemia where they were forced to wear a yellow patch with the "Star of David." Propaganda from Sweden told the story that the Jews in Denmark were required to wear the Star of David and that King Christian also wore it in defiance to the Nazis. It's a good story but my information claims that it never actually happened.

The Nazis sent the Danish Jews to Auschwitz in Poland for extermination. Two events saved some of them from the crematories. The Russian army had broken through on the Eastern Front and Count Folke Bernadotte of Sweden persuaded the German authorities to allow a convoy of white buses to bring them back to Sweden. Scandinavian pastors in Germany aided the project. On April 15, 1945, 423 Danish Jews and a few from Norway were brought out of Germany on thirty-five buses which were marked so that Allied military planes would not attack them. The advance of the Allied forces on the Western Front frightened many Nazi leaders. They were afraid of being tried as war criminals. Some were willing to cooperate in those last days of the war.

It wasn't only the seven thousand Jews who went to Sweden for asylum, but twenty thousand Danes also left their homeland to carry on the resistance. The Swedish government provided jobs, food, and shelter for them, as well as education for the children. More than five thousand Danes were given military training. There was also a woman's auxiliary corps.

If you ever go to Copenhagen, visit the Danish Resistance Museum. Most tourists don't get to see it. But for those of us who remember that terrible time in history, the events of the past bring back chilling memories. We hope that future generations will not forget the price that freedom demands.

Danish guard.

CHAPTER 12

Joan Haaland Paddock —
Fulbright Scholar In Norway

I T WAS NOT LONG AFTER arriving in Minot in August 1974 that I met Olaf Haaland, the Sheriff of Ward County. We worked together on the Community Traveler's Assistance program, helping people in need when going through Minot. In the summer of 1976, his wife Doroles worked energetically with many of us in the resettlement of Kurdish refugees.

Besides being community-minded people, the Haalands had in their family of four children a daughter, Joan, who was very musically talented. Joan was a frequently-featured trumpet soloist for musical programs in Minot. After completing high school, she went to Indiana University to continue studies in music, with the trumpet as the principal instrument.

Olaf retired from being a peace officer in 1978 and moved to Salem, Oregon, the following year. One day in the summer of 1986, Joan called at my office to ask about Norway. She had been awarded a Fulbright scholarship to study there. The Fulbright Act of 1946, an international exchange program administered by the United States Department of State, was established to increase mutual understanding between Americans and students of other countries. It was sponsored by Senator William Fulbright of Arkansas. Joan learned of the scholarship through a classified advertisement in the university's student newspaper. She had almost completed a doctorate in music at Indiana and was going to Norway to do research for her dissertation. Joan also asked for information on the American Evangelical Church in Oslo, in which she participated.

Arriving in Norway on November 10, 1986, Joan got right to work on her research project: "Twentieth Century Trumpet Music of Norway: Representative Selections with an Approach through Performance and Pedagogy." I was not aware how advanced Norwegian musicians were. However, having heard some excellent Norwegian musicians perform on summer concert tours and at the Norsk Høstfest, I shouldn't have been surprised. Joan quickly became acquainted with some of the country's leading trumpet teachers and began attending concerts and seminars.

Recipients of Fulbright scholarships are required to send progress reports to the United States Educational Foundation in Norway. These reports deal not only with the educational activities, but also with cost of living, health facilities, travelling and whatever was a part of the experience abroad. Joan shared these reports with me as information for this story.

Even with generous scholarship grants, students quickly learn how to budget their money carefully. Living costs in a university area tend to be high. My son Christopher learned this when living near the University of Minnesota. Joan lived at the Kringsjå Studentby (student housing) where she paid 1,000 kroner a month (about $150) for a room which included water, electricity, heat and local telephone. She shared a kitchen with six other people and a bathroom with one other person. It was about a four minute walk to a train which would take her to the center of Oslo.

Joan soon learned, as we had, to figure out which things can be bought in Norway that are government subsidized. Among these are bread, butter, cheese, milk, fresh meats and train tickets. Norwegians make transportation convenient and economical as a way of encouraging people not to drive cars. Joan bought a coupon good for six months of train rides anywhere in the city or suburbs. Norwegian trains can be depended upon to be on time. I remember the train in Mosjøen (not far south of the Arctic Circle) being an hour late once. The depot agent apologized because there had been a snow slide which covered the track. But otherwise, you can almost set your watch by their arrival.

During her months in Norway, Joan kept busy playing her trumpet, especially in churches. Of special interest was when she played in the Høyland Church where both of her Haaland grandparents had been baptized and confirmed and in Korgen in northern Norway from where her maternal grandmother, Barbara Watne Sullivan, has family roots. In February 1987, she gave her first concert of Norwegian trumpet music. Joan also gave trumpet lessons. In March, she was requested by the students to be the specialist that helped to prepare them for their annual concert and competition. It had been a unanimous request.

Joan was not formally enrolled in a regular class schedule in Norway, but was granted "part-time" status as a student at the Norges Musikkhøgskole (Norwegian State Academy of Music). While there, she entered a music competition and won a $100 prize. To show her appreciation for the privilege of studying at the school, Joan returned the prize money. She took trumpet lessons, participated in trumpet classes and in brass ensembles.

In April, Joan was invited to be a guest at a school where her mother's cousin, Ellen Finbak Ottmar, is a teacher for the blind. Besides playing the trumpet, she talked about America and North Dakota. They celebrated her visit as an "American Day," and had a special "All-American" meal. The children loved it.

One of the fun events was a meeting with other Fulbright students in Lillehammer in Gudbrandsdal. This is where the 1994 Winter Olympics will be held. Anyone who has been to Lillehammer will not soon forget the beauty of the Lake Mjøsa and its wooded countryside.

A high point in Norway for Joan was a visit to the Royal Palace and an audience with His Royal Highness Crown Prince Harald. She wrote to the Crown Prince for an audience and stated that her parents would be visiting Norway in May and would be in Oslo for the Constitution Day celebration on May 17.

To Joan's delight, an invitation arrived a week later from Colonel Langlete, Head of the Palace, inviting Joan and her parents to an audience with HRH Crown Prince Harald at the palace on May 4 at 11:30 a.m. The invitation requested that she send detailed biographical data about herself and her parents.

In her reply, Joan asked permission for her parents to bring a small gift to the Crown Prince. She also offered to play a tune on her trumpet for His Royal Highness. Even though she walked past the palace daily, she asked which door they ought to use upon entering. Joan also asked about proper protocol for the visit. In the biographical information on her parents sent to Colonel Langlete, she related that her father had served in the Viking Battalion in World War II. This was the 99th

Infantry Battalion Separate of Norwegian-American Ski Troops, which served as the honor guard for the return of King Haakon VII after his exile in England during the war.

The Royal Palace is at the west end of Karl Johansgate (Karl Johan's street). At the east end of the street is the Storting or parliament building. This is the famous street where a much photographed "Syttende Mai" parade takes place every year.

Joan and her parents entered through the main entrance and, after questioning, were escorted up red carpeted stairs to the office of Colonel Veil, adjutant to His Royal Highness. Upon arrival, HRH Crown Prince Harald greeted them with a handshake and they were seated around a small table. They began their conversation by bringing a special greeting from the Norsk Høstfest. The Haalands presented their gift to the Crown Prince and then gave him a copy of my book, *The Scandinavian Heritage.*

HRH Crown Prince Harald asked Joan about her trumpet studies and work with Norwegian composers for her Fulbright project. Her father, Olaf, spoke to the Crown Prince in his Stavanger dialect and was surprised to have him reply both in Norwegian and English. Commenting that the Crown Prince could speak perfect English without any Norwegian brogue, he replied, "Vel, I can turn it on ven I vant to."

They talked about a number of items, including Olaf's service in the Viking Battalion and the Crown Prince's time in America during World War II. Their fifteen minutes went by quickly and comfortably. Then His Royal Highness escorted them to the door and wished them well on their visit in Norway. He also sent a special greeting back to Minot. They thanked the Crown Prince for the visit and expressed best wishes to the Royal Family. On the way out, her parents were photographed by the King's guard. Joan said, "Our royal visit is one we shall never forget."

When the Minot Symphony Orchestra gave its 1988 Høstfest concert, Joan, now married to Paul Paddock and living in McMinnville, Oregon, was guest trumpet soloist. She played selections by Norwegian composers. Those of us who knew Joan while she was a high school musician, could only be amazed at her relaxed poise and flawless performance before an appreciative audience. We look forward for her returning to play for us often.

CHAPTER 13

Nels Kleppen —
Prairie Patriarch

MOST OF THE SCANDINAVIAN immigrants who came to America brought few worldly goods with them. Usually there were the clothes they wore plus a wooden trunk. Among the goods were some articles of faith such as the Bible, a hymnal, a devotional book and the catechism. Most of them didn't have much money, just enough for the one-way passage and the $25 that the immigration laws required. Often that had to be repaid to a relative in the New World who acted as sponsor.

Nels Kleppen was one of the 800,000 who left Norway for a better life across the sea. Nels was born Nils Jakobsen Birkeland in 1877 on a island northeast of Bergen called Østerøy. I was fortunate to secure a copy of his autobiography which he spoke into a tape recorder in September 1965 at the home of his granddaughter, Helen Silseth of Minot. Even at eighty-eight his memory was sharp and his speech coherent for the two hour narration. He died in April 1968.

When "America Fever" hit those northern lands it had about the same effect as stories of Constantinople in the Viking days. It was pictured as a land of abundance where everybody could get rich quickly. A few eventually did, but not very many and almost none quickly. But the enthusiastic letters written back to the homelands, loaded with a degree of propaganda, had the desired effect. Whole communities sometimes joined the caravan of wagons to the seaport cities. The passage across was usually in the worst of travelling conditions. All except those who were experienced at sea usually became ill before the voyage was completed.

It was common practice in Norway that if a man moved to the farm where his wife came from he changed his name to hers. That's how Nils Birkeland took a different name. His wife's name was Kleppe. However, when he got to America, he changed it again to Nels Kleppen because there was another Nils Kleppe where he homesteaded. Their mail kept getting mixed up. (My grandma Thompson's brother John changed his name from Johnson to Olson for the same reason.)

When Nels came to America in 1903, he left behind his wife, Katrina, and three children. Two other children had died and Katrina was expecting at the time of his departure. Like so many others, he was enticed by the hope of making a better living. Katrina's brother, John, sent a ticket for Nels to try his luck in the new land. It took another four years before the rest of the family could make the journey. One of his friends said, "I thought when I came to America that I could sweep the money up very easily but I find it different, you have to work for it." A lot of people made that same discovery.

They entered the New World in Quebec and travelled through Sault St. Marie and ended up at Emerado, North Dakota, after two more weeks of travelling. It takes only about eight hours of flying time to make the same journey today. But fifty years earlier it often took up to three months travelling with sail-driven boats. The first thing they noticed was the hot weather. The woolen clothes packed in their trunks weren't suited to the summer climate of the New World.

Money was hard to come by but Nels was willing to work to save enough money to bring his family over here. Fortunately, there was plenty of farm work at harvest time. Shocking grain for $2.00 a day was the average pay and maybe they could get $2.50 during threshing. But when winter came farm workers were lucky to find someone who'd give them room and board to do chores. That hadn't changed during the 1930s when I was growing up. My father never lacked help on our farm during the winter months. It was the surest way to get a job when field work began in the spring. Shovelling grain was another of the jobs that took strong backs and arms. One of the things that Nels discovered during threshing was that one of the other workers had lice. From then on, Nels slept in straw piles. There he heard mice crawling all over. But mice were preferable to lice.

After working at Emerado and Hatton the first year, Nels heard about homestead land available near Columbus, North Dakota. He filed for land twelve miles south of town in December 1905 and built his 10 X 12 shack the next summer. It took fourteen months to "prove up" the land before legal ownership took place.

Sometimes it seemed to Nels that he'd never get his family to America. It was so hard to save money. Finally, he decided the only way was to borrow the money to get them here. To his surprise, he got a letter saying that Katrina and the children were arriving at Vassar, Manitoba. Besides taking care of her family, Katrina earned the money to purchase passage to join her husband. When Nels went to meet them, no one showed up. You can imagine his feelings of helplessness. So he went back to Winnipeg to look for them at the railway station. They weren't there. He even checked the register in a Scandinavian hotel. Then he took to walking the streets in search for them. Suddenly he looked up and there they were, heading straight for him! For the first time he saw his little daughter, Nelsie. It was a happy reunion.

Times were hard for the early pioneers. Nels told about the time he had to ask the grocer in Columbus for $40 credit. He paid 10% interest on the loan. Interest was 15% in some places. In the 1930s, Nels had an $840 seed loan. Not until about 1939 did the rains return and were there good crops again.

The flu epidemic of 1918 hit the Kleppen home. They only had a three-room house. Eleven people were down sick in seven beds. The flu was complicated by pneumonia and nose bleeds. Fortunately, they all recovered. At one time, Magne, Helen's father, was so ill that Nels feared he was dying for sure. Then Magne raised up his arms and his parents thought "there he goes." But they continued praying for him and Magne lived. He told of seeing three angels at his bedside when he raised up his arms.

Prairie life was often hard on women. Katrina was no exception. In 1939 she became deathly ill and Nels was advised by three different physicians that there was no hope for her. After the others had left, he knelt by her bedside and prayed, "Lord, isn't it possible that we can have her with us yet? She has been so dear and is so dear yet." While still kneeling, he heard a voice saying to him, "not yet." The next morning he touched her face and said, "how are you feeling this morning, Mama?" She was much better and lived for another 21 years. Shortly afterwards, they left the farm and bought a house in Columbus.

After Katrina died, Nels used to visit his family, staying about two weeks at each place. Sometimes he didn't sleep well at night, but he told his family not to worry about him as he had so many people to pray for as he lay in the dark. He used to tell his family "my best advice for you is to raise up your child in the Lord, as your children are the only things that can go to heaven with you."

The Kleppens had eleven children, besides the two that died in Norway, all living within a fifteen mile radius of Columbus. Everyone of them sang in the church choir. At the time of Nels' death, there were forty-two grandchidren, one hundred great grandchildren and four great-great grandchildren. Today there are six daughters and one son still living, including Magne, Helen's father. Magne was the youngest of the sons who travelled to America with his mother.

During those visits to her home, Helen remembers that "Grandpa Kleppen," as they called him, spent a great deal of time reading the Bible and singing hymns. I listened to Nels' singing on the tape. Even at age eighty-eight, he carried a tune quite well. Those pioneers who claimed this country for future generations were a hardy breed, made of the same tough stuff as the Old Testament patriarchs. "Prairie Patriarch" is a fitting epitaph to mark the memory of Nels Kleppen. Fortunately, there were more like him in those days of land-claiming and community building.

CHAPTER 14

Oak Grove Lutheran High School — Norse 'Alma Mater'

WHEN IN FEBRUARY 1943 the Colfax Hi basketball team went to Fargo for a game with Oak Grove High School, I never dreamed that I would be transferring to Oak Grove the next year. As I recall, we lost the basketball game, and that was the last time I thought about the school until the following July at the Red Willow Bible Camp near Binford, North Dakota.

In the meantime I had decided on my career goals. After my last year of high school, I planned to attend Concordia College, Moorhead, and then Luther Theological Seminary in St. Paul to become a pastor. Nine more years of school seemed a long stretch of time to a farm boy who had spent most of his available time driving a tractor.

Rev. Thor Quanbeck (1899-1966), president of the school, visited the Bible Camp and encouraged me to transfer to Oak Grove in the light of my career goals. Those were the days of World War II and class "C" schools like Colfax Hi had a difficult time getting qualified teachers. The high school had only two teachers. Despite the smallness of the school, we still got a pretty good education, but with many of the men teachers off to war and women working in defense plants, it wasn't possible to get all the courses required for college entrance. I wasn't interested in taking high school make-up courses while in college.

When I returned to the farm at the end of the week and told my parents about these plans, there was solid silence. It would mean a sacrifice on their part, both for the costs and because I was needed for farm work. Fortunately, Oak Grove started three weeks late in the fall and got out three weeks early in the spring as a way to help the war effort. We made up the time by going to school for an extra hour each day. Since many of the students lived on campus in the dormitory, that wasn't a problem.

Another advantage of Oak Grove in those days was that classes were held from Tuesday through Saturday noon. This made it easier to get a job on Mondays when there was no competition with students of other schools. Since I was interested in journalism, work was arranged for me with the *Fargo Forum*. My job was re-writing obituaries from the county newspapers to shorter size.

Oak Grove was established by the Lutheran Free Church in 1906 as the "Oak Grove Lutheran Ladies Seminary." It was common in those days for private academies of high school level to call themselves seminaries. Today, we mostly think of seminaries as post-graduate professional schools to study theology and prepare for a career in the church. The school opened on Reformation Day (October 31). Twenty-four young women began their studies in domestic science, Norwegian, music and Bible, with a faculty of six teachers.

In the early 1920s there was a proposal to turn Oak Grove into a women's college. Augsburg was the men's school of the Lutheran Free Church with high school, college and seminary departments. However, Oak Grove became co-educational in 1926 and was renamed "Oak Grove Seminary." Augsburg also made the transition to coeducation. That same year Oak Grove was approved for accreditation by the North Central Association of Colleges and Secondary Schools. This made it easier for its graduates to be accepted into colleges and universities.

The purchase of the Barnes estate's "castle" provided the original home for the school. In 1922 the first major building was constructed and is known today as Jackson Hall, named after Ida Jackson, who was a Bible teacher and spiritual leader on the campus for many years. After World War II, a fund drive was held and a gymnasium-boy's dormitory building was erected. It was named after Rev. Jens E. Fossum (1872-1960) who served Oak Grove from 1907 until 1949. He was president from 1907-1925 and 1930-1937; and Treasurer from 1937-1949. He also served as a teacher.

Another name change took place in 1952 when the school became known as "Oak Grove Lutheran High School." The school originally got its name from the Oak Grove Park which borders the Red River and is adjacent to the campus. A classroom-administration was built in 1960 and a new gym in 1972. In 1977 Oak Grove expanded its curriculum to include Junior Hi. The latest building is the "Center" built in 1985, which houses both the food services and a chapel.

A number of foreign students have traditionally been enrolled at Oak Grove. In some past years, children of missionaries have also been enrolled if there were not adequate educational facilities where their parents worked.

It was quite a change for me to leave the farm at age 16 to live in a dormitory while finishing high school. It was the life of luxury not to have to go out to the barn and do chores before going to school. We started classes at 8:30 a.m. and finished at 4:30 p.m. After supper in the dining hall, we were free until 7 p.m. Then we had to be in our rooms to study until 9. Between 9 and 10 p.m. was free time, but 10:30 was "lights out." We were allowed one night a week to leave the dorm with permission. The dean of boys did room checks to make sure that there was no unnecessary noise or fooling around, and that no students were absent without leave.

To my surprise, I was elected president of the senior class of 1944, though I had been on campus but a few weeks. Attending Oak Grove made it possible for me to get the math and science requirements for college, besides voice lessons and choir. The choir took a tour of northern Minnesota after graduation. War time restrictions made a longer tour impossible. That gave me my first chance to see Bemidji's Paul Bunyan statue.

Since that time, North Dakota schools have been reorganized and offer adequate preparation for college. North Richland High School now stands in the place of the Colfax Hi that I knew. But there were many communities in the state that had no high school in those days. The choice was between renting a room in a town with a high school or not going further in education at all. A lot of good students lost out on education for that reason. Schools like Oak Grove offered the alternative of a home away from home with some degree of supervision and guidance, while getting a high grade education.

Oak Grove has a strong policy on students using alcohol, drugs and tobacco, not just because they are illegal, but because the swift academic pace requires students to be at their best. The Student Handbook requests those who can't get along without these things not to apply.

Because Oak Grove is a church related academy, some people expect it to have a "behavior modification" program for youth whom neither parents nor the public school can discipline. Oak Grove expects its students to have a high degree of self-discipline and maturity.

Today Oak Grove is a part of the Evangelical Lutheran Church in America and has its own corporation elected from congregations in North Dakota and Minnesota. The Oak Leaves Club, an association of graduates, former students and friends, has worked actively in support of the school in the Fargo-Moorhead area. Oak Grove is the only one of the many high schools established by Scandinavian immigrants which is still operating.

A new alumni directory was published in 1989. It brought back a lot of nostalgia while I was paging through it. It's a full evening of entertainment just to discover where one's schoolmates and other graduates are living and what they are doing today. High school friendships are held close to the heart and the prestige of an Oak Grove diploma grows with the years.

I suppose that those of us who graduated nearly a half century ago were pretty naive by comparison to the sophistication of today's high school students. Many today have had foreign travel and are taking courses in high school not available in universities in those days. But schools like Oak Grove did a pretty good job to prepare us to take our place in society. Much has changed since I was an Oak Grove student, but it still has a strong spiritual emphasis with a campus pastor to guide young people with seeking minds.

When you're in Fargo, drive over to the campus and see this exciting school founded by Norwegian immigrants.

CHAPTER 15

Gen. Keithe E. Nelson — Chief Air Force Lawman

I HAVE A LOT OF FRIENDS and acquaintances who are lawyers, and some are on large city staffs. But none of those legal partnerships compares in size to the firm headed by Gen. Keithe E. Nelson, the 9th Judge Advocate General of the U.S. Air Force and who is commander of the Air Force Legal Services Center.

Gen. Nelson is in charge of 1,385 military attorneys, plus 200 civilian attorneys and approximately 1,100 Reserve attorneys. This has to be one of the largest law firms in the world. It functions on more than 160 locations around the globe.

When he entered the University of North Dakota as a transfer student in 1954, Nelson had never planned on an Air Force career. A native of Grand Forks, he graduated from Concordia High School in St. Paul and continued his first year of college in the Twin Cities also at Concordia, an institution owned and operated by the Lutheran Church - Missouri Synod. He had originally planned to become a pastor.

Languages were a special interest to the future Air Force attorney. Two special events crossed Nelson's life while at UND. One was his marriage 1955 to Shirley Jordahl, also of Grand Forks. The other was joining the ROTC program, required of underclassmen at Land Grant universities at that time. His undergraduate degree in philosophy had to be delayed until he'd completed the ROTC program in 1958. He received his law degree in 1959.

Being married while going to college is nothing new, but Nelson remembers those student days as being pretty busy. During those four years, he held down a full-time job in addition to classes and homework. Three years were spent as a night watchman and janitor at the Vets Club. While doing the janitor duty at night, Nelson could study for three to four hours. Then he went directly to classes and slept in the late afternoons and evenings. He comments, "Naturally, our social life was limited." But he attributes his success as an Air Force Attorney to the discipline learned in his student days together with the "fine personalized education I received at UND."

The first assignment for the new Air Force lawyer was at Lake Charles, Louisiana. Moving into that hot and humid climate in the summer of 1959 was tough on the young North Dakotan who was accustomed to the mildly warm days and cool night breezes of summer on the northern prairies. January was more welcome than July to the Nelsons while in the South.

Nelson had planned to leave military service after his three year enlistment and return to North Dakota to put up his shingle to practice law. Then he was offered an assignment in Germany if he'd stay an additional year. Nelson says he "jumped at the chance." They liked Europe so well that they stayed there four years. In Germany, they were stationed near Trier, the summer home of the Roman emperors. A number of my Air Force friends who've been stationed in that area have commented about the richness of that area's history.

Looking back on the European assignment, the Nelsons remember the travelling they did with their VW camper. They visited every country in Europe except Albania. Their travels took them from the far north of Norway to North Africa, and from Ireland to Moscow, and they made it a point to get acquainted with the people of the land wherever they visited. They became acquainted with the Laplanders of Scandinavia, the nomads of Turkey, the peasants of Romania and the working people behind the "Iron Curtain."

It was still Nelson's dream to return to North Dakota, so he informed the assignment officers that he would return to civilian life in 1965 unless they'd assign him to the Grand Forks Air Base. They must have thought highly of him because Grand Forks was home for the Nelsons during the next four years. He served as Senior Attorney of the Base Legal Office. Those were delightful years as he renewed friendships with the University and colleagues in the state. He also visited Minot for consultation with the Air Force Base.

Nelson again planned to leave military service after another year while at Grand Forks. But then another intervention took place. The senior officer in charge of legal matters for the base was removed. Nelson was named to be the acting head of the department while just a captain with only six years of experience. The commanding officer took a liking to him and intervened to have him appointed to the position permanently, even though a Lieutenant Colonel normally held the job. He spent three years as the Senior Attorney in his home town. He says, "it could not have been better." 1968 was spent at the Air Command and Staff College in Montgomery, Alabama. There he studied leadership management, geo-politics and military staffing.

The Nelsons spent 1969-1973 at two bases in England. The first year was at Wethersfield in Essex. This is near the ancient site of Bury Saint Edmunds, which commemorates one of England's revered kings who came to a violent end in combat with the Vikings. The second year was with the Royal Air Force at Bentwaters near Ipswich in Suffolk. That interested me since Fiske familes from Surnadal, Norway, migrated to Suffolk shortly after the death of King Olaf Haraldson (St. Olaf) in 1030. Nelson encountered the name while there.

The travel was professionally useful too. Nelson became acquainted with many European attorneys, including barristers, solicitors and judges in England. This brought an invitation to Queen Elizabeth's birthday celebration. Attending a royal birthday party required a certain protocol of dress. So he rented a top hat and morning coat with tails. As they walked down the streets of London, looking like "English gentry," tourists photographed them, not realizing that this was an American military family dressed for the Queen's party.

After the assignment to England, Nelson transferred to Washington at the office of Management of Manpower and the Judge Advocates worldwide. During that time, he remembers visiting the Minot AFB in February 1974. He has since made several more visits to the Minot base. In 1977 Nelson was commandant of the Air Force Judge Advocate General school, commonly known as JAG, at Maxwell AFB in Alabama.

What does an Air Force Judge Advocate General do? Nelson descibes his department's job as consisting of "Constitutional issues, environmental law and lawsuits, Government contracts, international law, space law, military justice and many other specialized areas of the law." Their staffs have appeared before the bar of many Federal courts, including the United States Supreme Court. He admits, however, that since assuming his present position that life has been a "roller coaster." Still, he impresses me as thoroughly enjoying it.

Besides his heavy schedule of Air Force work, Nelson is an avid tennis player. "My racket travels wherever I do," he states. He also enjoys shotgun sports and has done a lot of competition shooting. The busy Air Force attorney still finds time to hunt geese. What he especially likes about getting out in the fields is the "solitude of a goose pit and the beauty of one of God's most majestic creatures in flight."

Nelson shared with me some things about his Scandinavian heritage. His father's family emigrated from Sweden and his mother's family from Norway. Minot holds a special place in his heart because his grandfather was a carpenter in the Magic City and this is where his father was born. He's quite excited about his Scandinavian roots and likes to talk about them. His mother's family comes from Christiansand in the south of Norway and his wife's family is from Christiansund (the same place as Hubert Humphrey's mother), on the coast west of Trondheim.

Modern day Scandinavians show up almost everywhere, even in the Pentagon.

CHAPTER 16

A Christmas Tale
From Telemark

T
HE "OLD TIMES" IN NORWAY, about which we children of the immigrants often fantasize with nostalgia, was in many ways steeped in the Dark Ages. They had, however, a magic that is lost in our world of high technology. They didn't have either our conveniences or world view. They often lived a lifetime in the valley of their birth until the nurturing earth reclaimed them.

It was a world in which the imagination was allowed to grow without the limitations of scientific verification. The woods, valleys, rivers and ocean were alive with mystery. People who lived up in the mountains didn't worry much about world issues. They usually didn't hear of them until they had become history. Their world was often limited to a so-journer who lived by his ability to tell stories which regaled the listeners and held them spell-bound through the long and dark hours of winter.

The story of Jon of the Black Croft (a croft is a small enclosed field) is such a tale set in the mountains of Telemark, to the northwest of Skien. The magic of the tale centers near Morgedal, one of the beauty spots in that land of the North.

Jon's father had built his cottage on a high plateau overlooking the prosperous valley below. The farmstead consisted of a cottage, a low stable and a hay shed. Above the buildings were forests of fir trees. Like so many others, Jon's father went to the Lofoten Islands to risk his life in the hope of getting a good catch of cod.

Normally, the fish didn't start to run until the New Year, but sometimes they were lucky and the catch would begin a few weeks before Christmas. They called this "Advent fishing." The seas were often stormy. Many a man and boy did not return to home and family again. As a reminder of those out at sea, a model ship was hung above the nave or chancel in the parish church.

Jon's father also took to peddling and trading in the years of his youth before settling down to wife and child. Jon's mother had now been a

61

widow for many years and she feared for her son's future with the poor catch of cod in the Lofotens. The drought and poor prices for produce offered no encouragement either. But she kept on working, making clothes of "vadmel," homespun cloth. These could be ornamented with silver buttons fashioned from coins.

Jon's mother wanted him to emigrate to America where so many of their relatives had gone. But since she would not go along, Jon would not go either. Nothing she could say would persuade him otherwise.

He half-believed in the magic of the "old times" that could turn a person's fortunes around. Out of the dim past, the Nokken, Hulder and Fossegrim (sprites or fairies from the rivers, woodlands and waterfalls) might still emerge to dazzle the eyes of a weary traveller with a lovely farmstead if one acted quickly to claim it. His dream was to claim the legend of the "enchanted valley." It could become his if it ever appeared before his eyes and if he would immediately hurl a piece of steel into the wall of the building pictured in the mirage, and then recover the steel while it was still burning hot. The legend of the enchanted valley was an aspiration to people of Jon's time as Eldorado was to Spanish explorers in America.

It was Christmas eve, one of the most magical times of the year. The Yuletide menu at the Black Croft for Jon and his mother was spare that year, the cod harvest yielding hardly a thing. But yet they shared with the pastor and his family such as they had. Jon went into the woods to find trees for their cottage as well as the parsonage, plus some juniper branches to be strewn on the floor for fragrance.

When Jon delivered the tree to the parsonage ("presthus"), he was welcomed cordially, despite their difference in social classes. They did not send him home empty, but filled his stomach with julekake and fattigmand, favorite pastries to this day among Norwegians. The return trip on skis up the mountain side was slow because he was given a bundle of yule-sheaf (grain) for the birds and a side of pork for his Christmas dinner, plus two silver marks, equivalent to a day's wage in the woods.

It was dark when Jon returned home. His mother was out in the stable milking the cows. Jon finished the chores and gave each animal an extra measure since it was Christmas eve. Legend had it that when the farmer locked the barn that Holy Night all the animals and feathered creatures were given the gift of speech to praise the Christ-Child. Then they went to sleep facing Bethlehem. The wise farmer would also remember the "Julenisse," the jolly bearded Brownie, with milk and porridge, or else a strangled animal might await him on Christmas morning.

On the way from the stable to the cottage, he stopped to look into the heavens for the Bethlehem star, like a lantern in the distance peering over the wooded mountains. Upon entering the cottage, Jon was greeted by the light of the Yule Candle and the fresh scent of juniper.

On Christmas morning Jon was up early to attend matins at the parish church. The rich and the wealthier classes came in their cutters pulled by prancing horses ringing with bells. Skis were the transportation of the poor. Jon racked up his skis and entered the candlelit nave.

As Jon left the church, he met Kirsti, a friend of the pastor's lame daughter, Ingeborg. They hadn't seen each other since confirmation. She had stayed at the parsonage to help with the household duties while being instructed for the rite of passage. But her home was not in that parish.

Several years went by and Jon was now twenty-five, looking for work as he was hiking near Morgedal (the home of Sondre Norheim, father of modern skiing). A lost kitten, pure white in color, caught his eye as he travelled in the dusk. It was lonesome and hungry, like Jon. This formed a bond of companionship. Around the next bend was a farmstead. In the fading light of day he recognized a voice, but not the face.

It had been several more years now since he had seen Kirsti and he could scarcely recognize her at first. The kitten was hers too. It turned out to be a happy meeting as well as a welcome meal. Kirsti's father was unable to do farm work. He walked with a cane and moved about the farmstead with care, his sight having failed. He had advertised for help, but no one responded. The harvest of hay was too much work even for a strong girl like Kirsti to cut, dry and stack, and to feed the cattle when winter came. So Jon found a job waiting for him.

The hay harvest went well until Kirsti hit a rock and bent the scythe. When they attempted to straighten it, the blade broke. As they returned to the farmstead, the landscape took on a new appearance before Jon's eyes. It was like magic, the magic of the mountain fairies. Kirsti walked ahead while Jon was held spellbound by the vision. Right in the midst of the glowing sun, Kirsti appeared as radiant as a princess. Was this real or was this an illusion conjured by the Hulders?

Quickly, Jon took a piece of steel from the broken scythe and hurled it into the farmstead. Then he hurried with all his might past Kirsti and her aged father. "Do you believe in the tale of the Echanted Croft, Kirsti?" he shouted. "If you truly do, then come and help me find the sign." They found the piece of broken blade firmly lodged in the stable wall. It was too hot to touch.

In his excitement, Jon exclaimed, "Now I have won the farmstead, field and the magic princess from the Hulders, Kirsti!" She stood staring at him in amazement, wondering what all this meant. Reality returned to Jon in a moment and he said apologetically to her, "But twas only a fairy tale, Kirsti. This only happens in the world of make-believe that the poor boy wins the prize. Only in storyland does Askeladden get half the kingdom and princess to wife. In real life the cotter's son wins only poverty and hard days."

Jon was about to walk away in his disillusionment when Kirsti called: "But wait, Jon. Perhaps it is no fairy tale. What if I told you...?" He turned to look at her again and realized that the legend of the enchanted croft was for real.

It was stories like this that kept life interesting and made the imaginations sparkle in the "old days" of Norway. If you were to visit the enchanting scenery of those mountains, rivers and valleys, you'd begin to wonder, as only children are able, that maybe the fairy tales are true.

I'm indebted to Olav K. Lundeberg's book *The Enchanted Valley — A Story and Legend of Christmas in Telemark in the Old Time*, published in 1937, for this fascinating tale. The book was about to be discarded from a church library in Arlington, Ohio, where my son Paul was interning. Recognizing its worth, he sent it to me in time for my Christmas reading.

CHAPTER 17

Lake View Church
Of Chicago

OLE MUNCH RAEDER was a Norwegian scholar who visited America during 1847-48. He was sent by the king to study the American jury system. The letters he sent back to Norway were lost for almost eighty years in the University of Oslo's Library until found by a Norwegian-American researcher. As a result we have a better understanding of what life was like when the early Scandinavian settlers came to America.

Munch was quite impressed with the good reputation that Norwegians had in America, except for Chicago. He wrote in 1850 that "there are many bad characters among the more than six hundred Norwegians in Chicago. I have not been there and consequently cannot speak from personal experience." Among the vices to which some Norwegians had fallen were drinking, gambling and fighting. He was impressed with the fact that in Illinois a Norwegian had been elected to be a justice of the peace.

They were not all rowdies, of course, perhaps only a small minority. Among the new immigrants from Norway were the people who organized Lake View Lutheran Church in 1848, the first Scandinavian congregation in Chicago. It's still a viable congregation.

The beginnings of Lake View Church go back to 1834 when it was a mission station and Sunday School. A building fund was started in 1847. They received $600 from Trinity German Lutheran Church in St. Louis, which is the best known of the early Missouri Synod congregations. The pastor, Dr. C. F. W. Walther took a strong interest in the ministry among Norwegians. He is remembered as the "grand-daddy" of the Missouri Synod and a founder of Concordia Seminary in St. Louis. The gift from Trinity was put together with a local fund drive and a building was begun.

Then tragedy struck. The leader of the fund drive absconded with the building fund money and a wind storm badly damaged the building under construction. Discouraged but not defeated, they contacted Paul Andersen, a student at Beloit College in Wisconsin who had come from Norway in 1843. He accepted the challenge on condition that Norwegian and English would be used on an equal basis. The congregation was officially organized on February 14, 1848, as "The Scandinavian Evangelical Lutheran Church of Chicago." Andersen was ordained the following year. One of the charter members was Iver Lawson, the father of Victor F. Lawson who was the founder and publisher of the *Chicago Daily News*.

When a boatload of Swedes arrived in 1852, they were struck with a cholera epidemic and had no money. The Norwegians responded to their needs and nursed them back to health. Jenny Lind, the great Swedish singer, heard about this kind treatment to her countrymen and in appreciation gave the congregation a silver communion set. The communion set is now on display at the Vesterheim museum in Decorah, Iowa. The Swedes and Norwegians worshipped together for a while, until it became apparent that they would do their work better separately. The Norwegians sold their building to the Swedes and in 1854 built a large brick building for $18,000 which seated over nine hundred people. It was called the "cathedral church" of Norwegian Lutheranism in Chicago.

Then another crisis came. Pastor Andersen had not worn the traditional vestments, including the "krage," the ruffed collar worn by clergy of the Norwegian state church. Pastor Peterson who came in 1861 liked the traditional vestments. Unfortunately, a church fight occurred and even though Peterson's side won, it split the congregation, with many people quitting church altogether. The unhappy affair was put to rest in the great Chicago fire of 1871, just a month after the split resulting from a court case in favor of Peterson's side. It wasn't only the church building that burned, but also the homes of many members.

Still they didn't give up. In November 1874, they erected another building also seating nine hundred. Special offerings were taken to erase the debt with its 10% interest. Times were difficult and in 1891 a small group of this original congregation moved into the Lake View area, north of downtown near Lake Michigan. This is how the name "Lake View" became attached to the congregation. Their first pastor in this neighborhood was Rev. Olaf Brandt, who later became a professor of theology at Luther Theological Seminary in St. Paul.

I first became acquainted with Lake View Church in 1950-1951 during my internship in Chicago. When I returned to the metropolitan area in 1967-73, Lake View was beginning a new direction. My son, Mark, attended worship at Lake View Church from 1981-84 while attending DeVry Institute of Technology. By this time it was no longer a Norwegian congregation. In 1972 a new Spanish ministry began together with the English. Pastor Julio A. Loza of La Paz, Bolivia, arrived to minister to the people of the community. While many of the north European background people have moved to the suburbs, Lake View has stayed in their building constructed in 1961. Now they are back to two languages again, but this time Spanish has replaced the Norwegian.

Lake View Church has opened up its facilities to four Alcoholics Anonymous groups, a Narcotics Anonymous group, Girl Scouts and other community agencies. They started a "Ministry Center" in January 1988. This has formed networks with community agencies to avoid duplication in needed services to the hungry, sick, poor, homeless and oppressed of all ethnic backgrounds. They also work with other congregations to develop the resources necessary to plan and underwrite the needed programs.

One of these services is the Volunteer Resources which provides bulk and mass mailing services to small not-for-profit organizations in the community together with giving support to needy individuals. They also give professional services such as financial and computer services to organizations and congregations, with oversight from a qualified accountant and staff trained in computer systems.

I'm impressed that Lake View Church has entered into a joint venture with the Lutheran General Medical Center in suburban Park Ridge to have a "Parish Nurse Program." A registered nurse on the staff helps provide health education and support services to a network of eight congregations and social service agencies of the community. This program was pioneered by Dr. Granger Westberg, author of the best-seller *Good Grief*. There is now a national parish nurse program affiliated with Lutheran General which trains nurses and congregations to do this kind of work. I became acquainted with Dr. Westberg in 1950 when he was the chaplain at the Augustana Hospital in Chicago.

Lake View Church is involved in the "Northside Ecumenical Night Ministry" which goes out on the streets at night to minister to people in need. Among these are the homeless and those involved in drugs, alcohol, prostitution and abuse. They have a "Youth Street Outreach" which concentrates on reaching youth who have no homes. They provide AIDS education to many of them. They cooperate with a "Genesis House" which provides hospitality for women, offers job counseling and health education. The "Exodus Homes" is a demonstration project which provides foster home care and support services for homeless and high risk youth.

They are also involved in the Street Volunteer Program and the Lake View Community Shelter. About twenty-five people sleep in their building every night between October and April, supervised by volunteers. They also have a day time drop-in center where people can get warm, have coffee and receive counseling. The Lake View Emergency Relief Project, which provides both shelters and food pantries, is also headquartered at the church. Lake View Church belongs to a network called Volunteer Attorneys for the Homeless and the Center for Sibling Loss of the Southern School.

I find it especially interesting that the "Church of South India Congregation" uses the building every Sunday evening. Most of these people are new immigrants to the United States.

They do all this work for a budget of less than $100,000. But that's pretty good for a congregation with less than one hundred adult members. $17,700 of their 1988 budget was income expected from renting out their parking lot for Chicago Cub baseball games. With the Cubs now playing night games, they'll be busier than ever.

Who would ever have dreamed back in the year 1848 that this congregation started by Norwegian immigrants to Chicago would have ventured into such an innovative ministry almost 150 years later. I take my hat off to the people of Lake View Church for resisting flight to the suburbs and doing ministry where they are. May they continue to prosper.

CHAPTER 18

Ukrainian
Reader Responds

I N THE EARLY PART OF 1988, I wrote a story on the 1000th anniversary celebration of Christianity in Russia. It relates to the Scandinavian heritage because the ruler, Prince Vladimir (Valdemar), was a Scandinavian. In response, I received a letter from a Ukrainian reader in Oregon. He'd read the story in the *Columbia Press* of Warrenton, Oregon. He also enclosed copies of the *Ukrainian Weekly* and the *Ukrainian Orthodox Word*.

During World War II, my Ukrainian friend was in the Coast Guard out on the West Coast and liked it so much that after the war he left Pennsylvania so he could breathe some "clean air."

The Ukrainians have good reasons to be proud of their heritage. Their land was the first to have an organized government among the republics which now make up the Soviet Union. They were also a part of the Scandinavian trade world as early as 650 A.D. According to the "Russian Primary Chronicles" written in the twelfth century, the leaders of Kiev, now the capital of the Ukraine, invited the "Rus" (Swedish Vikings) to be their leaders about 860 A.D. The Chronicle reads: "Let us find a king to rule over us and make judgments according to the law, for our land is large and rich, but there is no order in it. So come and be king over us." A rich collection of artifacts for this period is kept in the Hermitage Museum in Leningrad. Recently the Ukraine has gotten publicity from the Chernobyl nuclear disaster.

1988 was a special year of celebration for the Ukrainians. The *Chicago Tribune* carried a full color picture on August 1, 1988, of Ukrainian-Americans going to a prayer service in their elaborate costumes in a park near Lake Michigan to remember Prince Vladimir who established Christianity for them in August 988. These people have kept the faith for 1,000 years, despite invasions, oppressions and persecutions.

My friend in Oregon shares the Ukrainian-American distrust of the Soviet government. They have good reasons. During the 1930s, over five million Ukrainians died during Stalin's blood-bath because they resisted the collectivization of their farms. The irony is that before the Communist revolution of 1917 Russia was a wheat-exporting nation. Since the collectivization they have had to import food for their people and livestock.

A part of Russia's high productivity during this time may also be attributed to the progressive farming done by German colonists, especially in the Black Sea area. As a result of the oppressions in the latter days of the Czars (Caesars) and under the Communist rulers, large numbers of these farmers emigrated. North Dakota and South Dakota became the new home for many of them.

The Ukraine lies in the southwest part of the Soviet Union, bordering on both the Sea of Azov and the Black Sea. It has a temperate climate and consists of level plains which average 570 feet above sea level. It is one of the richest areas in the world for manganese and has an abundance of iron, coal, petroleum, bauxite, salt, potash and other minerals. The Ukraine produces almost half of the Soviet Union's cast iron and 40% of the nation's steel. The Soviet Union also depends on the Ukraine for a great deal of its manufacturing. They produce 60% of the country's sugar. It also has health spas with mineral springs. Though comprising only 2.7% of Soviet territory, the Ukraine produces more than 20% of Soviet industrial output and 25% of its grain.

Agriculture is a major industry of the area. There are about 8,000 collective farms and 1,700 state farms, producing large quantities of cereal grains, cattle, milk and sugar beets.

The Ukraine was a founding member of the United Nations as a nominally sovereign nation. It is ruled by the Communist Party which chooses the officials to run the government. The Ukraine became a republic in the Soviet Union in 1924.

Education is required of everyone between seven and seventeen with Ukrainian as the main language, though many other languages are also taught including Russian and English. They have more than 140 institutions of higher education. Among the universities are those at Kiev with 20,000 students, Kharkov with 12,000, Lvov with 13,000 and Uzhgorod with 10,000. Health services and education are free. All the news media, including more than 2,000 newspapers are under the strict control of the government.

The Ukraine covers 233,100 square miles (almost the size of Texas) with a population of about fifty million. It has a rich cultural history. The Ukraine is the most densely populated republic of the Soviet Union and has the second highest population. The great majority of the people are Ukrainians, though one hundred other ethnic groups live in the republic. By 1835, this included sixteen hundred Mennonite families who fled persecution in Germany and Switzerland. They established seventy-two villages and farmed a half million acres of land. While living in Chicago, I also met Jews who had lived in Kiev.

The early Scandinavian connection with the Ukraine was highlighted in the *Ukrainian Orthodox Word* (July-August 1977) with the front cover picture of Princess Olha, grandmother of Prince Vladimir. Known as "Saint Olha" (Olga, also Helga), she is described as "Equal to the Apostles, Great Princess of Kiev, Sovereign Rus-Ukraine - 945-969." It's a heroic story, and she's remembered by the Orthodox on July 11 and by Lutherans on July 15. A special festival was held in Manhattan's Ukrainian Village which honored both Princess Olha and Prince Vladimir. A concert held at St. George's Ukrainian Catholic Church was filled to capacity.

The Ukrainian Orthodox Church, established by Prince Vladimir one thousand years ago, was under the jurisdiction of the Greek Church in the beginning. It maintains close relations with the rest of the Orthodox world. Vladimir wisely made Slavic, rather than Greek or Scandinavian, the language of the church. In this way it became a church of the people rather than of foreigners. The conversion of the Slavic world to Orthodoxy strengthened the eastern church in its power struggle with the church of Rome.

The political and religious history of the Ukraine is highly complicated and it's not always easy to understand. Despite the controversies that have developed through the centuries, the church remains important to the Ukrainian people, both in Europe and in the New World. The Ukraine came under the political control of Poland in the sixteenth century, when Poland and Lithuania were jointly ruled. Pressure was put on the Orthodox Church to unite with Rome. At the synod of

71

Brest-Litovsk (Poland) in 1596, eight of the ten Ukrainian Orthodox bishops recognized the primacy of the Bishop of Rome, while retaining their liturgy and the right of the clergy to marry. This church today is know as "Uniate" (Ukrainian Catholic Church) or "Eastern Rite."

There was a backlash to this agreement, and after military battles and political maneuverings, many of the Ukrainians returned to the Orthodox fold. The Muslim government of Turkey participated in the "liberation" of the Ukraine. Finally the Turks were removed. The Swedes, under Charles XII, also became involved in the Ukrainian struggle for freedom; but the Czars brought the Ukraine into the Russian Empire in 1709.

The first Ukrainians came to North Dakota in 1896 and settled north of Belfield, and in the Wilton area in 1897. Other settlements are in the Max-Butte-Kief area and northwest of Williston. Most of the Ukrainians in the Belfield and Wilton areas are "Uniates," following the Byzantine-Ruthenian Rite, although Wilton also has a Ukrainian Greek Orthodox Church.

The Kief community reflects their point of origin in Kiev, arriving in 1899. The Ukrainians in the Max-Butte-Kief and Williston areas are mostly Protestant, belonging to Baptist, Seventh Day Adventist and United Church of Christ congregations. The Ukrainians in the Williston area arrived about 1905. The only settlement in eastern North Dakota is a small Ukrainian Orthodox congregation organized in Pembina in 1927. There are large settlements of Ukrainians in Canada, with a Ukrainian Information Center in Ottawa. Eastern United States also has large Ukrainian settlements.

In the New World, Ukrainians have been fiercely loyal to their heritage and slow to assimilate into the "melting pot" of our society. Neither are they uncritical of the Soviet government's treatment of their homeland. A *Wall Street Journal* editorial of June 20, 1988, reflected on the "arrogance" of Moscow towards Kiev, by taking credit for Prince Vladimir's baptism of the land 1,000 years ago.

The currents of history have many intertwining movements. You may call them accidents, fate or Providence. But they still remain a mystery. The Scandinavian settlements in eastern Europe were never large, but they played a decisive part in the development of the Kingdom of Kiev which was to influence a whole nation. Scandinavians still love adventure, so you can be sure we haven't heard the last of them yet.

Facade of an Orthodox church in the Ukraine.

CHAPTER 19

The Challenge
Of The Prairie Winds

THERE'S NOTHING LIKE an old fashioned three-day snow storm. The early pioneers were soon to discover this special feature of prairie life. Evelyn Dale Iverson of Canton, South Dakota, has written a delightful book about these wintry storms. The story centers on her grandfather, Nils A. Dale, who immigrated to America from western Norway in 1868.

The book, entitled *Prairie Wind, Blow Me Back*, is the story about one immigrant, but it's typical of thousands more. The book had a special interest for me since some of Nils' grandchildren attended Concordia College when I did in the 1940s. Their father, Hans (Nils' son), was on the college administration staff.

The immigrants were surprised how hard the wind blew across the prairies of the New World. Once when we were visiting with a cousin of my wife in northern Jutland (Denmark), he asked, "Does the wind blow in North Dakota?" We assured him that it did. Then he asked, "But how can it when you're so far from the ocean?" But blow it does, as anyone who lives on the prairies can attest.

Nils came from Breimsvatn, in the Westlands of Norway, about twelve miles northwest of Skei in Jolster. That's an area where some very beautiful folk music has been preserved. Musicians from the area have appeared at the Norsk Høstfest in Minot. Not far to the east are snow-capped mountains. Living on small farms along the fjords was a challenge. Fishing, farming, and often carpentry were all needed to keep families alive.

It was a time of "America Fever." Letters from the New World inflamed the imaginations of those Norse folk in whom the spirit of adventure had been latent since time immemorial. When Nils turned twenty-five in October 1867, it was apparent to all the family that he had set his mind on America. Many emigrating from western Norway usually left from Bergen and sailed to Quebec, which is what Nils did. Before leaving, he signed the Church Book as Nils Amundsen Stokke. The name was taken from his mother's parents farm. He was born while she was visiting there. Later, however, he took the name "Dale" from his father's farm.

Nils travelled to America with a friend named Arne. During the first winter, they worked at a lumber camp in Wisconsin, where they experienced a classic midwestern snow storm. Out in the woods when it started, they had no idea how frightening such a storm can become. With the help of more experienced woodsmen, they made it to shelter and safety. Arne's right foot became white and was frostbitten. The foot was saved, but it left him with a limp.

One winter in the woods was enough for Nils and Arne. They went off farming near LaCrosse. Like many other bachelor immigrants, Nils and Arne kept their eyes open for new arrivals from the Old Country. They were lonesome and hoped to meet the girls. When Nils met Rakel, it was love at first sight. To his proposal, she answered: "Oh, I'm only sixteen, my father wouldn't let me marry so young." "Well," Nils replied, "How old would you have to be?" She answered, "At least seventeen." They were married four months later, four days after her birthday.

The immigrants were eager for news of the outside world. The great Chicago fire of 1871 shocked them, especially since there was a Norwegian community which burned out. There had also been fires in Brown and Manitowoc counties in which three thousand homes were destroyed and thousands of people killed. This raised the concern for fire protection. After that, Nils always plowed a wide strip around his buildings.

The year 1872 was a good year for farming. But in 1873, a hailstorm took Nils' largest wheat field. In 1874 grasshoppers darkened the sky. They tried everything they could to protect their garden. Nothing helped. The hoppers came back in 1875, but were not so bad. While all these things were going on, they were also rearing a family. Times were tough, but there was still a little money squeezed out to give to St. Olaf College, begun in Northfield, Minnesota, in 1874, and for Luther Theological Seminary in St. Paul in 1879. It turned out to be a good investment since two of his sons attended St. Olaf.

THE SCANDINAVIAN ADVENTURE

The great "Dakota Land Boom" was on by 1879. Nils was now thirty-seven years old. With a group of seven other land seekers, he rode the train to Sioux Falls, Dakota Territory, and ended up in Volga. They got a room in a hotel (barracks style) and then set out looking for homestead land. It was out in these Dakota prairies that they discovered the full fury of the west winds. Its force was so hard that it nearly blew their coats off while prospecting for land.

It was a long trek to Dakota Territory travelling in covered wagons and leading their cattle. Oxen are slow, but they can face any wind. Not too many years before, earlier settlers had encountered hostile Indians. The Native Americans could not always understand the peaceful intent of these newcomers. Many of their earlier encounters with the white people had been with traders, soldiers and shysters. How could they know the intentions of these aliens who had come to their ancient homeland? And the newcomers had not been informed about the trail of broken treaties. But as luck would have it, they didn't meet any of the "hostiles."

A 10 X 12 building was required to "prove" a claim. Nils, however, built a 14 X 16 sod house. The strips were one foot wide, three feet long and about four inches thick. The flat prairie land was so different from what they had known in both Norway and Wisconsin. They told their children, "Mr. Wind has blown away the hills, and leveled the land all the way to the edge of the sky." There was also good fishing and hunting.

On October 15, 1880, a fierce blizzard caught the small colony of Norwegian settlers unprepared for winter. Nils' house was the only one completed and some of the men were gone to find work elsewhere. So everyone crowded into Nils' sod house. There wasn't much room for anyone. The air can get pretty stuffy at a time like that. To keep their up courage, they sang songs about Norway, its trees, waterfalls, lakes, fjords, mountains, fields and oceans. They recited Psalms, learned by heart in the Old Country schools. They prayed, and they prevailed. This storm went beyond the three long days we've heard about. Then followed bitter cold and more wind. Heavy snowfalls continued until spring and many animals starved or froze to death.

By 1882, a Ladies Aid Society had been formed and by 1885 they had put aside $450 towards building a new church. These women met twice a month in their homes and the meeting always included coffee and Norwegian pastries. Some walked for many miles carrying a baby while knitting all the way. The church was built on six acres of donated land. Included was land for a fenced cemetery and a buggy shed.

Nils returned to Norway in 1883. His father was still living, but his mother had died twelve years earlier. Such reunions were happy ones but they also had some sadness. Not only were things changed in the homeland, but the new ideas garnered in America had changed the Norse immigrants.

Some years were good. One of them was 1886. But 1887 was the beginning of many disasters. Drought dried up the streams. Dry winds ripened the grain prematurely. Prairie fires were a constant threat. Then came the famous blizzard of 1888. Snowdrifts were so high that farmers had to make tunnels from house to barn. Those winters seemed to last forever. And in the midst of it all, citizenship papers had to be filed.

Nils returned to Norway again in 1892. Rakel went along this time. Less than two years later, his father died. It was a bitter cold day in January 1894 when the grave had to be dug for the funeral. The church choir sang "Den Store Hvide Flok," a favorite hymn of Norse folk to this day, also in America.

Back home in Howard, South Dakota, disasters hit. The town had burned down. A recently built flour mill exploded from combustible grain dust. A diphtheria epidemic broke out. Nils and Rakel lost an eight-year old daughter. Nils built the pine coffin himself. The next year they lost another child shortly after birth. Still they had eight healthy children for which they were grateful. That year on Christmas eve, Nils suddenly died of internal bleeding from falling out of a tree while looking for lost cattle. Rakel was left a widow at forty-three, yet that same evening she read the Christmas story from St. Luke to her children.

The winds blew hard on the prairies. They still do, but we have better shelters now, including better communications and, medical care, better built highways and heated automobiles. Our homes, schools and churches are more comfortable too. But we must never forget those courageous people who bucked the west winds to build communities that have become good homes for us.

CHAPTER 20

'Odin's Ravens'
And The Scandinavian Press

THE OLD NORSE GOD, ODIN, was way ahead of his time. He had a great passion for information and knowledge, even sacrificing one of his eyes for more knowledge. In order to keep informed about the events of the world, he had two ravens which sat on each of his shoulders. Their names were Hugin and Munin. Each morning he sent them out to fly all over the world and they'd return to his home in Valhalla each evening. Then they'd report to him all that they had seen and heard.

Odin would have been interested in our "information age" and would have taken a keen interest in the way the press operates today in Scandinavia. The three hundred year history of the Nordic press has had a lot to do with promoting democracy in those lands.

Printing presses reached Sweden in 1483 and Iceland in 1526. In 1624 a news sheet entitled *Hermes Gothicus* was published for King Gustavus Adolphus. Denmark had Scandinavia's first public newspaper in 1634.

Freedom of the press is a high concern for any democracy. The First Amendment to the US Constitution (1787) states that "Congress shall make no law . . . abridging the freedom of speech, or of the press." Sweden had such a law in 1766. The principle of citizen rights has been a part of the Scandinavian heritage since before Christian times when they had local assemblies (Things) at which every free man had the right of speech and a vote.

The Norwegian constitution of 1814 provided for freedom of the press. The constitution reads: "There shall be liberty of the press. No person shall be punished for any writing . . . unless he willfully and manifestly has either himself shown or incited others to disobedience to the laws, or resistance to their orders, or has advanced false and defamatory accusations against another person." Only rarely will a journalist have to identify a source in Scandinavia.

Sweden has strict laws protecting the public from scandal. They've created an "Ombudsman" position which acts as a citizen advocate to protect people's rights against government bureaucracy. If a person is accused of breaking a law in Sweden, it's illegal to mention the name in the media. The name is protected from publication until conviction. This is to protect a person's reputation and to assist in rehabilitation. Libel suits against editors are not as numerous in Scandinavia as in America, partly because the awards are small and the plaintiff's risk is high. It includes paying the editor's legal costs.

Morgenbladet, a morning newspaper founded in 1819, is the oldest Norwegian newspaper. Because of its liberal political views, circulation was forbidden in Denmark. The word "liberal" in Norway meant that they wanted their political independence. Denmark didn't have a constitution until 1849, when freedom of the press became guaranteed.

The Swedish king tried to suppress the *Aftonbladet*, published in Stockholm, for its liberal views. Each time it was banned, it reappeared with a new name such as *Aftonbladet the Second*, *Aftonbladet the Third*, etc. After 14 such attempts, the harassment stopped. *Aftonbladet* was regarded as the "Bible of the Swedish people."

The largest newspaper in Norway today is *Aftenposten* with a circulation of 230,000. It publishes both morning and afternoon editions with a conservative point of view. While having only the eighth largest circulation in Scandinavia, *Aftenposten* is regarded as the most influential, followed by the conservative *Berlingske Tidende* (Denmark's oldest, founded in 1749), and Sweden's *Dagens Nyheter*, an independent paper with a centrist political position. *Expressen*, a Liberal Party paper published in Stockholm with a circulation of 531,000, is the largest Scandinavian newspaper. It's followed closely by *Helsingin Sanomat*, a conservative paper with a circulation of 450,000 published in Helsinki.

I visited *Dagbladet*, a daily Norwegian tabloid with a circulation of 140,000 in 1983, hoping to interest them in the "Scandinavian Heritage column." The editor liked the articles but explained to me that as a tabloid they were interested in entertainment and highly sensational stories with lots of pictures. Time didn't permit me to visit the Morgenbladet. That remains for a future visit.

THE SCANDINAVIAN ADVENTURE

Finland was dependent on Swedish as its cultural language until the mid-nineteenth century. It wasn't until 1847 that a Finnish language newspaper appeared in Helsinki. This was during the Russian period (1809-1917). Three years later, the Czars started to impose a strict censorship. The Finns managed to get some freedom of the press by 1855. However, about 1900, in the latter days of the Czarist rule, the government again imposed heavy censorship.

Iceland got its first daily newspaper in 1910. The Icelandic people are the most interested in world news of all the Scandinavians. Their little island republic depends on international connections.

During World War I, both the British and German governments tried to influence political views in the Swedish press. The Swedes resisted these attempts in their determination to be neutral. The role of the newspaper in Sweden has been described as being a "watchdog" on the government.

Scandinavian newspapers are privately owned as in America, but many of the weeklies have government subsidies so they can inform and educate the public. Norwegian newspapers have public education as their primary goal and carry a lot of essays and in-depth discussions. It's not uncommon to find carefully researched articles on philosophy, theology, history, architecture, economics, social policy and heritage in the Nordic newspapers. The newspapers often are the vehicles of public debates. They are expected to practice restraint on publishing articles that would harm the government's foreign policy, especially in Finland.

Denmark has the tradition of having a four-newspaper system: Conservative, Social Democrat, Liberal and Radical Liberal. Copenhagen has 12 daily newspapers today, whereas Chicago has only two and Minneapolis one. Scandinavians have the highest per capita readership and many homes take two or more daily newspapers. In Finland 98% of the people read a daily newspaper.

It's interesting to read the well-known American comics in the Scandinavian newspapers. Among these are Peanuts, Donald Duck, Hagar the Horrible, Sad Sack, Garfield and Blondie. Humor, however, in a foreign language is more difficult to understand than informational reading. So a foreigner is apt to miss the punch line even when translated.

World War II was a time of special importance to newspapers in Denmark and Norway. "Underground journalism" sprang up in newspapers which were permitted to stay in business. Articles were written in such a clever way that the Nazis had difficulty catching on to what was being said between the lines. There were over three hundred underground papers circulating in Norway during the War.

Patriotic newspapers were operating all over Denmark during the Occupation. 166 newspapers with a circulation of 2,600,000 were were printed in 1943. In 1944 the Nazis made mass arrests of journalists and printers. The Communist newspaper was banned, but it also went underground. Oppression increased the newspapers to 244 with an incredible circulation of 11 million. Since the war, the number of newspapers has declined but the readership has remained high.

My favorite story of the war in Denmark was when the British bombed the rail yards at Fredrikshavn in northern Jutland. The Nazis ordered the newspapers to report that the bombs fell harmlessly in a pasture killing a cow. Two days later, the press reported that "the cow that was killed in the R. A. F. raid two days ago is still burning." The Danes used ridicule as an effective weapon against the invaders.

If Odin were around today, he'd be reading newspapers too, besides tuning in on all news radio and TV stations. But then, what would he do with his ravens?

An excellent study on Scandinavian newspapers is *The Ravens of Odin: The Press in the Nordic Nations* by Robert G. Picard (State University of Iowa Press, 1988).

CHAPTER 21

The Norwegian-American
Press Today

O
UT OF THE FOUR HUNDRED Norwegian language
newspapers that once were published in America, there are
only two left today. They are the *Western Viking* in Seattle and *Nordisk Tidende (Norway Times)* in Brooklyn.
They have stories in both Norwegian and English.

During pioneer days in the Dakotas and Minnesota, the *Decorah-
Posten* was standard reading in every Norwegian home. The comic strip,
"Han Ola og Han Per," (He's Ole and He's Per) was awaited every week.
But in 1972, the Iowa paper's subscription list was sold to the *Western
Viking*. They still carry "Han Ola og Han Per."

The editor of the *Western Viking* is Henning C. Boe, born in 1914.
His is not a desk job by any means. Each week finds Boe putting
together the pages of the newspaper. He started in the printing business
at age fifteen to support his family. A native of Oslo, Boe came to the
New World in 1951. Not caring for the Big Apple, he went to the Middle
West to set type for the *Decorah-Posten*, then the largest Norwegian
language newspaper in America. He returned to Norway the next year.

Boe went to Seattle to work for the *Washington Posten* in 1954. In
1958 he purchased the newspaper and changed its name to *Western
Viking*. Even though Boe knew the printing business well, he enrolled
at the University of Washington's School of Journalism to study writing
for two years. In his office he proudly displays the certificate showing
that he was decorated by King Olav V, receiving the "Order of St. Olav."
He has also been recognized by St. Olaf College and the Sons of
Norway.

A big day for the Norwegian language papers is when they carry the
stories about the upcoming "Syttende Mai" (17th of May) which cele-
brates the Norwegian constitution of 1814. Norwegians love to re-tell
the story of Eidsvoll and how they hoped for a while that they might
even have independence. But it was not to be for another ninety-one

years as the British forced the king of Denmark to give Norway to the king of Sweden. But they kept their constitution! For the first time they'd have a national parliament in their own country. Norwegians in the New World have not forgotten the meaning of this event.

Nordisk Tidende is published in Brooklyn. On a trip to New York City in 1970, I was interviewed by a reporter of the paper. I was living in Chicago at the time and they wanted to get some reflections on Norwegian heritage from someone whose roots were in North Dakota. Brooklyn has a strong Norwegian community. The Brooklyn Norwegians are more apt to go to Norway for a vacation than to visit Yellowstone Park or the Grand Canyon.

Like the *Western Viking*, the *Nordisk Tidende* has an eye for the events going on among Norwegians in the Middle West. The Brooklyn paper had a big story in September 1988 when the Bismarck (North Dakota) City Auditorium was renamed in honor of the late Belle Mehus, a Norwegian-American music teacher and cultural leader. She had died the previous January at age ninety-one. The dedication tribute called her "Bismarck's First Lady of Music."

The Norsk Høstfest regularly advertises in both newspapers. People attend the Høstfest from both Brooklyn and Seattle. Many people read the paper as much for its advertising as for the news. If there is anything Norwegian to be found, these papers are likely to tell you how and where to find it.

The *Nordisk Tidende* is quick to report news that shows Norwegian genius. One of the stories that broke in 1988 was the charge that the American polar explorer Robert Peary (1856-1920) did not really reach the North Pole in 1909 as reported. According to Perry's own notes, it was claimed, he had not gotten closer than 115 miles from the pole. The *National Geographic*, however, has since affirmed Peary's claim to discovery. If Peary had not discovered the North Pole, Norway's Roald Amundson would get credit for this achievement. In 1911, Amundson crossed over in a dirigible. The *Nordisk Tidende* put this story on front page.

One of the interesting stories reported in the Brooklyn paper was how Norwegian sailors after World War II gathered intelligence information for the CIA and for the British M16. They took photographs and made sketches in Communist bloc countries of warships and defense installations. Though illegal for Norwegians to do, it was kept up for about thirty years.

Norwegians are intensely interested in the Olympics and are excited about the Winter Olympics to be held in Lillehammer in 1994. When athletes from Norway brought home two gold and three silver medals from the Summer Olympics in Korea in 1988, they were welcomed as heroes.

When I've visited in Norway, people have always asked me questions about politics in America. They follow the presidential elections as if they were their very own. They watched the candidacies of Humphrey and Mondale with great interest because of their Norwegian heritage. It happened again in 1988. Though there were no Norwegian candidates, Sen. Lloyd Bentsen, the Democratic candidate for Vice President, was of Danish rootage. Norway generally favored Dukakis. They were, however, quick to express their congratulations to President Bush and some of their press have called him "America's most underestimated politician."

The Chicago based *SCAN USAMERICA*, a successor to *Vinland*, was short-lived. It was even-handed in its reporting for the five Scandinavian countries: Denmark, Finland, Iceland, Norway and Sweden. They gave an excellent report on the Norwegian pavilion at EPCOT Center when it opened at Walt Disney World in Florida. They also gave Art Lee, history professor at Bemidji State University, a good review of his books with Lutefisk titles. A full page ad invited the public to attend a concert which featured seven outstanding Scandinavian stars, including Victor Borge and Arve Tellefsen, both of whom have performed at the Norsk Høstfest. The paper in 1988 carried an abundance of Swedish-American stories in celebration of 350 years of Swedish settlers in America along the Delaware River.

One ad caught my special attention in the Chicago paper. The Norwegian Lutheran Memorial Church (Mindekirke) in Logan Square advertised its church services, "English translation of Norwegian sermon available," and "Security guard outside the church." The old neighborhoods aren't like they used to be. Street gangs have taken over in some of the sections where Scandinavians once lived without fear of personal safety. Despite having their memorial church where it used to be, most Norwegians in Chicago have moved to the suburbs. So have many other people.

I'm glad that there are still at least two of these Norse ethnic newspapers being published. They help keep the heritage alive and give us some understanding that we'd otherwise miss.

CHAPTER 22

Andreas Ueland — 'Recollections Of An Immigrant'

THE NAME UELAND, pronounced "UU-eh-lahnd", was well known in Norway during the 19th century. Ole Gabriel Ueland (1799-1870) was a travelling rural schoolteacher from 1827-1852. He was elected to the Storting (parliament) in 1833 and remained there until 1869. Ueland, though conservative in outlook, demanded "ruthless economies at the expense of the official class," according to historian T. K. Derry. In the parliament he became a powerful leader for the farmers and called for the jury system in the courts.

Ole's son, Andreas, had the same dogged determination as his father. In his memoirs written in 1929, he told of his beginning education. It was from listening to his father talk with neighbors during the long winter nights by the light of flickering candles. He told of watching the travelling tailors and shoemakers work at their farm between Egersund and Flekkefjord.

Despite the strong influence of Hans Nielsen Hauge in the Ueland home, Andreas remembered that there was still some remembrance of the old Asa religion. This became most apparent at Christmas time when nights were the longest. Many people were sure they had seen the devil along the lonely mountain roads at night. Judgment day was their greatest fear.

Growing up as a young boy in those days meant certain duties. Most important was to memorize the catechism explanation by Bishop Pontoppidan, Bible verses and hymns for confirmation. There was also farm work to do. It was common for ten-year-old boys to herd sheep up in the mountain pastures (seters) during the summer.

One of Andreas' delights was travelling to Oslo with his father when he went to Storting meetings. There young Andreas met many famous people who took a liking to him. He might have had a political career in Norway had he wished, but Andreas set out for America after his father died in 1870. The following year, at age eighteen, he travelled on an English steamer from the Stavanger harbor. His destination was Rushford in southeastern Minnesota, home for many other Norwegians.

The young men from Norway looked for farm work as soon as they arrived at their destination. Andreas might have become a farmer if someone hadn't told him about Minneapolis. Ueland moved to Minneapolis and set about learning English. After three years of hard manual labor, he started studying to become a lawyer (advocat). In those days, it was common to be apprenticed to another lawyer and take the bar examinations when ready. Of the five who passed, Ueland had the highest marks.

Starting out to be a lawyer often provides an income near the poverty line. Ueland was no exception. As a law-clerk he earned only $3.50 a week, if he got paid. As a full fledged lawyer, he started at $7 a day and earned $1000 his first year. That was considered pretty good.

One of the most controversial Norwegians to visit America was Bjørnstjerne Bjørnson (1832-1910). Bjørnson was thoroughly disliked by most of the Norwegian Lutheran clergy for his criticisms of the church. Most of it was directed against the state church clergy of Norway. However, this criticism spilled over against almost all the Norwegian pastors and theologians in America. His religious expressions often mixed Christian aspirations with the pagan mythology of Old Norway. Bjørnson, however, had high praise for Andreas' father, regarding him as a champion of the common people.

In June 1885, Ueland married Clara Hampson whom he had first met ten yers earlier when she was only fifteen. It was love at first sight. She was beautiful, highly talented and had a strong community consciousness.

Ueland told of holding court at Medora, North Dakota, in 1906. Minneapolis lawyers were often invited to travel to the frontier. That was real cowboy country in those days. He described the town as having about a half dozen houses and half a dozen "blind pigs." According to Ueland, Prohibition didn't dry up this Badlands community. He commented that the lawyers and jurors looked sleepy during the trials, but were wide awake at night when playing poker in the bars.

He told of a blacksmith, who, while under the influence, had insulted a storekeeper with an unusually rich vocabulary of scorn. Some local lawyers advised him that he would be justified in shooting the blacksmith. But because he was running for the legislature, he didn't want to give his opponent a chance to distort the facts during the campaign. He had to settle for seeing his adversary spend fifty days in jail instead.

Ueland used to write his letters while riding the trains. In 1907 he wrote his daughter while riding on the North Coast Limited past Dickinson about the beauty of the North Dakota prairie in late March.

The theological struggles in the Norwegian Lutheran Church in the New World involved Ueland. He criticized the church for holding on to Norwegian, charging that this blocked progress among the immigrants in becoming Americanized. This meant that they wouldn't get good paying jobs and that their children would be hindered in the New World.

During the controversy for control of Augsburg College and Seminary in the late 1890s, Ueland represented the United Church (Forenede kirke) against the "Friends of Augsburg." In 1917, he did the legal work for organizing the Norwegian Lutheran Church of America, which united most of the Norwegian Lutherans in this country.

On a trip to his homeland in 1909, he wrote that in Norway all the women voted. American women had not yet been granted suffrage. During the thirty-eight years since he emigrated, Norway became independent and was learning how to be a free nation of the world.

In 1913, Ueland returned again to Norway, this time on the same ship as the St. Olaf College Choir. A highlight of the trip was an audience wih King Haakon VII. For the visit he bought a silk hat and a pair of brown gloves, and wore his Prince Albert suit. The king acknowledged Andreas' father and engaged in small talk. A royal concern was that too many Norwegians were leaving their homeland. Ueland assured him that this would diminish since the free land was all gone.

During World War I, Ueland went to Cooperstown, North Dakota, to visit his uncle's farm. The farmers in those days were challenged to raise enough wheat to feed the soldiers. It took two days for the war news to reach Cooperstown from Minneapolis. He pointed out that the American-born Germans were highly patriotic Americans.

Ueland was a highly regarded lawyer and citizen of Minneapolis. When the Federal Reserve Bank was organized in the city in 1914, he became its general counsel. In 1926, Ueland came to Minot to defend the Federal Reserve Bank against a decision by the Supreme Court of North Dakota.

Many people in Minneapolis still perk up their ears when the name of Ueland is mentioned. Two sons, continuing in the law profession, were also highly regarded in the community.

In North Dakota, another Ueland, Lars, a farmer from Edgeley, was a member of the state's first House of Representatives. He championed the citizen's right of initiative and referendum. The "Ueland Bill" finally became law in 1914. Lars was accepted into the Norsk Høstfest's Scandinavian-American Hall of Fame in 1986.

I was fortunate to get a copy of Andreas Ueland's *Recollections of An Immigrant*. My son Paul obtained it for me when it was being discarded by the Luther Northwestern Theological Seminary Library in St. Paul. A few pages were missing which I was able to replace. Ueland was an interesting person, someone I'd like to have known.

CHAPTER 23

Scandinavian Crusaders
In The Middle East

I SHOULDN'T HAVE BEEN surprised when reading Joinville and Villehardouin's *Chronicles of the Crusaders* to learn that the Scandinavians joined the thousands of warriors and pilgrims to wrest the holy shrines of Jesus from the Muslim "Infidels" (Unbelievers). The Danes and Norwegians got in on the excitement of the two hundred year period from 1096 to 1291. The military expeditions to the eastern end of the Mediterranean Sea were the main pre-occupation of western Europe during those days. Even though their losses were catastrophic, building ships, stockpiling food, making armor and forging weapons contributed heavily to the economy of the times.

Actually, the Norsemen's part in these wars was quite small. The Germans, French, Italians, Dutch and English furnished most of the soldiers and war material. Still the Scandinavian part in the Crusades has some points of interest.

After the armies of Islam captured Jerusalem in 638 and then swept across North Africa and up into Spain, Christian Europe was on the defensive. The high point of the Muslim invasions was at Tours in France (130 miles SW of Paris) in 732 when they were defeated by Charles Martel. The Song of Roland also glorified the Frankish knights who had fought the Saracens (Muslims) in Spain, but were annihilated by the Spanish Basques as they returned across the Pyrenees.

The stage for the Crusades had been set for centuries. The Muslim Arabs had been quite tolerant of Christian pilgrims who visited the land of Jesus. It was good tourist business. When the warlike Seljuk Turks overran the Middle East and threatened Constantinople, Emperor Alexius I Comnenus asked help from Pope Urban II in 1095. He suggested that this military force might also go on to liberate Jerusalem. There were reports that Christian holy places were being violated by the Seljuks. Pope Urban's response was to sanction a "holy war." Four years later Jerusalem became the capital of a Crusader's kingdom and a cross was placed on the Dome of the Rock, the third most holy shrine in Islam. This is the site where the Jewish temple had once stood and where Abraham was supposed to have brought Isaac for sacrfice.

Then many confusing things happened. The Muslims responded with their own "jihad" (holy war). Holy wars are always the worst kind of wars since they often result in everybody on the losing side being massacred. But it wasn't long before the Emperor in Constantinople broke with his allies, the Frankish knights. The Muslims also became divided. There were times when Christians and Muslims were allied against other Christians and Muslims. It's a wonder that anybody was left alive.

The Norsemen's ancient love for warfare was rekindled by the call to rescue the "Holy Land." There was adventure to be had and perhaps a fortune to be gained. This was enough for at least two kings from the north to join the action.

Denmark's King Eric Egode (reigned 1095-1103) responded to Pope Urban's call. He was the first European king to sail for Jerusalem. On the way, he stopped in Constantinople to visit the Emperor's Scandinavian Guard, the "Varangians." The Varangians were "soldiers of fortune," mainly Danes and Norwegians. Unfortunately for Eric, he died at Cyprus en route to the Holy City. His wife, Bodil, continued the trip but she also died on the Mount of Olives before she could enter Jerusalem.

One of the prizes of war for the Muslims was to capture a Danish battle axe. There was a sizeable group of "Assassins" in Syria who carried these axes. The word "assassin" comes from "hashish." These terrorists were so named because they smoked hashish before doing their executions. The Danish axe was regarded as a prestige item of armor.

The most publicized of the Scandinavian crusaders was King Sigurd (1103-1130) of Norway, known as "Jorsulfarer" (Jerusalem traveller). Before leaving his country, a king usually went through a religious ceremony in which he "took the cross." In exchange for prostrating himself before the bishop, he was promised a full remission of all his sins for making the journey.

Sigurd left Norway in 1108 with sixty ships. They didn't conduct war the way we do today. There was a lot of pomp and circumstance along the way. Sigurd first stopped in England to visit King Henry, son of William the Conqueror. After a series of celebrations, he went to Sicily to visit the Norman Duke Roger and made him a king. That meant more parties. Finally, he got to Jerusalem were he was welcomed royally by King Baldwin.

The Norse king got into one battle. Together with King Baldwin, he laid siege to the ancient Phoenician city of Sidon. It capitulated on December 4, 1110. But unlike so many of the other places where a city was captured, at Sidon there was no massacre of the population. Instead there was a massive exodus to Tyre and Damascus. The Sidonians had sent a delegation to the kings, pleading for their lives in exchange for surrender. It was granted. By contrast, when the Frankish knights captured Beirut the previous May, they massacred all five thousand of the inhabitants. This was their normal procedure. The Arab historians of the time did not distinguish between the Scandinavians and the Franks. They referred to Sigurd as a "Frankish king."

Sigurd's reward for capturing Sidon was a true "splinter of the cross of Christ" which had been held "hostage" by the Muslims. This was the most highly valued of all trophies. He took it back to Trondheim where it was placed in the shrine of St. Olaf at Nidaros Cathedral. This enhanced tourism to Trondheim. It became the third most visited European shrine in the Middle Ages.

Everywhere Sigurd went, he was received with honor. The Emperor in Constantinople entertained him sumptuously. In Denmark, his aunt, who was married to the king, gave him a fully outfitted ship for returning to his homeland. He gave much of the wealth gathered on the trip to churches in Norway.

The returning crusaders came home with a wealth of learning as well as gold, silver and jewels. The Muslim lands of the Middle East were advanced in medicine, literature, architecture, astronomy, chemistry, geography, mathematics, paper-making and other industries. They had a higher standard of living than Christian Europe. The Crusaders also brought back plants previously unknown in Europe such as apricots, oranges and watermelons.

Norway, however, did not reap the benefits of this new knowledge; it remained in the Dark Ages. On the continent, however, universities absorbed the new knowledge and even surpassed it. The Crusades did not permanently wrest the holy places of the Bible from the Muslims, but they did bring back knowledge that was the beginning of a new Europe. And strangely, the Muslim world went into decline.

The Crusades remain a sore spot in Christian-Muslim relations. On May 13, 1981, Mehmet Ali Agca, a Turk, attempted to assassinate the Pope. He had written in a letter: "I have decided to kill John Paul II, supreme commander of the Crusades." It may take many more generations of attempts at reconciliation before the Crusades cease to be a cause of division between these two large sectors of society.

Christians and Muslims have lived in peace, however, over long periods of time. It's been the "hot-heads" on both sides that have continued to provoke the "holy wars." The vast majority of the people want peace.

Another Scandinavian, Count Folke Bernadotte from Sweden, did manage the miracle on June 11, 1948, when he arranged a cease-fire in Palestine. Unfortunately, he was gunned down by soldiers three months later. Despite the setbacks, let's hope that we'll never stop trying to realize the dream.

CHAPTER 24

The Martyrdom
Of St. Magnus

YOU DON'T HEAR MUCH about the Orkney Islands in the news today. However, if you had lived in Norway a thousand years ago, you may even have had relatives living there. The Orkneys are a group of about seventy islands and islets, of which about twenty are inhabited today. They are located about twenty miles north of Scotland and were formed by glacial erosions. The hard blowing westerly winds have made trees scarce.

The Orkneys were inhabited in prehistoric times by a civilization that has disappeared. In the seventh century A.D., Norwegians settled on the islands. Celtic missionaries from Ireland and Scotland attempted to Christianize the Norsemen, but this was not accomplished until 994 when it was done forcibly by King Olaf Tryggvason. The Orkney and Shetland Islands came under the control of Scotland in 1472 when the king of Denmark defaulted on a dowry that was to accompany Princess Margaret in her marriage to King James III. Since the mortgage wasn't paid, King James foreclosed. They are a part of the United Kingdom today.

We know a surprising amount about this windswept island from the "Orkneyinga Saga" written about 1200 by an Icelander. The Icelanders were the great Scandinavian scholars of the Middle Ages. Some later additions were made to the original writing.

The stories of all the wars and pagan practices of these early Norsemen is too detailed for a short story. But there is one event in the saga which deserves attention. It concerns Magnus Erlendsson, an earl of the Orkneys. The title "earl" (called "jarl" among the Danes and Norwegians) had to be conferred by a king and it ranked just below royalty. An earl was something like a governor general.

The king of Norway, Magnus Bare-Leg (1093-1103), claimed sovereignty over the islands. Magnus Erlendsson was beholden to the king. After a battle in which the earl refused to fight, the king took him prisoner. He escaped from the ship one night by making his bunk to look like someone was sleeping in it. Then he went overboard and swam to shore. In the morning, men with bloodhounds went in search of the earl. A dog found him up in a tree, but he gave the dog such a blow with a branch that it ran away yelping. So he escaped to Scotland and England. Scotland's King Malcolm offered him sanctuary. He didn't dare return to the Orkneys as long as Magnus was king.

King Magnus kept on the move, raiding and pillaging wherever he could find some easy money. He was killed in Ireland while plundering in Ulster. This was the signal for Magnus Erlendsson to return to the Orkneys. The farmers liked him and welcomed him back. Haakon Paulsson, a loyal follower of the king, was made an earl and laid claim to the islands. Fortunately, some of the farmers mediated a truce between them and avoided bloodshed. Earl Haakon and Earl Magnus became good friends and there was peace on the island. Norway's King Eystein gave his approval.

The saga writer paid a fine tribute to Magnus Erlendsson. They said he was "a man of extraordinary distinction, tall, with a fine, intelligent look about him. He was a man of strict virtue, successful in war, wise, eloquent, generous and magnanimous, open-handed with money, sound with advice, and altogether the most popular of men. He was gentle and agreeable when talking to men of wisdom and goodwill, but severe and uncompromising towards thieves and vikings, putting to death most of the men who plundered the farms and other parts of the earldom." Magnus was impartial in judgment, taking no bribes from the rich. The saga writer continued, "He lived according to God's commandments, mortifying the flesh through an exemplary life." Yet he didn't make a show of his piety.

Everything looked good until some troublemakers caused distrust to come between the two leaders. This led to the mustering of soldiers and attacks commenced. But the farmers intervened for peace again. They didn't want any trouble, especially during Lent.

Haakon offered to meet Magnus during Holy Week at a place called Egilsay. It was to be a "peace meeting." They were each to sail to the island with two ships and an equal number of men. Having complete trust in the agreement, Magnus sailed with his two ships full of the best-natured and peace-loving men on the island. The sea had unusually high waves and Magnus said, "I think it forbodes my death."

Haakon, on the other hand, put together a fleet of eight ships, fully manned for battle. When Magnus learned of the treachery, he would not flee. His men offered to protect him, but he refused, saying "I don't want you to risk your lives in saving mine. If there's not to be peace between me and my kinsman, then things must go according to God's will."

Earl Magnus went ashore on the island to the church where he spent the night. He prayed devoutly and had Mass sung for himself. In the morning Haakon and his men went searching for Magnus. They found him at prayer. He rose and crossed himself and addressed Haakon: "You have not done well to break your oaths." Magnus offered Haakon three choices. First, Magnus offered to go on a pilgrimage to Rome and to the Holy Land, thus giving up his claim to the Orkneys. It was refused. Second, he offered to be mutilated, blinded and put in a dungeon for the rest of his life. Haakon agreed but the soldiers refused, threatening to kill both of them, saying "We're having no more joint rule." So Haakon said, "Better kill him then, I don't want an early death; I much prefer ruling over people and places."

Magnus knelt in prayer. The first soldier angrily refused to strike the death blow. The cook was ordered to do the deed. He began to weep aloud. Earl Magnus prostrated himself on the ground and prayed for his enemies, forgiving them. He made confession of his sins, received the sacrament and walked away with his executioner.

He told the executioner, "Stand in front of me and strike me hard on the head, it's not fitting for a chieftain to be be beheaded like a thief." Then he said, "Take heart, poor fellow, I've prayed that God grant you his mercy." He crossed himself and the blow was struck. The saga writer wrote, "So his soul passed away to Heaven."

The spot of execution was said to have turned into a green field and miracles took place which were attributed to Magnus. The date of death was probably April 16, 1117. People claimed to have been healed as they visited his grave. Later, when his body was exhumed, it appeared as bright as gold. His bones withstood the test of fire three times. This was a test of sainthood. The ruins of a church named after St. Magnus still stand on Egilsay. Magnus' body was taken to Kirkwall on the mainland

and buried in the Christ Church Cathedral. In the course of time the relics were lost.

On March 31, 1919, during the restoration of the cathedral, a wooden casket was removed from within the wall and put to scientific investigation. The skull was broken, likely from an axe blow. Could it be the remains of St. Magnus? The historians and scientists agreed that it was. The bones were placed in a new lead-lined casket and replaced within the wall. And so ends one of the most interesting stories told from the Norse sagas.

I've not visited the Orkneys, but I've seen them from 30,000 feet. They don't look large from the air. But according to Magnus Magnusson, author of *Vikings!*, it was "the major staging-post of the northern seas, where many trade — and raid — routes met."

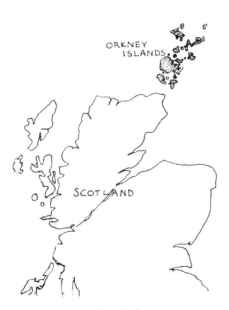

The Orkney's

CHAPTER 25

Iceland —
The Enchanted Island

THERE IS MUCH MORE that's happened in this world than we'll ever know. The best historical research through archaeology, literary sources and oral tradition has merely skimmed the surface.

Iceland is a case in point. In the southern part of the island Roman coins dating to about A.D. 300 have been found. How did they get there? One of the best guesses is that during the Roman occupation of Britain (B.C. 55 - A.D. 410) seafarers visited this distant outpost known as "Ultima Thule." The copper coins are on display in the National Museum in Reykjavik.

Iceland has always been a place where the cause of freedom has been championed. It's a part of the world that people seeking peace and solitude have sought as a refuge. The Althing (parliament) dates to 930 and is called the "Grandmother of Parliaments." Christianity was adopted as the religion of the land in 1000 during the assembly of this legislative body.

Among those seeking the quietness of Iceland were some Irish monks who settled there shortly before 800. They travelled in skin boats called currachs. The monks, however, left hurriedly when the Norwegians came in the late ninth century. It may be that they did not want their privacy disturbed or that the pagan Vikings were a threat both to their spiritual quests and personal safety.

The Norwegians, under the leadership of Ingolfur Arnarson, a chieftain from west Norway, emigrated during the tyranny of King Harald Haarfagre (872-930). They might have emigrated to the Shetland and Orkney islands, but Harald also laid claim to these lands. In the beginning they lived largely by fishing, but in a short time they began sheep farming. About 90% of the people are Nordic; most of the rest are of Celtic origin. About 97% of the people belong to the Lutheran Church. Between 1870 and 1900, a large number moved to Canada and the United States.

Iceland is a young island which grew up through volcanic action. There are about two hundred volcanoes today. The newest island in the area, called Surtsey, was created between 1963 and 1967 off the southwest coast. Alkaline hot springs and gasses are an important industry of the island. The largest of these hot springs produces the equivalent of 1,500,000,000 watts of power. As you would expect, earthquakes are also frequently felt. The volcanoes are among the most spectacular in the world. Snaefellsnes Glacier was made world famous by Jules Verne's science fiction novel, *Journey to the Center of the Earth* in 1864.

Today Iceland has a population of about 250,000. Fishing continues to be a leading part of the island's industry. Between 1950 and 1976, three "cod wars" were held between Iceland and England. Finally the British recognized Iceland's two hundred mile claim from its shoreline for fishing rights, even though Iceland has no military to enforce the claim. They depend on NATO's deterrence for their security. Other sources of income come from potatoes, woolens, livestock and mining. Their gross national product is about $2,500,000,000. Over 40% of Iceland's export trade is with the United States and the United Kingdom. Other countries with which they have significant trade include West Germany, Denmark, Sweden, Netherlands, the United Kingdom and Norway.

But Iceland's most popular recognition in recent years has been the beauty of its women. In 1986, Holmfridur Karlsdottir, a schoolteacher, was elected Miss World. The Norsk Høstfest was one of her stops in world travel. She paid high compliments to the Minot celebration. Just to show that history can repeat itself, another Icelandic beauty, Linda Petursdottir, went to London to compete for Miss World 1989 and came home with the prize. She won $8,750 first prize money and the chance to earn another $175,000 from endorsements and modelling assignments.

During the Middle Ages, Island's great contribution to society was literature. In the relative isolation of the North Atlantic, they researched and wrote the best histories of Scandinavia. The famous of these writers was Snorri Sturluson who wrote the *History of the Norse Kings* (*Heimskringla*).

Iceland became the center of the world's attention in October 1986 when the Reagan-Gorbachev summit took place. The Hofdi House,

99

where the meetings were held, was shown on TV screens throughout the world. Nixon and Pompidou also held an important American-French meeting there in 1973.

Jon Pall Sigmarsson, who looks like a super Charles Atlas, has several times won the title as the "Strongest Man in the World." Besides the fame of Sigmarsson and the Miss Worlds, Iceland has become better known today through the American operated NATO base at Keflavik. Many American Air Force personnel have been stationed there. Keflavik is also a favorite place for shopping by travellers between Europe and America, especially for the famous Icelandic woolens.

Iceland has achieved fame in international chess tournaments. They hosted the famous Fischer-Spassky World Championship in 1972. In 1988 Johann Hjartarson, an Icelander, defeated Victor Korchnois in the Candidates Match in Canada.

Iceland's official name is "Lydhveldidh Island," pronounced "LID-vel-did EES-lund," and means Republic of Iceland. Iceland declared its independence from Denmark in 1944. The name "Iceland" is credited to Hrafna-Floki, an early Norwegian visitor, who climbed a mountain-top and saw a rare sight, icebergs drifting in a fjord. Another contemporary visitor disputed this description and referred to it as a land in which butter dripped from every blade of grass. Earlier names for the island were Thule, Snaeland (snowland) and Gardars-Holmi (farmer's island).

Even the language of Iceland carries with it a ring of nostalgia for Scandinavians. Modern Icelandic is the closest to the Old Norse spoken one thousand years ago. At the airport in Copenhagen, I visited with a family from Iceland and was able to converse with them in Norwegian. In fact, it was fun to hear words spoken that aren't ordinarily used by Norwegians today.

It comes as a surprise to many people that Iceland, though located at the Arctic Circle, has a fairly mild climate. The average temperature in July is 52° and 30° in January. Mostly the weather is changeable. There can be a gale, clear sky, calm, sunshine, rain and snow all in the same day. The air is clean and unpolluted. I flew over it in September 1985 in clear sunshine when every building in Reykjavik could be clearly seen. Even Capt. Leif Hansen, who was the pilot of the SAS flight, commented on the clearness of the day.

Iceland is a land of charm and enchantment. It's the one country where everyone's ancestry can be traced back to the original settlement over 1,100 years ago. It has been called a "poor country where poverty doesn't exist." Education is important to these islanders. The University in Reykjavik, founded in 1911, is open to every qualified citizen free of charge. Even one of the Hardy Boy's adventure books was written about it. Progressive in politics, the Icelanders elected Madame Vigdis Finnbogadottir as President in 1980, the first woman in the world to be elected president of a republic. A former actress, she has a Ph. D. in English.

Though it's off the main travel routes, a visit to Iceland is well worth the extra planning needed to get there. Even though Iceland is an isolated island in the North Atlantic, its history and volcanic nature hold a fascination for all who visit it.

A stone and turf hut typical of the type lived in by Vikings on Iceland.

CHAPTER 26

The Volsunga —
National Epic Of The Northmen

OLD STORIES NEVER DIE, but they may take new shape and form. The Volsunga saga is such a literary creation. This national epic of the Scandinavians, British and Germans even found its way into the story of Beowulf (A.D. 675-725). The Volsunga saga is the story of the Volsungs and Nibelungs which belong to the early legends common to the northern world.

The Icelanders wrote this saga about 1200. It furnished the background for Richard Wagner's opera *The Ring of the Nibelung.* The entire opera was premiered at the Metropolitan Opera in New York in March 1889. The first of the four cycles, "The Rhinegold," had been performed in Munich twenty years earlier. Wagner's opera has a cycle of four musical dramas which still draws excited crowds to its performances of heavy Germanic music fitting to the story.

The two outstanding characters in the story are Sigurd and Brynhild. Sigurd's father, Sigmund, was a mighty warrior of the Volsung family descended from Odin, the "All-Father" god of the Norsemen. Because Sigmund was killed before Sigurd's birth, his mother, Hjørdis, married Alf, the king of Denmark. Sigurd grew up as a handsome warrior, full of wisdom and courage, with a head of heavy blond hair. He mastered the skills of blacksmithing, music, carving runes, learned several languages and was eloquent in speech — the basic attributes of a Scandinavian warrior.

As Sigurd reached manhood, his friend Regin urged him to ask King Alf for a war-horse. He found one that was a descendant of Sleipner, Odin's eight-footed steed, fabled in the sagas. In Vancouver, British Columbia, there's even a Sons of Norway lodge named after Odin's horse.

Every good story has to have a conspiracy at its heart. Even the Gospels have such a theme. Regin's father, Hreidmar, had become very rich with gold. He was the envy not only of political rivals and the gods, but also of his sons. Greed for gold has been the undoing of many people. Fafnir, the oldest son, murdered his father to claim the treasure. Then he changed himself into a dragon to guard his hoard from Regin.

Fleeing for his life, Regin found Sigurd and convinced him to avenge his wrongs by slaying the dragon. For this task, Sigurd needed a sword worthy of the deed. The fragments of Sigmund's sword were forged so skillfully that it split the anvil without even suffering a scratch. Sigurd was now ready to challenge the dragon, Fafnir.

The struggle with the dragon recalls Beowulf and St. George, both of whom had slain dragons. The Volsung saga tells the story of the battle with the same concern for details as Wagner's opera, *The Valkyrie.* The struggle took Sigurd into the dragon's cave. As the slimy dragon moved to his watering place, Sigurd delivered the death blow by thrusting his sword under Fafnir's left shoulder.

As in an opera where dying takes a long time, there was an extended conversation between Sigurd and the dragon. After the death blow, Fafnir, who had been a mighty warrior before turning himself into a dragon, wanted to find out all there was to know about his slayer. Finally, Fafnir tells him to get on his horse and ride with haste to find the gold.

At this point Regin became surly and jealous, being afraid to lose the treasure to Sigurd. Feigning friendship, he asked Sigurd to roast the dragon's heart on a spit for him to eat. Suspecting nothing, Sigurd carried out the request. In touching it to see if it was tender, Sigurd burned his fingers so severely that he put them in his mouth. As soon as the dragon's blood touched his lips, Sigurd was able to understand the language of the birds. That's how he learned that Regin was planning to kill him. Whereupon Sigurd slew Regin.

Sigurd's greatest challenge was yet to come. He found a beautiful warrior-maiden fast asleep on a mountain. With great effort he woke Brynhild and it was love at first sight. She was a goddess who had been banned to the world of mortals. They were married, but did not live happily ever after. In the stories of mythology and in operas, as also in real life, fate frustrates the best laid plans.

Sigurd went off to do more battles. Having been bewitched, he forgot the beautiful Brynhild and sought the hand of Gudrun in the land of the Nibelungs. She was the "most beautiful of maidens" in the land. An alliance of blood was sealed between Sigurd and the Nibelungs. During the wedding feast, Sigurd gave his bride some of Fafnir's heart to eat. The moment she tasted it her nature changed to become cold and silent.

Gudrun's eldest brother, Gunnar, became king of the Nibelungs. Since he was not married, his mother counseled him to seek the hand of Brynhild who had been left with family but no husband. There was, however, a ring of fire around her house. She had vowed that she would marry only the warrior that dared to brave the flames. Sigurd, having forgotten Brynhild, went with Gunnar. However, the horse would not ride through the flames. So Sigurd and Gunnar changed armor and it was Sigurd who rode through the fire disguised as Gunnar. This is perfect story material for an opera.

The surprised Brynhild agreed to the marriage and promised to appear in ten days for the wedding. During the ceremony, the spell that had been cast over them was broken. But it was too late. The vows had been made. Brynhild's warrior spirit returned and her heart was fierce with anger. The two queens, Brynhild and Gudron, became bitter enemies. Gudron then produced the ring that had originally been given to Brynhild by Sigurd. She became deathly ill from frustrated love and anger. Her pride being crushed, she conspired for Sigurd's death. Then she committed suicide and her body was burned on the funeral pyre with Sigurd's.

In Wagner's opera, the death scenes are even more dramatic. Brynhild, mounted on her horse, leaped from the flames and led her battle-maidens back to Valhalla (Heaven), passing forever from the sight of earth and men. In a short time, Sigurd died and Gudron fled to the home of King Alf where she spent the rest of her life embroidering the great deeds of Sigurd on a tapestry, and attending her daughter Swanhild who reminded her of the great Sigurd.

In those days when people didn't have theater and television, they found entertainment and philosophy of life in the sagas. Strange as they are to us, and often horror-filled, these stories are probably no more tragic than the world in which we live today. We may not turn ourselves into dragons and cast spells on our enemies, but we try every form of magic at our command to get the best of each other. Some day, a saga may be written about us and an opera about our times. I wonder what they will say and what kind of music will they play.

Sigurd Volsunga

CHAPTER 27

Lillehammer And
The 1994 Olympics

EXCITEMENT IS ALREADY building up in Lillehammer, Norway, for the 1994 Olympics. This quiet little city of 22,000, nestled along the east bank of Lake Mjøsa, the largest lake in Norway, is busy getting ready for the world's biggest winter sports spectacle.

Lillehammer is located near the lower end of Gudbrandsdal, one of the largest and most scenic valleys of Norway. Many people from this valley immigrated to America. The Gudbrandsdal Lag (Lodge) meets every summer to keep the fellowship alive.

You would think that the people of this valley would be delighted to host this prestigious winter sporting event, and they are. But it's not all that simple. It takes an enormous amount of planning and building to get ready. In the sheer speculation that they might be selected for the Olympics, a giant hockey rink was built.

Lillehammer is an ideal site for these winter events. The mountains have a gentle slope, reminding one of the 1980 Olympics at Lake Placid, New York. They're not like the jagged and rough mountains of Norway's Westlands. It's a popular place for skiers in the winter and hikers in the summer.

Like Americans, Norwegians enjoy their weekends and holidays outdoors. But unlike Americans, they close their shops at noon on Saturdays and many do not open up until Monday afternoon. It's the same way all over western Europe. The question of having department stores open on weekends, much less Sundays, is not an issue in Norway's parliament. They'd rather go off to the mountains. You can see it by looking at them too. They have a healthy look and usually have slim waistlines. Most Norwegians don't lie around on Sundays with TV, newspapers or going out to eat. They go hiking.

Because Norway has so many forests, most houses are built of wood with charming design and colorful decor. You'll see wooden houses in strong and vibrant blues, grays, reds and other colors, but not pastels. It's especially attractive during the long days of winter when there isn't much sunlight. While tile is often used for roof covering (icicles don't hang from tile), some roofs are covered with thin overlapping sheets of slate. I've seen huge slabs of slate along the Sus River in Hattfjeldal, near the Arctic Circle.

Visitors to Lillehammer will want to visit Maihaugen (May Hill), an outdoor museum with one of the finest collections of folk art. Founded in 1887 by Anders Sandvig, a dentist, this ninety-acre open-air museum has more than one hundred buildings from the seventeenth and eighteenth centuries which show what life was like in those times. A stave church from the thirteenth century is also a part of the collection.

Two Nobel Prize winners come from the Lillehammer community. One of these was Sigrid Undset, famed for her novels of the medieval period. The other was Bjørnstjerne Bjørnson, a controversial critic of the nineteenth century who wrote Norway's national anthem, "Ja vi elsker dette landet" ("Yes, we love that land").

Bringing the Olympics to this "fairyland" that some people call "Trolltown" has some risks. Lillehammer will change, but I hope not too much. I like it the way I've seen it. But change has already begun. In 1988, the first "convenience" gas station and fast-food places arrived.

Norwegian author Pål Espolin Johnson (quoted in the Des Moines Register) said, "I feel shaky. I have been against it all the way, though not very actively so. But now, when we have got it, I feel we have got to make the best of it. What will this bring to our little Trolltown?"

The Olympic games are the oldest sports tradition in the world. They began in the vicinity of Mt. Olympus in Greece. This has long been associated with the Greek gods, chief of whom was Zeus. The first records were begun in 776 B.C., though it's believed that the games were probably five hundred years old by that time. Originally these were one-day festivals, but later were extended to five. Now they last several weeks and are international television extravaganzas.

There were other sports festivals in as many as 150 different cities throughout the Mediterranean world during the ancient times. The games were banned by Emperor Theodosius I in 393 A.D., probably because of their pagan religious connections. The temple of Zeus was the largest and most important building at Olympia, the site of the ancient Olympic games, having been built about 460 B.C. It was richly decorated with sculptures and had a large gold and ivory statue of Zeus. There was also a great altar dedicated to Zeus.

In 1887 Baron Pierre de Doubertin of France began the restoration of the Olympic games and the International Olympic Committee was founded in 1894. Two years later the first games were held in Athens. Thirteen nations sent almost three hundred athletes to participate in forty-two events of ten sports. The Lillehammer event will mark the hundredth anniversary of the modern Olympics.

The Winter Olympic Games were approved in 1924 and the first games were held in France with sixteen events. Oslo held Norway's first Olympics in 1952. Not many Olympic watchers expected Norway to be awarded the 1994 event and some international politics played into it. Sweden also made a bid. The Soviet Union was a key factor in choosing Norway because Sweden and Russia were having disputes over Russian submarines invading on Swedish waters. The Swedish protests drew Soviet reprisal.

One of the main changes in the modern Olympics is the participation of women. That would never have happened in the days of ancient Greece. Norway's Sonja Heine held the figure skating crown for ten years (1927-1936). She also made a few Hollywood movies, but it's agreed she was better on ice. In the early days of winter sports, even before summer and winter games were separated, Scandinavians often won the majority of first prizes. That's no longer true. Other countries, Switzerland, France, the USA and the USSR, have been in keen competition. For a complete record of the modern Olympic events and contestants, see the Encyclopedia Britannica.

How does author Pål Espolin Johnson now feel about the Olympics coming to Lillehammer? He has since written, "A good night's sleep and I feel somewhat excited about this."

Minot, North Dakota, has a special interest in the 1994 Olympics. The "father of modern skiing," Sondre Norheim (1825-1897) emigrated from Morgedal in Norway to Denbigh, North Dakota, about 25 miles east of Minot, where he lived the last nine years of his life. He was posthumously inducted into the Høstfest's Scandinavian-American Hall of Fame in 1985. The Olympic torch will surely either be lit in Morgedal near his statue or will make a stop there in respect to his great achievements on skis. There is also a statue of Norheim in the Scandinavian Heritage Park in Minot. Another Norwegian skier of fame was John "Snowshoe" Thompson (1827-1876) who carried mail over the Sierras before the Pony Express. (See *The Scandinavian World*, Chapter 23.)

Now is the time to plan on attending the Winter Olympics in Lillehammer. You're in luck if you have relatives or friends that can put you up. Why not invite them to America for the Høstfest. They will be sure to return the hospitality. Summer or winter, Lillehammer is one of the world's delights.

Olympic ski jumper.

CHAPTER 28

Hans Nielsen Hauge And 'Liberation Theology'

T HE STRUGGLE OF THE working classes to break free from economic and political oppression has always been a part of human history. Most such attempts have failed either because of inadequate preparation or from brutal repression by the oppressors. Peasant movements, slave uprisings and social justice movements are not new, but they have received much greater attention in the twentieth century.

One would not ordinarily identify the Norwegian religious reformer, Hans Nielsen Hauge (1771-1824), with "Liberation Theology" of Latin America today. But there are some interesting points of comparison which may come as a surprise to the people who look upon Hauge as their folk hero as well as religious leader.

Liberation Theology emphasizes social justice, freedom from economic and political oppression, and calls for giving power rather than charity to the oppressed. This is in contrast to the classic Christian tradition of concern for liberation from sin and fear of death. Liberation Theology isn't satisfied with better things to come in the spiritual realm. It wants full freedom in the present secular order. It wants a piece of pie now, not "pie in the sky by and by."

Sometimes Liberation Theology is confused with Marxist Communism because both claim to be concerned about the liberation of the oppressed lower classes. There have been times when Christians of this persuasion have made common cause with Communism, just as the Danish Underground did in World War II to oppose the Nazis. But once the revolution took place, Marxism created a new class of capitalists, as Milovan Djilas wrote in his book *The New Class — An Analysis of the Communist System* (1957).

While Liberation Theology is politically popular in the Third World, especially Latin America, it's also an ideological force behind the Civil Rights Movement in America and the opposition against apartheid in

110

South Africa. The Feminist Movement and concern for the poor white also employs the dynamics of Liberation Theology. Liberation theologians claim that their goal is to liberate the oppressors from their need to oppress.

How does Hans Nielsen Hauge relate to Liberation Theology? I'm indebted to Rev. Kenn Nilsen of Jericho, Vermont, for calling this to my attention in an article he wrote for the Trinity Seminary Review (Columbus, Ohio) Fall 1987. Hauge was an activist who believed that Christians ought to be involved in the political process.

That's in contrast to traditional Lutheran quietism, or the belief that the church shouldn't offer direction or criticism to the affairs of state. Hauge became involved in community life and this got him into trouble with the bishops and sheriffs in Norway. It cost him both imprisonment and health, but the movement he started changed Norway to this day and strongly influenced the political views of the immigrants in America.

Hauge was influenced by the pietist movement identified with two German church leaders, Philipp Jakob Spener (1635-1705) and August Hermann Francke (1663-1727). Its goal was to fill the moral and social vacuum following the Thirty Years War (1618-1648) with a theology of the heart rather than the head, and was a challenge for moral integrity and care for one's neighbor.

Hauge was a self-educated farmer from southeastern Norway. He was a hard worker and gifted at manual skills. He also had a good business head. His outstanding skill was as a communicator. When Hauge talked, people listened. He was not a shouting sensationalist, but a serious and quiet conversationalist who drew heart-felt responses out of people. At age twenty-five, while working in the field, he was overcome by a deep spiritual conviction, and he believed that it was his life's calling to preach the gospel to all Norway.

There was no lack of religion or preaching in Norway when Hauge began his travels. But the state church pastors educated in Copenhagen during the "Enlightment" period tended to intellectualize the gospel, including the explaining away of biblical miracles. Some of the sermons preached at the time were entitled, "How to Grow Potatoes," "On Vaccination," and "Love of the Fatherland." A widening gulf grew up between the clergy and the people. When Hauge appeared, the people recognized him as one who spoke with authority.

Hauge's social ideas wouldn't satisfy a liberation theologian today, but they were radical in Norway during his time. He was a firm believer that the church was a people called by God and not an hierarchical structure. More than that, Hauge believed the church was made up of members to be equally valued. This meant that the rich farmer and his poor tenant were to be treated as brothers. He even believed that people should share all their worldly goods. This didn't sit well with the upper-classes in Norway. Most Norwegians were poor. The good government jobs were filled by Danes and Germans who were wealthy friends of the king in Copenhagen. Hauge naively believed that the ruling classes were as concerned about the need for social reform as he was.

Once his eyes were opened to the entrenched self-interests of the ruling class, Hauge wrote: "The worldly minded have become rich and powerful in the world, and by their wicked wisdom have made the good people their slaves while they themselves live in luxury, splendor, and sensuality." He further wrote, "we must encourage the weak." How? Hauge believed that cultivating the soil was the most honorable occupation. This way one did not oppress one's neighbor to gain a living.

Hauge was one of Norway's earliest folk leaders. But he was different from the revolutionaries. He believed that "if individuals, parishes, and states would deal in love with everyone and try to serve them, then peace would be established. All people could use their gifts with diligence to earn their daily bread. No one would have to rob or beg. No one need remain in idleness and ignorance. Everyone would have enough to do."

He started a paper mill and trained farmers in the skills of the business. A part of the daily schedule was Bible study and devotional meditation. The profits were shared. He also started a brick factory to benefit the workers. During the English blockade of Norway, the authorities had to let him out of jail so he could build a salt factory. When it was completed, he was put back in prison.

How was Hauge's work like the modern liberation movements? Both claim a biblical basis in their concern for the poor. Both criticized the civil and religious authorities for their neglect of the poor. Like Hauge,

Gustavo Gutierrez, a leading liberation theologian from Peru, emphasizes "doing" theology rather than just "reflecting" on it. But there is one major difference. Hauge was "non-violent," while the Third World movement recognizes degrees of violence to obtain its goals.

Nilsen states "the irony is that the thrust of Hauge's work is now more likely to be embraced and appreciated by Roman Catholics in Central and South America than by Protestants in North America." While Nilsen cites no direct linkages between these two movements, they have a lot in common and we haven't seen the end of them yet.

Hans Nielsen Hauge

113

CHAPTER 29

Stoughton's 'Syttende Mai'
Celebration

WHEREVER THERE ARE NORWEGIANS, there will also be a "Syttende Mai" (pronounced SIT-tende MY) celebration. This simply means "May 17th" and it's the day which commemorates Norway's constitution of 1814.

Some people refer to it as "Independence Day," but this was short-lived wishful thinking by some signers of the constitution. No nation recognized their self-proclaimed independence and before the year was over, Norway was forced by its neighbors to elect Sweden's king as their ruler. In return, he promised to respect the new constitution, with a few changes. This gave Norway considerably more self-determination than they'd had under the rule of Danish kings. Denmark didn't get a constitution until 1849.

The Norwegians clung to their constitution, modelled after the French constitution of 1791 and the American constitution of 1787 with some additional ideas from English law. They made some revisions along the way to their full independence of 1905. However, they did have more freedom under Swedish rule than they'd had under Denmark, for the Danish kings had no constitution at the time and made laws as they pleased.

Stoughton, Wisconsin, was founded in 1847 by a Vermont Yankee named Luke Stoughton who built a dam and sawmill on Catfish River. I'm indebted to Eugene and Beatrice Kalland of Stoughton for much of my information on the community. They're active at the Stoughton Historical Museum. Beatrice is also the president of the Wisconsin State Rosemaling Association. We visited at the Nordic Fest in Decorah, Iowa, in 1988.

Stoughton is located just fifteen miles southeast of Madison and has a population of 7,600. The first Norwegians arrived in Dane County in 1839 in the Koshkonong community a few miles to the northeast of where the city was established. In his book *Normaendene i Amerika*

(Norsemen in America), Martin Ulvestad, in 1906, referred to this as the "first and best known Norsk settlement in America."

The Koshkonong community attracted a large number of Norwegian settlers. One of the first things they did was to build churches. Among the well known pastors who ministered there were Herman Amberg Preus and J. W. C. Dietrichson. The Norwegian Synod and Luther College in Decorah had much of their early support and leadership from these congregations. They also had the distinction of electing one of their people as the first Norwegian in the Wisconsin legislature, Gunnulf Tollefsen in 1868. Knut Nelson, the first Norwegian to be elected a governor in America, also grew up in the community. Besides serving as Minnesota's chief executive, he also was elected to both the U.S. House of Representatives and Senate.

At the turn of the century, Stoughton was the home of the famous Mandt wagon factory, where up to 35,000 wagons a year were made. They also had ten passenger trains daily, with hourly connections to Madison and the nearby resorts. They advertised that "labor troubles are unknown, rents and living expenses reasonable and surroundings healthy and wholesome." (See *The Scandinavian World*, Chapter 21.)

It's no wonder then that these Stoughton Norwegians are proud of their heritage and celebrate with colorful pageantry and emotional fervor. The celebration is held on the closest weekend to "Syttende Mai." They have a king and queen for the celebration, as well as junior royalty. They claim that Norse ancestry is not required for being chosen as royalty, but my guess is that most of them are.

The Stoughton Hall of Fame also inducts new members at the Syttende Mai event. In 1987, the 140th anniversary of the city's founding, Dr. Michael Iversen (1861-1929) was chosen. A native of Norway, Iversen was the founder of the Stoughton Hospital. Before coming to America in 1891, he'd studied medicine in both Norway and Germany. His fame as a highly skilled surgeon spread far from Stoughton. Way back in 1896, he operated on a six-year-old boy who was born blind. The newspaper story reported that he could "now see perfectly with both eyes."

The Chamber of Commerce sponsors a trip to Norway for two as the "grand prize" of the festival. Of course there is food. Not only the restaurants, but special food stands are set up in the streets. You wouldn't need to ask if they have lutefisk, lefse and lots of coffee. Rosemaling is also a favorite event.

Besides these they have folk dancing, arts and crafts, a quilt show, a canoe race, a "Syttende Mai Run" of twenty miles beginning at the state capitol and ending at downtown Stoughton. The people of Stoughton love parades and even have a youth parade. Over one hundred entries participate, including the local chapter of SADD (Students Against Drunk Driving). Representatives of their sister city in Norway, Gjovik, also ride in the parade.

Concerts, worship services with Norwegian music and liturgy (the sermon, however, is in English), and a costume show are part of the program. Stoughton High School even has a Norwegian Dancer's group which entertains with up to five performances. The high school Madrigal Singers also sing a concert of Norwegian music, as well as the Grieg Chorus. They have some extra fun with their "Ugliest Troll Contest." The "village theatre" which puts on several performances of a play with a Norwegian theme. They hold the raffle drawing on the trip to Norway at the very end of the last day. That keeps the crowd. The local Sons of Norway gets into the act too with food services, besides helping out all over town.

My earliest acquaintance with Stoughton came in the late 1950s, through the Skaalen Sunset Home, a highly rated nursing home. Two friends, Arne Bjorke of Rugby and Keith Anderson of New Rockford, have been administrators. The Skaalen Home chooses their own king and queen for the event.

The whole state recognizes Syttende Mai. The Governor makes an annual proclamation recognizing all Norwegian communities in Wisconsin and the constitution of 1814. The proclamation reads: "We are pleased to salute all Wisconsin citizens of Norwegian heritage and join them in celebration of their honored traditions during this rich, colorful, cultural festival weekend."

For those who can't be in Stoughton for this event next May, you'd find the Historical Museum an interesting stop at any time. Stoughton is easy to find if you should be driving to Chicago from the north. It's just off Interstate 90 south of Madison. Stoughton is an example of a community that loves the New World but still carries a torch in their heart for their heritage in the Old World.

Luke Stoughton, founder of Stoughton, Wisconsin.

CHAPTER 30

Favorite Hymns
Of Scandinavia

MY SON, MICHAEL, while a student at Wartburg Seminary in Dubuque, Iowa, asked me, "Why don't you write a story about Scandinavian hymns?" It sounded like a good idea since the Scandinavian hymns have a distinct character and have been a powerful influence on the life of those northern people.

I first heard these hymns sung by my father, Oscar (1903-1969), who had a beautiful tenor voice. Listening to him sing hymns and nursery rhymes while I sat on his lap as a small child is how I came to appreciate good music. The hymns were sung mostly in Norwegian. The tunes and lyrics still ring in my soul. One of the reasons that they've become so much a part of me is that they were sung to the melodic folk tunes.

Scandinavia was geographically isolated from much of the world until modern times. Now, of course, there are hardly any places that aren't heavily influenced by what is going on in the rest of the world. It was in this setting of isolation that some of the world's most beautiful folk music originated. Fortunately, many of these hymns were collected into hymnals so that we still have access to them, even if most of them aren't sung any more.

The Reformation is credited with introducing the congregational singing of hymns first in Germany. This spread to Sweden through the Petri brothers, Olavus and Laurentius. Sons of a blacksmith, they studied at Wittenberg University and brought back many of Luther's hymns to Sweden. Their fiery zeal for the new learning in Germany was not without risk, however. They might have been massacred in the Stockholm "bloodbath" of 1520, if some Germans in the city had not saved them. When the Swedish revolution of 1523 placed Gustavus Vasa on the throne, the Petri brothers were given important positions in both church and state. Most of their hymns, however, are translations of German and Latin originals.

Hymnody was given a great boost by the pietist movements in the Scandinavian countries. This was an appeal to a religion of the heart that emphasized "living" the faith. E. E. Ryden, in his book *The Story of our Hymns* (1930), called Johan Olof Wallin (1779-1839) "Scandinavia's greatest hymnist and perhaps the foremost in the entire Christian Church during the Nineteenth century." Born into poverty and with poor health, Wallin earned a Ph. D. at Uppsala University when he was 24. His poetic talent produced 128 original hymns, plus 23 translations and 178 revisions in the Swedish *Psalm Book* of 1819. He has been called "David's harp in the Northland."

A well known hymn of Swedish background is "Children of the Heavenly Father" (Tryggare Kan Ingen Vare) written by Lina Sandell Berg (1832-1903). She wrote 650 hymns. Her father, a parish pastor, drowned when the ship on which they were travelling gave a sudden lurch and he fell overboard. She discovered her comfort in writing hymns. Her hymns were popularized by Jenny Lind, known as the "Swedish Nightingale."

Another Swedish hymn which has become popular in America is "How Great Thou Art" (Den Store Gud), written by Carl Boberg (1850-1940). Inspiration for the hymn came one evening when he was struck by the beauty of nature and the sound of church bells. The Swedes have popularized a Christmas hymn of German origin so that almost everyone thinks it's a Swedish carol, "When Christmas Morn is Dawning" (Når Juldagsmorgon Glimmar).

Denmarks's three most famous hymn writers were all bishops. Hans Brorson (1694-1764) wrote a Christmas hymn that I remember from earliest childhood "Your Little Ones, Dear Lord, Are We" (Her Kommer Dine Arme Smaa). I still get a thrill out of singing it in Danish each Christmas. Brorson wrote the best loved of all the hymns of Norway, "Den Store Hvide Flok." We use it so frequently in the original that it's hardly sung in the translation, "Behold, a Host." The music, based on a Norse folk tune from Heddal (home of Norway's largest stave church), was arranged by Edvard Grieg (1843-1907), Norway's most famous musician.

While visiting the St. Magnus' Cathedral in Odense on the island of Fyen, I saw the statue of Thomas Hansen Kingo (1634-1703), the first

119

great hymn writer of Denmark. Two of his hymns, "On My Heart Imprint Your Image" and "All Who Believe and are Baptized" are sung in many American churches today. His paternal family had come from Scotland, as had Edvard Grieg's.

The greatest hymnwriter of Denmark was Nikolai Severin Fredrik Grundtvig (1783-1872). Two of his Christmas hymns are sung every year, "The Bells of Christmas" (Det Kimer nu til Julefest) and "O How Beautiful the Sky" (Dejlig er den Himmel Blaa). Of the one thousand hymns he wrote, two of them frequently sung today are "Built on a Rock" (Kirken den er et Gammelt Hus) and "O Day Full of Grace" (Den Signede Dag). Grundtvig was also famous for his work of establishing "folk schools" which were forerunners to public education in Denmark.

Iceland's most famous hymnwriter was Valdimar Briem (1848-1930). He is remembered in America by his hymn "How Marvellous God's Greatness." One of Iceland's hymns which became its national anthem, "O Gud Vors Lands" (O God of our Land), was written by Matthias Jochumsson (1835-1920).

Finland's most celebrated musician, Jean Sibelius, is best known for his "Finlandia." It's the tune used for the hymn, "Thee God, We Praise." Among the Finnish hymns used in America are J. L. Runeberg's (1804-1877) "I Lift My Eyes Unto Heaven;" "Your Kingdom Come, O Father" by Kauko-Veikko Tamminen (1882-1946); and "Lost in the Night" from an unknown secular source. The Finns have contributed many more tunes to which hymns have been set.

Norway's mountains, valleys and fjords have been an inspiration to many musicians, including hymn writers. The best known Christmas carol from Norway is "Jeg er saa glad" (I Am So Glad Each Christmas Eve) written by Marie Wexelsen (1832-1911). Two of the greatest names in Norwegian church music are M. B. Landstad (1802-1880) and Ludvig M. Lindemann (1812-1887). Landstad's hymnals were found in nearly every trunk that came with Norwegians to America. The hymn for which he is best known in America is "I Know of a Sleep in Jesus' Name." Lindemann's original family name was Madsen, which may have been Danish. His grandfather, a physician in Trondheim, changed his name to Lindemann (German). This was a popular thing to do about two hundred years ago. (I have discovered people of Fiske ancestry in

Norway who changed their name to Fische.) Lindemann wrote the music for many hymns including "Come to Calvary's Holy Mountain," "Built on a Rock," "Jesus Priceless Treasure" and "Hallelujah! Jesus Lives!"

Besides "Den Store Hvide Flok," hymns that I remember my father singing to me as a small child include "I Himmelen, I Himmelen" (In Heaven Above) and "Velt Alle Dine Veie." The words of the latter still speak to me, "Thy way and all thy sorrows, give thou into his hand. His gracious care unfailing, who doth the heavens command. Their course and path he giveth to clouds and air and wind. A way thy feet may follow; he, too, for thee will find." It's been over two decades since my father last sang among us. His love for Scandinavian hymnody has been an enriching legacy.

There was an enduring quality to these hymns and we'd do well to take a second look at them today. And if given a chance, many of the tunes would keep singing in our minds and hearts forever.

CHAPTER 31

Carl Larsson's
Home In Sweden

I T'S A "MIRACLE" how a talented artist can take what is plain and ordinary and transform it into a thing of exquisite beauty. Carl Larsson (1853-1919) was such an artist. Carl and his wife Karin took a small house "laying bare on a heap of slag" and turned it into one of the best known and most beloved homes in Sweden, if not "of all times," according to Ulf Hard, author of *Carl Larsson's Home*.

It was in 1889, when migrations to the New World from Sweden were claiming most of the country's attention, that the Larssons moved into a house which they named "Little Hyttnas" (cottage) in the village of Sundborn in the province of Dalarna in the central part of the country. The house was a gift from Karin's father. It had just two rooms, an attic and an attached woodshed. Over the next two decades many rooms were added, and it still has not lost its quaint appearance of comfort and warmth, but no one would have recognized it.

Nineteenth century Sweden was an underdeveloped country and its capital, Stockholm, was a relatively small city with many poor neighborhoods. It's a wonder that a boy born in Gamla Stan (Old Town) should become the outstanding representative of the "new art." I've visited the community twice. Today it's a model of cleanliness and beauty. The old buildings have been renovated in magnificent style.

Carl's father has been described as a "ne'er-do'well" who abandoned his wife and family when Carl was a small child. His mother supported the family by washing and ironing. They were forced to move into a slum-section in the East End of Stockholm. Things were so bad that Larsson wrote: "If I say that the people who lived in these houses were swine, I am doing those animals an injustice. Misery, filth and vice — every kind of vice flourished there — seethed and smouldered cozily; they were corroded and rotten, body and soul." He later wrote that he could remember nothing of happiness from his childhood. No wonder that he loved the peaceful woods of Dalarna.

When only thirteen, Larsson was encouraged by his teacher in the "poor school" to apply to the school where his maternal grandfather had studied art. Because of his background in poverty, he was shy and handicapped by an inferiority complex. After about three years, his shyness wore off and his artistic ability began to blossom. It was when he was editor of the school paper that his talent was discovered. He was hired by a humor magazine to draw. It wasn't long before he was earning a respectable salary. Then he supported his mother and a younger brother who was also artistically talented.

It wasn't long before Carl was travelling all over Sweden and even abroad as a sketching reporter. It soon became noted that wherever anything of importance happened, two people could be counted on to be present, Larsson and King Oscar II. When one of the students who had been a great inspiration to Larsson in Sweden died in 1877, he went to Paris with a heavy heart. Going to France was the fashionable thing to do for art students in those days. France was in low morale too, having been disastrously defeated by Germany in the war of 1870-1871. Larsson travelled to France several times before finding his niche. On one of his return trips to Sweden he did art illustrations for August Strindberg, a famous playwright.

Larsson continued to be afflicted with depression. A turning point in his life seems to have been when he made new friends at Gretz-Armain-villiers, a village outside of Paris where Scandinavians used to get together. He also made the acquaintance of some of Sweden's finest future artists there. Grez was a quaint village "full of charm," with an ancient arched bridge, a medieval church with moss-covered walls, and the ruins of a castle. Stone walls in front of houses, gardens with flights of stone steps and trellises with grape vines, plus fruit trees, made the village an artist's paradise.

It was at Gretz that Carl met Karin Bergoo, who had come from a well-to-do Swedish home with a liberal outlook on life, evidenced by the fact that she was allowed to be educated as an artist. They were married in 1883.

Larrson described the site of their house in Sundborn as having just a few small birch trees and some lilacs, plus a potato patch. Having limited means, they improved it by putting away extra savings whenever they could. With the help of some village carpenters, a blacksmith, a bricklayer and a painter, they put together a house which has become part of Sweden's pride. At first, it was just a summer house, but eventually, it became their permanent home. Today it is known as "Carl Larsson's Home" and has become a noted tourist attraction.

Carl and Karin were internationally oriented, but retained their romantic views of Sweden. Besides Paris, Carl had also gained artistic impressions in Berlin, Vienna and London. While Carl became famous as a painter, Karin gained her fame for weaving and embroidery.

The rooms in the Carl Larsson home look small to visitors today, but Larsson's painting had the effect of making them look larger than they were. Simplicity marked the interior planning. The main additions to the original log house began in 1890. It included an art studio with pictures to the front, and a large fireplace which added elegance. By 1900, more space was need for the studio, so the original one was turned into a family room where Karin could do her work while the children did woodwork or played.

Sundborn became their permanent home in 1901. The woodshed was torn down and a two-story addition was added to make room for eleven persons. In 1912, a cottage was attached to the studio for the display of paintings. Author Ulf Hard claims that their home "became unique and exemplary and has so remained" as "a vital part of the culture at the turn of the century." Since 1943, the buildings have been administered by a family society. Above the door there is a wood carving, commonly done in Scandinavia, which reads: "Welcome to this house, to Carl Larsson and his spouse."

We're fortunate to have several books on Carl Larsson. In addition to the one on his house, he wrote six others. The best known are *Carl Larsson — On the Sunny Side* (1910) and *The World of Carl Larsson*. *On the Sunny Side* contains pictures of his paintings of the rooms in the house, about the children. Flowers were everywhere in the home. It reads as an autobiography and a story of life in the home. I have never run across anything quite so charming. *The World of Carl Larsson* deals with his art works, which are displayed in museums around the world.

I'm always amazed at human potential popping up in unexpected places. Here was a poor boy who became Sweden's greatest painter and illustrator of all times and was acclaimed internationally. Known as the "sunshine man," Larsson occupies a place in Swedish consciousness which is shared by no other artist.

Carl Larsson

CHAPTER 32

Denmark's
Famous Porcelain

ONE OF THE ARTISTIC benefits that came to me when marrying a Danish wife was to discover the beautiful Christmas plates made in Denmark. They're for sale in gift shops all over America, as well as in Scandinavia. There's quite a story behind these plates and the other porcelain products made in Copenhagen.

Two manufacturers, Royal Copenhagen and Bing & Grøndahl, are the best known. We have some of both, as well as a number of Porsgrund plates from Norway. The Lutheran Brotherhood home office in Minneapolis has a complete set of the Danish Christmas plates on display, which is open for the public's view.

Originally, the arts and crafts were the special privilege of royalty and the very rich. The Danish royalty became seriously interested in art works during the reign of Christian IV (1588-1648). He worked feverishly to promote national industry and to improve Denmark's economy by producing more goods for export. The king was concerned about his country's balance of trade deficit. He believed that the best way to improve the economy was to make Denmark competitive in world trade. Christian IV was never successful in war, but he was one of the best builders Denmark has ever had on its throne. You can see his statue in front of the Vor Frelsers (Our Savior's) Cathedral in Oslo. He rebuilt it after Oslo had been destroyed by a fire.

The first factory to produce decorative earthenware was established in 1722 by Johann Wolff of Holstein, a Danish province now a part of Germany. The project was financed by King Frederik IV. Even then the color of the manufactured products was blue, as is the dominant color today in Danish porcelain. The color probably was borrowed from Dutch stoneware. The early patterns were influenced by the German artists at Meissen. There were also Japanese and Chinese influences in the designs. The following year Wolff went to Germany to hire more potters. Then he absconded from Denmark with his stock of cobalt dye to establish a factory in Sweden.

Though disappointed, the Danes didn't give up. Several attempts were made, some of which were short-lived. They induced more German potters to come to Denmark. It was quite common in those days for enterprising Germans to go to Denmark to look for work. Many of them ended up working for the king, both in Denmark and Norway. One of the challenges was finding the right clay. Kaolin deposits, a white clay, were found on the island of Bornholm. It took years to perfect their products to the satisfaction of the king. Besides the right quality clay, they also had to discover how to put on a glaze with graceful decoration. A. G. Moltke, a powerful patron of the arts, hired a French modeller who brought the desired results. It wasn't until 1780 that the Danish porcelain business turned a profit. That year they produced 100,000 pieces.

To begin with, the porcelain products were a royal monopoly. Members of the royal house were also among the best customers. The porcelain was often purchased as gifts given to foreign dignitaries. It was common for the donor to have large vases with his own portrait on the porcelain as gifts.

Whereas the Meissen works in Germany were the pace-setters in the eighteenth century, the Danes came into international prominence in the late nineteenth century. The first public showing of these porcelain products was at the Nordic Exhibition in Copenhagen in 1888. At the World Exhibition of 1889 in Paris they won the grand prize. In 1900, Bing & Grøndahl (organized in 1853) also won the grand prize.

Philipp Schou (1832-1922), an engineer who was also a brilliant businessman and a member of parliament, was a successful promoter of Royal Copenhagen after it was sold to private industry in 1864. Under his leadership, which began in 1882, many changes rapidly occurred. He modernized the factory buildings and recruited younger staff. His leadership helped bring Danish porcelain into international recognition.

Two of my favorite Christmas plates are the 1972 Bing & Grøndahl and the 1982 Royal Copenhagen. The Bing & Grøndahl plate is entitled "Christmas in Greenland." It shows nine dogs pulling a sled, being driven by two men returning to the village on Christmas eve, the sky being lighted by the Christmas star. The 1982 Royal Copenhagen plate is entitled "Waiting for Christmas." It shows a little girl looking longingly out the window of her warm home. The Teddy Bear is on the floor, the tree is decorated and a rabbit is sitting out in the cold wintry snow. The expressions on both of them are so life-like and friendly.

What makes Danish porcelain so beautiful? It's a combination of the raw materials used, the exquisite glaze which covers them and the high quality and technique of the artists who apply the decorative patterns.

Originally, the porcelain was primarily used for dinner services. Later, a full line of vases and figurines were added. Because the Danes have had such a love of Christmas, Bing & Grøndahl started to produce a Christmas plate in 1895. Each year a new and distinct pattern is manufactured. The mold is destroyed after the production is completed. Royal Copenhagen followed with their own design of a Christmas plate in 1908. You can easily tell the difference between these two lines because Royal Copenhagen has a darkly bordered edge. The patterns on these plates include landscapes, churches and Christmas scenes.

Other plates have been added. Mors Dag (Mother's Day) plates are now a regular product of these lines. They also manufactured a special plate for the 1972 Olympic Games in Munich and another for the 1976 bicentennial of American independence. Danes are greatly fascinated by America.

We discovered a shop on Gaagaden (Walking Street) in Copenhagen named "Chicago" which has a large selection of Danish porcelain products at competitive prices. In addition to some Christmas plates, we also purchased the Olympic plate. The most economical way to buy the plates is to go to Copenhagen. Their prices are lower than in any other place we found in Scandinavia. But if you are not going there (or, having a friend pick some pieces up for you), the best thing is to look them over in a local gift shop. They are rather expensive, but if you really like these exquisite pieces of art, you may decide they are well worth the price. Besides, you'll have a status symbol once enjoyed only by royalty and the wealthy.

I am not an expert connoisseur of the arts. I can only judge by my feelings. But I have to admit that Danish porcelain appeals to my eye and heart. They've done more with the color blue than I could ever have imagined. And since blue is one of the much loved colors of Scandinavia, I suppose that I've got a prejudice for those shades of color. The next time you go into a gift shop or Scandinavian specialty store, ask to see the Danish plates, vases and figurines. I'll wager that you'll fall in love with them too. In my case, I fell first in love with a Dane.

CHAPTER 33

The Movies Of
Ingmar Bergman

A S A YOUNG CHILD, I was fascinated with movies, even though I didn't get to see many. I remember going to town Saturday nights at Colfax, thirty-five miles southwest of Fargo. There'd be free movies, the silent kind, with the words printed below the pictures. During the intermission periods, dixie cups of ice cream were sold which had pictures of movie stars under the covers. I had a collection of them. We'd trade them as baseball cards are exchanged today. I didn't see a "talkie" until I was ten years old at a theatre in Wahpeton, thirty miles away. It starred Shirley Temple in *Wee Willie Winkie* and took place in India. I still like to watch it. Movies made a big impression on my youthful mind.

Ernest Ingmar Bergman was born July 14, 1918, in Uppsala, Sweden. His father was a Lutheran pastor who became chaplain to the royal family. Reared in strict discipline which included corporal punishment and isolation, Bergman found his escape in movies. He saw his first movie at age six.

While staying at his grandmother's house in Dalarna, Bergman became acquainted with the projectionist at the local theatre. He was allowed to sit alongside of the projector and watch movies. When only nine years old, young Ingmar obtained a magic lantern and projected light on cut-outs which cast shadows on a screen. He'd do his own narrating while his younger sister was a captive audience.

At nineteen, Ingmar entered the University of Stockholm to study art history and literature, and there he directed a campus drama group. After a bitter argument with his parents, he left the parsonage home, dropped out of school, and went to work as an errand boy at the Royal Opera House. At age twenty-four, he got a job with the Swedish Film Industry (Svensk Filmindustri) which today produces his movies.

Bergman did so well that he won the Grand Prix at the Cannes Film Festival in France in 1946. This is the world's most famous place for reviewing movies. If the Cannes critics give a good rating, it usually assures a success at the box office. Not all his early movies went so well, but he made his mark on the industry and worked harder than ever to make good.

The early Bergman movies were black and white. *Smiles of a Summer Night* won the prize for "Most Poetic Humor" at Cannes in 1956. It's the story about a Swedish lawyer and his mixed up love life. His son was a theology student preparing for the ministry who became quite confused between his concern for "virtue" and his father's libertine life. It's a genuine soap opera with a far more interesting plot than you'll find on TV. It was a satirical spoof on the morals and social conventions of his day.

The following year Bergman made it big in Cannes again with *The Seventh Seal*. The title, taken from the Apocalypse of St. John (Revelation 8), is an allegory on man's relation to God and how he tries to cope with death. Max von Sydow played the part of a knight recently returned from the Crusades in the Middle East. Having participated in that terrible debacle of death and destruction, he returned to Sweden in search for the meaning of life. Throughout the play, the knight plays chess with the devil for his life. Only after the devil, in the disguise of a priest during confession, prodded him to reveal his secret for winning, did he lose. The central theme is the dichotomy between God in his silence, appearing to be our enemy, and yet self-proclaimed as the creator and lover of life.

Since it was the Middle Ages, everything had to do with religion. Will Durant described that time as "the age of faith." The real struggle was for faith. The knight wants the devil to tell him what God may have told him about faith. As usual, the devil lied and he learned nothing. Several scenarios go on simultaneously: The burning of a young girl as a witch, shades of Salem in New England; "flagellants" preaching doom and the end of the world while administering torture to themselves as a way of atoning for their sins; and a travelling actor who got into all kinds of trouble because of religious visions. The movie has a contemporary psychoanalytic twist.

Wild Strawberries (1957) is built around a sequence of dreams filled with death tones by an octogenarian who has flashbacks. The elderly professor travels to Lund, an ancient university city in southern Sweden, to receive an honorary doctorate. This movie won first prize at the Berlin International Film Festival in 1958. In America *Wild Strawberries* was named the best foreign film in 1959 by the National Board of review. Bergman also received an Academy Award nomination in the category of best story and screenplay. The Oscar, however, went to Doris Day and Rock Hudson for their performance of *Pillow Talk*.

Bergman's *The Magician* also reached America in 1959, again starring Max von Sydow. It's the story of a magician who, pretending to be mute, fooled everyone about his identity. After several scrapes with the law, he ended up doing a performance at the palace in Stockholm. Several critics have wondered if this movie was really Bergman's own spiritual autobiography. There are parallels to it in the Passion Play.

The Virgin Spring, also starring Max von Sydow, made the deepest impression on me of any of the Bergman movies I have seen. Set in the piety of the Middle Ages in Sweden, it portrays beautiful country scenes. It has been called his "masterwork," the most lyrical, compassionate and lucid of all his productions. It's heavy stuff and will probably raise your blood pressure and temperature. I don't recommend it for weak hearts. But I've seen nothing which I think better portrays life in medieval Scandinavia. In 1960 it was honored as the best foreign film at the Oscar awards in Hollywood.

These are some of the early Bergman films, all in black and white and all in Swedish. However, the English sub-titles are adequate and if you have some knowledge of any Scandinavian language, you will understand quite a bit of the narrative. Bergman emphasizes acting rather than words in his serious movies. The background music is worth listening to even if you didn't watch the movie. The more recent Bergman movies are in color as well as in English. The best way to see them, especially the older ones, is to find a video shop that has a foreign film section. In the larger cities, you may find Bergman's movies at a theatre.

In 1976, while rehearsing a new production of Strindberg's *Dance of Death* in Stockholm, Bergman was arrested and charged with tax fraud. It took two months before the authorities were satisfied that he was innocent. He was so offended by this experience that he left Sweden to settle in Munich, not returning until December 1977 to accept the

Swedish Academy of Letter's "Great Gold Medal." Only seventeen people have received the award during the twentieth century. The following year he resumed the directorship of the Stockholm Royal Dramatic Theatre. Sweden was grateful for his return and established a prize for excellence in filmmaking to honor him.

Bergman's movies are not for everyone. He's both a showman and a moralist, both comic and serious. One critic describes him as a "film-maker of magic with an evangelical point of view — a Druid captured by Lutheranism." Watching his movies requires thinking and reflection. You won't get bored and need popcorn to stay awake. If you have rigid Victorian manners, you may be offended and find it difficult to watch. But if you can stand it, the plot of these movies will linger in your consciousness for some time. They may even appear in your dreams. I'm looking forward to more of his productions. Bergman's autobiography, *The Magic Lantern* (*Viking Press*, 1988), will fill you in on the other interesting details of his life.

Ingmar Bergman

CHAPTER 34

Vilhjalmer Stefansson —
Arctic Explorer

VIKING BLOOD FLOWED passionately through the veins of Vilhjalmar (VIL-yal-mar) Stefansson. Better known as "Stef," he became one of the world's great Arctic explorers. His parents had emigrated from Iceland to Manitoba in 1877. Vilhjalmar was born at Arnes, November 3, 1879. Baptized William, he changed his name to the Icelandic form, Wilhjalmur, when an adult.

Because a flood brought tragedy to the family in 1880, they moved to a small farm near Mountain, in northeast North Dakota. Two of the children were lost in the floodwaters. Young Stefansson's education was pretty skimpy. School attendance was infrequent, but he read avidly in the Bible, Icelandic sagas and an Icelandic newspaper called *Heimskringla*. His father died when "Stef" was thirteen. To lessen the burden for his mother, he went to live with a married sister and also went out to Montana with an older brother to capture wild horses. These were later sold to farmers in North Dakota. He also grazed sheep in Ramsey County.

In 1898, at age nineteen, Stefansson entered the Preparatory Department at the University of North Dakota. For some unclear reason, he was expelled in 1902. Some people asserted that it was for encouraging students to protest against the administration, but he denied this in his autobiography. It seems more likely that his independent attitude had upset the faculty. (At age fifteen, he had been reading Darwin, Ingersoll and Huxley.) Determined to get an education, he transferred to the University of Iowa, tested out in examinations, and graduated in just one year, 1903. They were impressed with his academic record. Besides taking all the math that UND offered, he studied German, Latin, English, Scandinavian and history. He learned Greek in a year with minimal tutoring.

Stefansson's strong interests were in religion and anthropology. Receiving a scholarship to study theology, he continued his education at Harvard. At the end of a year, he dropped his studies in theology and studied full-time in anthropology. Twenty years later in 1923, at the age of forty-four, he received a master's degree in it.

While at Harvard, Stefansson made two trips to Iceland. In 1905, Harvard sent him on an expedition to the Arctic. This was the turning point in his life. The polar mission was aborted because the supply ship failed to rendezvous, so he lived with an Eskimo family for 18 months and wrote a book about it, *My Life With The Eskimos* (1912). The story was first serialized in *Harper's* magazine. Stefansson's humane side is revealed in his comments about dogs. When treated kindly, he wrote, even the most snarly Huskies became gentle.

Stefansson adapted well to the Arctic regions. He learned the language (Inuit), their survival methods, culture and diet. In 1912, he wrote an article for the *Seattle Daily Times* claiming that he had discovered "blond Eskimos" on Victoria Island. He became quite taken up with them and believed that they were the descendants of early European explorers. He published these findings in the *Literary Digest* and the *Scientific American*. This is still an open question.

From 1913-1918, this hardy Icelandic-American led an expedition financed by the Canadian government to explore more of these northern regions. In 1914, he and two companions lived in the Arctic on floating ice for many months, surviving mainly on meat from polar bears and seals. They discovered several major islands: Lougheed, Borden, Meighen and Brock. For this work, he was recognized by the Royal Geographical Society, the American Geographical Society, the National Geographic Society, and the Philadelphia Geographic Society.

Not everything that Stefansson tried succeeded. His attempt to raise reindeer on Baffin Island failed. There was no lichen for the animals. However, he was an advocate of domesticating muskox, which others have since encouraged. The "Karluk," a refitted whaling ship, met with disaster, being locked in by ice, and drifted to Siberia with a part of his crew and supplies. At another time during his explorations (1921-1924), he claimed the island of Wrangel north of Siberia for Canada. This created an international incident.

After 1918, Stefansson began a career of writing. He made his home in New York City where he developed an Arctic library of 25,000 volumes and 20,000 pamphlets, which was later sold to Dartmouth University in Hanover, New Hampshire. Stefansson also assisted in setting up the University's "Northern Program" as a "living legend-in-residence," being available to students and visitors as a resource in the anthropology of the North.

In 1941, then sixty-one, Stefansson was married to Evelyn Schwartz Baird, who was twenty-seven. She had been on his library staff. They moved to Hanover, New Hampshire, in 1951, where he lived until his death from a stroke on August 26, 1962. They also had a farm near Bethel, Vermont, where they spent a great deal of their time.

Besides being an experienced authority on Arctic exploration, Stefansson had great visions for the future of the Northlands. He was one of the first to suggest a crude-oil pipeline between Norman Wells and a refinery in the Yukon. He was an early promoter of highway building that eventually led to the Alaska Highway of today. However, he did not agree on the routes used for either the pipeline or highway.

Besides research and writing, Stefansson also kept busy in public life. From 1932 to 1945, he was a consultant to Pan American World Airways on planning Arctic routes. During World War II he was an advisor to the United States military as an instructor in Arctic survival techniques. He was also an advocate of submarines travelling under the polar ice cap in order to connect the two great oceans, the Atlantic and the Pacific. On August 1, 1958, the Nautilus dived into the Pacific near Alaska and four days later emerged in the Atlantic near Iceland.

As you might expect, Stefansson was a controversial person. Some people believed he was the "prophet of the North," while others thought of him as "an arrogant charlatan." Another great explorer, Roald Amundsen of Norway, regarded him in the latter terms. Columnist Westbrook Pegler called him a "Commie." His one time colleague, Dr. R. M. Anderson of the University of Iowa referred to him as a "Windjammer," a term describing a Norwegian sailing ship used to train young boys for life on the sea. Anderson was referring to his sense of urgency about mission and impatience with the politicians, administrators and scientists involved in his work.

There is some risk in writing about such an international celebrity because there are many people living today who knew him well and many have written about him. Besides his own voluminous writings, he has several biographers. The most recent is *Stef: A Biography of Vilhjalmur Stefansson, Canadian Arctic Explorer* (1986) by William R. Hunt. It is one of the more sympathetic presentations. Mrs. Iver (Ruth) Iverson of Minot wrote an excellent monograph for a history seminar at Minot State University in 1952 which carefully documents his early lfe. It's in the Minot State University Library.

My reason for writing about Stefansson is that he belongs to the tradition of great Scandinavian polar explorers. I'm always interested in the early beginnings of people who overcame adversity to achieve greatness. There are far too many people sitting around waiting for the "breaks" in life. Stefansson made them happen. It's like the old saying, "the harder I try, the luckier I get." Stefansson continues to be an inspiration to many.

CHAPTER 35

The 'Windjammers'

I RECOGNIZED IT the moment I saw it. Right before my eyes in the Oslo harbor lay the "Windjammer," an ocean-going sailing ship that had gone the way of the dinosaur. Twenty-three years before, in 1954, I had seen the movie *Windjammer* at a theatre in Minneapolis. It was one of those serendipitous things. I had gone to the Mill City for business and discovered the movie playing in a downtown cinema. The fact that it was about Norway and Norwegians attracted me.

The "Windjammer," in this case, was a ship powered by wind that has become a school for Norwegian boys who want to learn the art of sailing. It's a point of pride for these teenagers to be chosen for this experience at sea, even though work on board ship is difficult and can have some risks. But the very thought of it rouses the Viking spirit for adventure that has never left these people of the North. After leaving the Oslo harbor, they sail southwards along the coasts of France and Portugal and follow the southern route across the Atlantic until they reach the eastern shores of America and then sail northwards to make stops at major ports. The visit to New York was always a highlight as many of them have relatives living there. The whole East Coast population of Norwegians gets excited over their arrival and they are entertained royally.

I must admit that I hadn't known of the "Windjammer" until seeing the movie, but curiosity has since moved me to learn more about it. The only use of the term "windhammer" I'd heard as a child was as a jibe about people who were always telling tall tales.

The taunt of "windjammer," however, was probably not so far from the truth about the way steamship sailors referred to these proud sailing vessels. The steamship crews gave them this name because they didn't believe that these "monsters," as they called them, could actually sail. They claimed that they were far too clumsy to sail neatly into

138

the wind, and that they would have to be "jammed" into the billowy gusts.

But the windjammers proved to be worthy competitors to the steam-powered ships for many years. In fact, many people with experience on the sea believe that they are the finest sailing ships ever built. Having acres of sail on their towering masts, they transported uncounted loads of nitrates, guano, coal, grain and lumber to all parts of the world. For about sixty years they gave the steamships a good run for their money. They outsailed them around the Cape Horn (the southern tip of South America) on their way to the west coasts of both Americas, to Australia and other distant ports.

The windjammers were successors to the famous clipper ships that had traversed the seas since the 1830s. Instead of being built of wood and iron as the clippers, the windjammers were constructed of steel and had improved equipment which required a crew of less than thirty, whereas the clippers needed fifty or sixty men while carrying a much smaller load. The windjammers were built up to four hundred feet or more in length, being more than twice as long as the clippers. The windjammer masts had up to five or six large sails and rose up to two hundred feet above the keel. The wire, chains and ropes used on them measured in miles. Even when dry, some of the sails weighed a ton. The "bottom line" for the owners meant more profits.

The windjammer era lasted for about sixty years, from the 1860s into the 1920s. There were attempts to make them profitable during the 1930s, but by that time steam had conquered. Then came the more powerful diesels. Several factors combined to end the windjammer's high place on the sea.

When the United States built the transcontinental railroads, it eliminated much of the need to travel around the tip of South America, which was a major run for the windjammers. When the Panama Canal was built, the steamers had the advantage of being able to go through the canal, whereas the sailing vessels had difficulty with such passages. Yet the windjammers were so cost effective that they lived until the advent of the much faster steam-powered ships. Wars improve technology and that happened in the shipping business too.

THE SCANDINAVIAN ADVENTURE

In their heyday, great pride was taken in the wind-powered vessels as they raced against their own records to shorten the time. In the early days, steamships moved at only about seven knots per hour. The windjammers could travel up to sixteen knots. The clippers could go up to about eighteen. The windjammers had an advantage in bad weather. Steamers ran the danger of having their propellers sheared off, their smoke stacks crushed and their boilers doused with sea water. The windjammers kept right on course.

There were dangers at sea that needed improved equipment and better designed ships. The most serious danger was having the crew washed overboard by high waves. The high waves were estimated to carry over seven hundred tons of water as they hit the deck. The German shipmasters were the first to rig life nets along the sides of the deck when they entered stormy waters. The helmsmen were always in danger on stormy seas, and were sometimes lashed to the deck. Just working the wheel was dangerous enough.

These sturdy ships were also called "floating storage bins." It reminds me of World War II days when some of the aircraft — those of twin tail construction — carrying military cargo were called "flying boxcars." By today's standards these are, however, pretty small.

Competition between countries to move freight the fastest was keen. Two firms excelled. They were the German firm of Reederei F. Laeisz and the French Antoine-Dominique Bordes et Fils. They kept breaking each others records. The cargo could also be a problem, especially nitrate hauled from Chile for fertilizer in Europe. It was extremely heavy, flammable and noxious.

After World War I, the Versailles Treaty deprived Germany of its magnificent merchant fleet, both steam and sail. This blow to the country's economy probably contributed to the depression which aided Hitler's rise to power. The German ships in the American harbors at America's entry into the war (April 6, 1917) were impounded and sold. The German windjammers were given Indian names and sold to companies that tried to make a business of hauling lumber from the Pacific Northwest to Australia. Though the windjammers were bought for a low price, the new owners went bankrupt. Gustaf Erikson bought the best of the windjammers for $12,000 after their failure in America and sailed it to Sweden.

The windjammers are now extinct except as museum pieces and for the one in the Oslo harbor. Though it is used as a school for training young sailers, look for it in the Oslo harbor if you visit there. You just might be lucky enough to see it when it's in port. Then remember those "thrilling days of yesteryear" when they sailed the seven seas in majesty.

Windjammer

CHAPTER 36

Edvard Grieg
Revisited

NO ONE HAS DONE MORE to popularize the folk music of Norway than Edvard Hagerup Grieg (1843-1907). No one has written a better book on Grieg than Finn Benestad and Dag Schjelderup-Ebbe. It was translated by William H. Halverson and Leland B. Sateren, and published by the University of Nebraska Press (1988). The book itself is a work of art with 441 large pages on high quality paper. There are 404 illustrations and many interesting notes printed on the outside columns. Also included are many musical scores. For anyone who would take music history seriously, or would know all there is known about the composer and his times, this is the book: *Edvard Grieg: The Man and the Artist*.

The name Grieg comes from the MacGregor clan in Scotland. Originally Grig, from MacGregor, it was changed to Grieg. Edvard's great-grandfather, Alexander Grieg, immigrated with his wife to Bergen, where some of the family had settled as early as 1600. There are some claims that he was a fugitive from the gallows. Edvard's paternal grandmother was Danish, the daughter of a violinist from Aalborg.

Edvard's maternal grandfather, Edvard Hagerup, was deeply involved in Norwegian politics and was one of the 112 representatives who signed the Constitution at Eidsvoll on May 17, 1814. Edvard Grieg was also a relative of Ole Bull, the great violinist. Grieg's mother was a highly talented singer and considered to be the best piano teacher in Bergen.

If you've ever been to Bergen on a clear day and seen the city from the adjoining mountains, you can't help but be impressed with its beauty. It was the center of the Hanseatic League in Norway, German merchants who dominated Norway's west coast fishing industry for hundreds of years during the late Middle Ages. Grieg loved the old houses, narrow streets, the harbor and the surrounding mountains, but he vigorously disliked its middle-class business mentality. He was hungering for more of the artistic and spiritual values.

The nineteenth century saw the awakening of Norway to become a part of the modern world. The change of government from the ruling class in Denmark to Sweden and the new Constitution called forth an unusual amount of energy and talent in such persons as Henrik Ibsen and Bjørnstjerne Bjørnson in literature, Iver Aasen in the revival of the Norwegian language (nynorsk), M. B. Landstad and Ludvig Lindeman in music, Jorgen Moe and P. C. Asbjornsen in folklore, the Sverdrups in politics and theology, and many more. Ole Bull became famous in America, but Grieg said he wouldn't cross the ocean for a million dollars. He got seasick easily.

Edvard — small of stature — was not known as an especially good student. The rote-learning method of education did not take with his creativity. He used a special trick to get out of school. Getting to class late brought punishment by making the student stand outside until the end of the period. One day he stood under a rainspout (it rains often in Bergen) and got soaked. When the teacher saw him all wet, he sent him home for dry clothes. Since it was a long walk, he had the day off. This trick worked well for a time, but one day he tried it when it was hardly raining at all. The suspicious teacher had someone spy on him and that was the end of that. He also repeated third grade.

But Edvard did have an unmistakable musical talent. So did several of the other children in the family. His mother recognized his special giftedness at the piano. While hating lifeless scales and exercises (so did I), he loved to daydream at the keyboard to create new melodies. He began piano lessons from his mother at age six. It was Ole Bull who took hold of him and said: "You are going to Leipzig to become an artist!" And so began the career of Norway's greatest musician.

In the course of his career and travels he met most of the great musicians of the time. He loved French and Russian music most of all, though he refused to perform in Russia because he detested the Czar's government. He said, "They are the worst criminals of our time." He had a special love affair with Copenhagen. It became his "artistic and spiritual home" rather than Oslo or Bergen. While the piano was the center of his musical studies, he also conducted symphony orchestras. In 1880 he became director of the Bergen Symphony. He saw his task as turning them into a first class organization. When several members failed to show up for a dress rehearsal in order to attend a large public dance, he dismissed them.

Grieg was a very private person. He couldn't tolerate having anyone near when he composed, so he built a private hut away from his house for this work. His famous summer home in "Troldhaugen," just outside of Bergen, has become a major tourist attraction. When there, you can peek in at the hut where he worked near the water's edge, as well as walk through the house where he and his wife, Nina, lived. The Bergen residence, however, was too hard on his health and they lived in it only during the summer months.

While Grieg was famous for his music, he was equally serious about politics and religion. He held radical political views, even favoring a republic over a monarchy. However, he soundly approved the new monarchy of 1905 with a Danish prince and an English princess for the new royalty. He reacted strongly against social injustice, lust for power and the snobbery that he saw in the ruling classes. Meeting royalty was a painful ordeal to Grieg. He felt that the required protocol was too full of vanity.

In religion, Grieg was a maverick. Though brought up under the influence of "orthodox" Lutheranism, he found that it was too confining for his doubts. On a trip to England, he became a Unitarian, which he remained for the rest of his life. His creed was summed up in "love" and the Sermon on the Mount. Yet he kept on good terms with a cousin who was a state church pastor. When buried, his ashes were put in a grotto where visitors may view the site today.

I was fascinated to learn from Clifford Rostvedt of Minot that he had an aunt, Marta Sandal Rortvedt (1878-1930), who had sung solos under Grieg's direction. Unlike Grieg, she crossed the ocean thirteen times and apparently never got seasick. She appeared as a soloist with Grieg in his last concert on October 17, 1906, in Oslo, before the new royal family. Grieg wrote a unique introduction for her singing in America. She introduced his music at Carnegie Hall in New York City. She was also presented at the royal court in Russia, but did not sing there. Grieg wrote: "I have no doubt that she will succeed in winning the hearts of the New World as she did in her own country." She was the only authorized "Grieg singer" before the public and received high praise in London, Berlin and Chicago.

In her last years during the 1920s, she lived with her husband, Gudmund Rortvedt, in Heimdal, North Dakota. While her husband farmed, she organized young talent from surrounding communities into a choir. They gave many concerts, including a trip to Minot in 1928. Her daughter, Sylvia, writing of her mother said: "She was always a 'lady.' I might say she was not the kind of a woman that was expected to 'help with the dishes,' though, if necessary, she could 'do menial tasks with her usual aplomb.'"

So Grieg did get to America and I get excited every time I hear one of his piano or orchestral compositions. The additional story of Marta brings it a little closer home. If you visit Troldhaugen in Bergen, look for her picture on a table in Grieg's home. And if your curiosity wants to find out the full story of Norway's musical genius, read the book: *Edvard Grieg: The Man and the Artist.*

Edvard Hagerup Grieg

CHAPTER 37

August Strindberg — Swedish Playwright

Y OU CAN NEVER ACCURATELY predict the future of any child. This is one of the exciting things about life. Whenever I read a biography, I am less interested in a person's achievements than in the childhood experiences which influenced the direction of a person's life. August Strindberg (1849-1912) is a case in point.

Strindberg was born in Stockholm when its population was just 90,000. Today there are over 1,500,000 in Stockholm and its suburbs. It was a time of change and upheaval. Though his family had been normally well off financially, August was born when money was scarce in the wake of financial reverses. This left a deep mark on his soul. But it also challenged him to achieve.

Strindberg's early life was marked with a great deal of repression and the feeling that he was not loved. Because his two older brothers developed faster and handsomer than August, his parents favored them over him.

At age seven, he was sent off to the Klara school in Stockholm, known for its strictness. It was a long walk from his home, especially in the dark days of winter. He later wrote: "Facts were crammed in by means of the cane and by the fear of it." At age eleven, he persuaded his father to send him to the nearby Jakob school, a place where most of the children came from poorer families. August liked this school well and forever became attached to those people.

When August was only thirteen, his mother died. While he never did feel fully approved by his mother, at least she was a way he could communicate with his father. Shortly afterwards, his father married the governess who was thirty years younger than himself, and just barely older than his oldest son. This caused more problems for young August as she was always resorting to pietism and puritanism to get her way. August rebelled against this repressive and suffocating religion. It showed in his writings for the rest of his life.

146

Still young August was a religious person. At age seventeen, he gave a sermon in church. He was very proud of his accomplishment but stated that he hated the regalia he had to wear when giving it, especially the stiff, ruffled collar.

At age eighteen, Strindberg went off to Uppsala University, north of Stockholm. He dropped out after a year and then went back for two more years. He left, however, without getting a degree. At the University he concentrated on sciences, especially chemistry. But his main interest was in the theatre. He wrote seventy-five plays, thirteen works of fiction and nineteen other books, some in more than one volume.

Strindberg is most famous for his plays. Some of these have been made into movies. In a Stockholm hotel, I watched one of his plays on TV. It was an exciting part of being in Sweden. His movies are hard to find in America, but you might inquire at a video shop. While regarded as a serious writer, he could also excel in humor.

It's always interesting to learn what the folks back home think of a local person who has become internationally successful. In Sweden, Strindberg was not only looked upon as a dramatist and a writer, but as a political figure, publicly controversial and anti-establishment. His older brother wrote that August was always trying to convince others that there were two sides to every issue. Then he'd try to persuade you about his way.

The Germans gave Strindberg a hero's welcome. They looked on him as having a religious calling to expose materialistic corruption. By the time of his death (1912), there were two hundred editions of his writings in German. His plays were hailed as the drama of the human soul. He disagreed with Freud's sexual understanding of life, but this may have been partly because he had trouble with his own sexuality. He looked for a higher (transcendental) reason to interpret life. His writings also coincided with the "expressionist" views of the times. The Germans regarded him as the poet of the middle classes.

By contrast, Strindberg found little support among the French, likely because of his popularity in Germany. Neither did he have much success in America or in England. This may have been in part because of the great popularity that Norway's Henrik Ibsen held in these places. These two famous dramatists differed especially in one area: Feminism.

While Ibsen had been "enshrined as the saint of the feminists and liberals," Strindberg vehemently opposed the feminist movement as "an aristocratic movement, a political upper-class movement, in which women were employed as agitators," according to Spinchorn in his book *Strindberg as Dramatist*. Strindberg warned women that this would eventually lead to a new slavery for them. He claimed that a change on women's social position would lead to a damaging political upheaval. Strindberg's own experience with women was anything but happy, starting with his mother and step-mother. He was married and divorced three times.

Strindberg was controversial because he tried to write about the world from a different point of view than was popular. He may have been misunderstood because people judged all of him for what was really just a part, or a phase, of him.

He shared Albert Einstein's theory of "relativity" with regard to life. While most writers of the time held to a "solid state" view of the world, Strindberg believed that everything is constantly changing. Einstein stated: "Body and soul are not two different things, but only two different ways of perceiving the same thing." Strindberg wrote: "Life would be pretty monotonous if one thought and said the same things all the time." He could also laugh at his own past work.

Strindberg's life was tragic from some points of view, but he worked hard to improve his skills. He would study dictionaries, read books on grammar and wrestle with linguistic studies. Curiously, he held that Hebrew was the original language of the world. So did my Hebrew professor in college.

He summarized his own life saying: "Thought about my life this way: Is it possible that all these terrible things I have experienced were especially staged for me, so that I could become a playwright, capable of describing all manner of psychic conditions and situations? I was a playwright at age twenty, but if my life had proceeded in a calm and orderly fashion, I would not have had anything to render into drama."

On approaching death, he gave specific instructions for his funeral. One of these was to place a crucifix on his chest when he died. His gravestone bore this epithet (in Latin) "O Cross, Be Greeted, Our Only Hope."

148

The funeral was meant to be a private ceremony at eight o'clock in the morning. The day of burial turned out to be a Sunday and thousands came to honor him, both from Sweden and foreign countries. Especially noticeable in attendance, because of their red banners, were the laboring people of Stockholm, for whom he had become a hero. The funeral liturgy was conducted by Archbishop Nathan Søderblom, head of the Swedish State Church.

Strindberg makes you think. That's a lost art in most of the entertainment media of today. I have another interest in Strindberg. His grandfather was a pastor. I'm always curious about how pastors' grandchildren turn out.

August Stringberg

CHAPTER 38

Attending A
Hallinglag 'Stevne'

GROWING UP ON A FARM seven miles south of Walcott in southeastern North Dakota, I took it for granted that most people in the world were Norwegian and that at least half of them were Halling. I knew some other kinds of people too, mostly German, but also a few English, Irish, French and Swedish. There were, of course, a few Native Americans (whom we just called Indians), and I'd heard about Danes, Chinese, Africans, Mexicans and Gypsies.

But of Norwegians, I soon learned there were many kinds: Hallings, Trønders, Sognings, Nordlings, people from Numedal, Telemark and some other places. They each had their own different way of speaking Norwegian, but if one listened carefully and they didn't talk too fast, it was possible to understand them.

In 1907, twenty years before I was born, the Hallings held a "stevne" in Walcott to organize their "lag" (lodge). A stevne is a rally where people get together to enjoy each other's company, mostly because they are glad to be Norwegians. In the old days, Walcott, Colfax, Kindred, Abercrombie and the other nearby towns were quite some places. You could buy practically anything you needed without having to go to Fargo or Wahpeton, except when you had to do some business at the courthouse. The general stores sold everything from food to salt blocks, overalls, shoes and material for the women to sew clothes for the family. These little towns also had banks, farm machinery, lumberyards and blacksmith shops, as well as churches and grain elevators. There were also shoemakers who could make harnesses for the horses. Those were exciting towns, especially on Saturday nights. A lot of the old buildings still stand, but many are boarded up today.

I visited my home community for a few days in the summer of 1989 to attend a Hallinglag stevne in Wahpeton, being invited to give the keynote address. All of the above recollections passed through my mind

150

as I looked over the changes that have taken place in the past generation. Good highways and fast automobiles are called progress, but they've made the small towns unnecessary. And there aren't many young people left.

The Hallings have changed too, according to what I remember about them from the days of my youth. They've tamed down quite a bit, if what I was told about them is true. They used to have some peppy parties, with spirits provided privately during the days of prohibition. The Hallings were also noted for wearing their knives, as a part of their dress-up bunads. Back in Norway, those knives were more than decorations at some of the week-long wedding parties. It's said that women used to pack their husbands' burial clothes when attending these events.

My earliest ancestry in America is Halling and I was proud to "stand tall" at the stevne. The Hallings may have slowed down with age and the civilizing process, but I like those good friends and hope to attend more stevnes.

My wife and I visited Hallingdal in 1985. It's a beautiful area northwest of Oslo. I didn't find any trace of relatives. It may be that they all went to America or won't admit they're related to us. My great-grandparents, Ole and Kari Bakken ("Hølle" in Norway), emigrated from Hemsedal in Hallingdal to Blooming Prairie, Minnesota, in 1867. Twelve years later, they obtained land west of Walcott. Their descendants still live on the land.

I was impressed with the friendliness of the people I met. About forty Hallings came from Norway. Some come every year. While travelling with SAS (Scandinavian Air System) on a trip to Europe a few years ago, I visited with the pilot who was a Halling. He'd been to Seattle to attend a stevne that summer. Many Hallings come every year to the Høstfest in Minot.

The stevne was called into sessions by the sound of a lur played by a twelve-year-old boy. The lur today is a long wooden instrument used in the mountains of Norway. Originally it was a bronze-age S-shaped trumpet developed by early Scandinavians — the oldest metal musical instrument. Its tones carry far into the valleys. Distance seems to enhance their beauty.

The sessions were held at the North Dakota State College of Science in Wahpeton. Besides the formal business sessions, there was a lot of music. A trip was arranged to visit historic Ft. Abercrombie, about twelve miles north along the Red River.

One of the very interesting events at the stevne, apart from just having a good time visiting with old friends and making new ones, was listening to songs played on a "stonophone." The only one in the world, it was built and played by Rolf C. Johnson, formerly of Carpio, North Dakota, who is now retired from teaching music at Montana State University in Bozeman.

What is a "stonophone?" You have to see it and hear it to believe it. Prof. Johnson had found some musical stones in Confederate Gulch to the northeast of Canyon Ferry Lake in Montana. He's rigged up six stones whose notes range from G through D. He thinks that the varying density of the stones is what gives them their tones and that the size of the stone has nothing to do with it. Johnson strikes the rock with a steel bar, while accompanied by guitar.

The first time the instrument was played in public was on April Fools Day, 1976, at the University. When Johnson and the guitarist joked around a while before hitting a note, the people in the audience were sure it was all an April Fool joke. But when they started to play, amazement overtook the audience, as it did us at the Halling stevne. A picture of the Stonophone with a recording was sent to a musician in Norway. It ended up being played on the Norwegian National Radio System. Johnson, who has spent a whole career in teaching music and directing both bands and choirs, spent seventeen years at Montana State University and sixteen years before that in public school music, besides being City Music Supervisor for the city of Bozeman for seven years. Johnson told me that he got his first real band experience under Prof. Arturo Pettruci at Minot State University.

The 1989 Stevne was the 150th anniversary of emigration from Hallingdal to America. In 1839, two people from Aal made the journey. Knud Gjermundson Gullstein, a bachelor, was thirty-five years old. Ordinarily, he should have inherited the farm and would have stayed in the Old Country. But his father was fined heavily for taking part in a political demonstration in 1818. Since the fine could not be paid, the government foreclosed and Knud had to find a new place to live.

The other Halling was Svein Torgeirson Tufto. He left Norway because his parents died when he was an infant (1814). The farm was sold at an auction and he was reared by an aunt. The boat on which Svein travelled transported sixteen unmarried girls emigrating to America. Though there were quite a few newly married couples, and some couples with small children, there were no "senior citizens."

They sailed from Drammen, southwest of Oslo, and settled near Jefferson Prairie, Wisconsin. Why did they leave Hallingdal? Overpopulation is the reason mostly given. Emigration kept the people from starvation. Most of the immigrants were young, between fifteen and thirty years old. Many immigrants sent money back to Norway to help others emigrate. Occasionally an inheritance returned to Norway and that was a happy day.

How long will the stevnes keep going? I don't know, but my observation of the Hallings is that they're having too good a time to stop. The president of the Hallinglag, Prof. Clarence Thompson of the Medical School at the University of North Dakota in Grand Forks, has impressed me with his keen perception of their task. If you are "Norwegian" and any part of your ancestry is from Hallingdal, it's not too late to join up. If you want more information, write to "Hallingen," Box 2263, Fargo, North Dakota 58102

CHAPTER 39

Scandinavian Influence On
The English Language

I'M IMPRESSED THAT SO MANY towns along the railroad across North Dakota from Grand Forks to Williston have English names. That should be expected, I suppose, since there was a lot of New England leadership and money in the development of this territory. One of these towns has special interest to people curious about the Scandinavian influence on the English language.

Rugby, North Dakota, founded in 1886 and named after a city in the Midlands of England, betrays such an influence. Cities in England such as Derby, Whitby, Woodthorp, Applewaithe, and Langtoft also show Scandinavian influence. More than 1,400 villages and towns in England have names which reflect Scandinavian origins. In some sections of England (Yorkshire, Lincolnshire, Cumberland, Westmoreland and Norfolk), up to 75% of the place names are Danish or Norwegian.

England and the English language have undergone many changes. The Anglo-Saxon culture, which established itself after the Roman armies left shortly after A.D. 400, had been transplanted from northwest Germany and Denmark. The island had been previously called "Britain." The name "England" came from the Angles of southern Denmark. They called it "Angle-land." The earlier Celtic culture survives mainly in Wales and Ireland today.

The Scandinavians started showing up in England in the late eighth century. Their arrivals to loot and plunder were a shocking experience. The longboats seemed to come out of nowhere. And as soon as their boats were filled with treasure, they left. The raids continued for 250 years.

This changed in the summer of 835 when the Vikings began to colonize these lands. They might well have conquered all of England except for an unusually gifted king, Alfred (871-899), whom the English still call "Great." He deserved the title. Alfred couldn't defeat the Danes, but he did make things so tough for them that they agreed to divide

England into the "Danelaw" (under Danish rule) and Anglo-Saxon. Alfred's own ancestors had come from Sweden three hundred years earlier.

Because the Viking devastation of England was such a disaster to literature and learning, we're indebted to Alfred for his writings which still survive. He was the most intellectual of all England's kings and was the founder of English prose. He has also been called the "father of English education." Nevertheless, the Scandinavians who settled in England began to change the language and the institutions of the land. There was some compatability between the languages as both had earlier Germanic background.

"By-law" is a word of Scandinavian origin common to English usage today. "By," a Danish word pronounced "bee," means a village, a town or a farm settlement. "By-laws," then are the laws of the community. There are more than six hundred places in England which have names ending in "by." The origin of the name comes from the Danish "byr" (village). There are seven communities named "Normanby" (village of the Northmen). There are four communities named "Irby," which means "Village of the Irish." But the Irish in this case are Norwegians who had moved from Ireland to England. It's similar to "Germans from Russia" in North Dakota.

The word "law" also comes from the Danish "lag" and means "that which is laid down." L. K. Barnett in his book, *The Treasure of Our Tongue,* states that this reflects the "profound influence that the Scandinavian system of jurisprudence had on the legal structure and legal terminology of England." Many of the Danish legal terms disappeared from use after the Norman conquest (1066). The Normans had developed their own terminology in France.

There are about three hundred communities in England today with the word "thorp" or "torp" which means "village." The word "thwaite," which means an isolated piece of land, is also found in about three hundred communities. The word "toft," which means "private property," is found in one hundred modern English places.

Other Scandinavian words which continue to this day in English place names are "beck" (brook), "brack" or "breck" (a slope), "fell" (hill),

155

"garth" or "gaard" (yard), "gill" (ravine), "keld" (spring), "mel" (a sand dune), "rigg" (ridge) and "slack" (a shallow valley).

Where the two languages, Anglo-Saxon and Scandinavian, lived side by side, sometimes the English prevailed and sometimes the Scandinavian. Hybrid words resulted when the two blended. One of the most interesting cases was in the words "shirt" and "skirt." "Shirt" was Old English and "skirt" was Scandinavian. But originally they described the same garment.

The Scandinavian "syster" (sister) replaced the Old English "sweoster." Other Scandinavian words which replaced Old English were "weak," and "window." Sometimes the Scandinavian word prevailed in popular use, and the Old English became a secondary word to mean the same thing. The Scandinavian "anger" is more commonly used than the Old English "ire." The Scandinavian "sky" has replaced the Old English "wolcen." In the case of "church" (Old English), it has replaced the Scandinavian "kirk" except in Scotland.

Sometimes the Old English form of a word survived, but a Scandinavian meaning became attached to it. The Old English "eorl" referred to a warrior or a just man (as all men were required to keep their swords sharpened at all times) and the Scandinavian "jarl," a governor or powerful nobleman. The "earl" of later English history was like the ancient Scandinavian "jarl" rather than the Old English "eorl."

The most beneficial influence of the Scandinavians on Old English was to simplify its grammar and reduce the confusion of meaning. Old English had difficulty distinguishing in the sounds between the singular and plural for pronouns, like "he" and "they," or "her" and "their" and "their" and "them." The Scandinavian plural forms helped clear up this problem.

When you write in English about religion, philosophy or intellectual concepts, you have to use words with Latin and Greek origins. When you write about art and social customs, you have to employ words of French origin. But for the everyday living, we use language of Scandinavian origin. Some of the nouns are axle, bank, birth, bull, calf, crook, dirt, freckle, guess, knife, leg, race, root, skull, slaughter, steak, and trust. Some of the adjectives of Scandinavian origin are happy, ill, muggy, odd, rotten, sly, tight, ugly, and wrong. Verbs include bait, call, crave, drawl, dangle, drown, gasp, guess, happen, hit, lift, rake, scare, scream, snub, take and thrive.

A lot of the little words that act as fillers in our speech come from the Scandinavian. These include: at, both, less, though, until, worse, hence, whence and thence. The verb "are" is Scandinavian and, according to Barnett, the expression "they are" is pure Scandinavian.

It has been a thousand years since the Norsemen made their impact on England. Not only blue eyes and blondness mark parts of England, but the language has affected the whole English speaking world. The children of Scandinavian immigrants to America have now reclaimed a part of the heritage that has survived the Scandinavians in England who have otherwise lost their identity. You just never know how something you started will affect future generations. It also shows how so few can influence so many.

CHAPTER 40

The Great
Viking 'Breakout'

THE SCANDINAVIAN PEOPLE were in serious trouble 1,200 years ago. They needed land. But where would they go? They couldn't move south because the kingdom of the Franks and their powerful ruler, Charlemagne, controlled the main part of the continent. As long as he lived, they were effectively blocked from southern expansion. He died in 814.

The chronist, Adam of Bremen (d. 1081), wrote of the Vikings in the tenth century that "forced by the poverty of their homeland they venture far into the world to bring back from their raids the goods which other countries so plentifully produce." Another chronicler wrote, "great armies of Norsemen like storm-clouds or swarms of grasshoppers" descended upon their countries.

The Vikings were experts in detecting weaknesses in their enemies, so they attacked where they had a chance of winning. The Danes swept into Frisia (Holland), southern England and northwest France. The Norwegians moved into the Orkney and Shetland Islands, the Isle of Man off the southwest coast of England, Ireland, Scotland, northeast England, Iceland and Greenland. They didn't stop until they reached the eastern coasts of North America. The Swedes went east into the Baltic regions (Latvia, Estonia and Lithuania), into northwest Russia and down its mighty rivers until they came to the gates of Constantinople.

What gave them such energy and what made the "breakout" impossible to stop by their neighboring lands? Having been isolated from the main currents of European society, they developed their own civilization. They broke out in their longships and moved up into shallow creeks and hidden estuaries. They could strike quickly on unsuspecting victims. That's why they were called "Vikings." The word "vik" is derived from the word "bay." The word was later found in the vocabulary of the Algonquin Indians of eastern United States.

Barbarians (literally, those who could not speak Greek, the cultural language of civilization two thousand years ago) normally have had a

158

military advantage over people who have become comfortable in their culture. The so-called "civilized" people forget that the "barbarians" didn't live by the same set of values and were not above using treachery. As a result the Germanic tribes finally broke through the defenses of the Roman Empire. The English and Irish, who had become comparatively gentle people under Christian influence, were completely unprepared for the onslaught of the raiders from the North.

The Norwegians found the green hills of Ireland much more to their liking than the rocky fjords back home. They controlled every river and stream with their longboats and built Ireland's first cities. Prior to their coming, the Irish communities — after Christianity came — were organized around monasteries. And being businessmen at heart, the Norwegians minted coins and traded with other countries. Eventually, they accepted the Christian faith and settled down to be farmers. But since they brought their families and livestock with them, they maintained a separate identity for three hundred years on the Emerald Island. The Norwegians also controlled northeast England and moved from Ireland into northern Wales.

The Danes concentrated on southeastern England and Normandy in France. Normandy was so named because of the Normen (northmen). The Danes had their greatest impact in England. They too accepted the Christian faith in these lands and brought the new faith back to their homelands.

The Swedes went east and established trading communities in Finland, the Baltic lands and Russia. Their goal was Constantinople, the capital of the Roman Empire of the east. While never conquering it, they did force the emperor to trade with them and they served as his palace guard. They also gave their name "Rus" to the land. It's from a Finnish word "Ruotsi," which means "rowing men." In the Ukraine they were invited to organize the first government in Russia (a claim challenged by Soviet historians). Like the other Norsemen who had gone into western Europe, they eventually melted into the native populations. In each case of expansion, they began as raiders but ended up as colonists and traders.

Despite their reputation as "barbarians," they brought with them a long history of democracy. Though they didn't have a concept of "nationhood" like the one which governed remnants of the Roman Empire, they operated by consensus rather than hierarchical structure. When an envoy of the king of France met to parlay with them, he asked, "Who is your leader?" They replied, "We are all equals." Seeing they had come with great fleets of hundreds of longships, he was astounded that no single leader claimed to be in charge of the operation.

Their laws were derived from the decisions of the "Thing," an assembly of landowning free men. Each district had its own assembly and the judgments of the Things were passed on orally from one generation to the next. They also had regional assemblies where representatives of the local assemblies met, usually in the summer. There they considered such matters as the election of kings, declaration of war and matters of religion. In Iceland these assemblies continued without interuption until 1798. The weakness of their system was that they had no executive branch of government to enforce their laws. As a result many of the individual complaints were settled by duels or other violent means.

Their democratic form of government didn't have an imperial view of nationhood, nor did they always have fixed borders between countries. They operated tribally. One time the Norwegians and Danes fought a fierce battle in Ireland.

Another feature of the Norsemen which showed that they really had a civilization, though vastly different from their neighbors, was their respect for women. Women were held in the highest esteem by the Norsemen and enjoyed rights of property and status unknown elsewhere until many centuries later.

The Normans, who settled in northwest France, learned French manners, customs and the French style of warfare. They also provided France's most vigorous leadership in military, statesmanship, law and religion. They ruled southern Italy and Sicily — their kingdom of the two Sicilies endured a hundred years and once they rescued the Pope from German invaders.

When Duke William of Normandy invaded England, he faced a strong ruler, Harald Godwinson, who was his relative. Harald did not lack leadership qualities or courage in facing the invasion. However, he had to march his soldiers 150 miles in five days after a fierce battle at Stamford Bridge in Northumbria with the Norwegian king, Harald Haardraade, the most powerful warrior of his time. The Norwegians were defeated after being caught napping and taken by surprise.

When Harald Godwinson arrived in 1066, to face William at Hastings, he was outclassed by a relatively small invasion force of twelve thousand. But the invaders were equipped with the most modern methods of warfare, cavalry and archers. Struck by an arrow, Harald was killed and his soldiers broke rank.

Individual courage and charisma may go a long way, but it's only when strength is organized that it's effective. It's teamwork, coupled with technology, that wins battles and builds communities. The Normans went on to change England by introducing uniform national laws, fixed taxes and a military loyal to the king rather than to local chieftains. The Vikings (the "bay men") disappeared from history and went back into their geographical isolation. Their passion for democracy never died, however, but emerged in the nineteenth century. This time as advocates of peace.

CHAPTER 41

The 'Great
Northern War'

INTERNATIONAL PROBLEM SOLVING is never simple. In the struggles of nations to achieve their "manifest destiny," there will always be conflict between what one nation perceives to be its destiny and what its neighbors suppose to be theirs. The result is often war.

When the Vasa family came to power in Sweden in the early sixteenth century, new energies were unloosed both in leadership and in the vision of their people. The most famous of the Vasa rulers was King Gustavus Adolphus (1594-1632), the "Lion of the North" who established Sweden's military power in Europe. Later Vasa kings also proved able leaders. As a result Swedish military power became dominant in northern Europe by the time of Charles XII (reigned 1682-1718).

Because of Charles' aggressive foreign policies, a tide of resentment rose up against Sweden, especially in Denmark, but also in Poland, Saxony and Russia. At the same time, Russia came under the rule of Peter I, known as the "Great" (reigned 1672-1725). Peter was determined to obtain access for Russia to the great oceans for trade. He fought a war with Ottoman Turkey (1695-1696) for rights to the Black Sea. Only Sweden stood in his way to establish Russian access to the Baltic Sea. He also waged war against Persia to acquire access to the Caspian Sea (1722-1723).

Peter had acquainted himself with the ways of western Europe and travelled through those lands which were well advanced over Russia. He had an eye for a vast Russian empire, even employing the Danish sea Captain, Vitus Bering, to explore the ocean between Siberia and Alaska.

To prepare for his struggle with the Swedes, Peter concluded strategic alliances with Sweden's neighbors. In 1699, he made alliances with Denmark and Saxony. The ruler of Saxony was also the king of Poland. They were only too eager for the opportunity to challenge their warlike neighbor. The following year, the Danish king, Christian V, attacked Holstein, an ally of Sweden. The Saxons moved against Livonia (Estonia and Latvia). Then after concluding a peace treaty with Turkey, Peter declared war on Sweden (1700).

This action resulted in what was called the "Great Northern War" (1700-1721), a war which outlasted both kings. It is also called the "Second Northern War," the "First Northern War" being fought (1655-1660) between Sweden and Poland over succession rights to the Swedish throne. As a result, Poland gave up its claim to Swedish power and Sweden acquired Skåne from Denmark.

It was a well coordinated attack. The Swedes, however, under the leadership of their energetic King Charles, and with the aid of the English and Dutch fleets, handed the Danes a swift defeat. The Saxon attack on Latvia was also broken and the Swedes defeated the Russians and their allies.

But then the tide of battle began to turn. Charles was moving in too many directions to encounter his enemy effectively. This gave them a chance to maneuver into better positions and be rested. Still the Russians and their allies feared to face Charles in battle unless they could have decided field advantage.

To establish his power more firmly in the North, Peter founded the city of St. Petersburg in 1703 as the seat of government, (after 1924 called Leningrad). He also built up a naval base at Kronstadt.

Charles suffered a series of defeats in Russia. The most decisive was at Poltava in June 1709. It had been his intention to capture Moscow. As with other invaders (Napoleon and Hitler), it ended in disaster. As a result, Charles fled to Turkey where he hoped to gain an ally based on anti-Russian policies. The Turks declared war on Russia in 1710, won a battle and then negotiated a truce. Angered, Charles issued a number of statements hostile to the Turkish government and his case began to fade.

Large countries like Russia always have a number of disaffected "minorities" who are looking for the opportunity to strike their own bargains. Of special interest was the promise that twenty thousand Cossacks were ready to join Charles. This caught the Russians by surprise and they stalled for time to re-group their forces. Unfortunately for Charles, only two thousand Cossacks showed up for battle and fled after a brief encounter.

Meanwhile, the anti-Swedish coalition started stripping away the Swedish empire in the Baltic. Charles was finally expelled from Turkey and he returned back to Sweden in November 1714 to try to save the situation. Other powers joined the coalition after the Swedish reversals. Both England and Hanover (northwest Germany) sided against Charles because he didn't honor his promises to give them territory in exchange for their neutrality in the war. Prussia entered the war against Charles in 1713, occupying nearby territories. Peter's diplomats were as effective as his armies, by signing treaties with Charles's enemies.

Charles met his end in southeastern Norway at the seige of Frederikshald on November 1718. There are some who said that he was shot in the back by one of his own officers who regarded him a tyrant. That's quite possible as there was a constant struggle in Sweden between the nobles and the king about how the government should be run.

Upon the death of Charles, his brother-in-law, Frederik, became king. Of German background and tired of Charles's policies, Frederik I of Sweden negotiated a series of peace treaties. The English recommended that Sweden sue for peace. Frederik took the advice and did quite well. Sweden, Saxony and Poland returned to their status as of before the war. Denmark returned its conquests to Sweden in exchange for a substantial amount of money. Sweden gave up claims to cities in Germany. The Treaty of Nystad was concluded on September 10, 1721. Russia got what it wanted, access to the Baltic Sea.

The "Great Northern War" was a turning point in the politics of northern Europe. Sweden began a decline in power and Russia was on the ascent in the Baltic.

The Great Northern War was a decisive factor in the development of Russian military science and was the start of a regular Russian army, with infantry, cavalry and artillery. They also built up a naval fleet. Peter wisely calculated his political goals before taking military offensive. His goal was access to the ocean for trade. He never wavered from this goal and won. Russian armed forces adopted the most advanced European military tactics under Peter's leadership, especially using the bayonet charge under fire. Peter achieved success by learning from Sweden's military tactics and armament. Peter, of course, toured western lands — Prussia, Holland and England — to learn what he could in order to defeat Sweden and gain his "window to the west."

If Charles had pursued an active foreign policy of negotiating with his neighbors, he might have defeated the Russians, because he was superior in the opening encounters. But because he did not "seek peace and pursue it" (the motto of the United States Air Force in 1988), he threatened his neighbors and they responded with an alliance against him.

Charles was the last of the real bellicose (warlike) Swedish kings. A tide of resistance began successfully to challenge the power of royalty. In another hundred years, Sweden joined the nations who became "peacemakers" and are still so today.

Of special interest to me is how polite and courteous the leaders of enemy nations can be to each other when signing peace treaties. If only they would hold a similar ceremony before the battles, perhaps many lives could be saved.

CHAPTER 42

The Myrdals Of Sweden —
Nobel Prize Winners

T HE NOBEL PRIZES are among the most coveted recognitions in the world. It's most unusual when a husband and wife each are recognized. This has happened only three times since the prizes were initiated in 1901. Pierre and Marie Curie shared the Nobel Prize for Physics in 1903, and Carl and Gerty Cori shared the 1947 award in medicine. But only once have a husband and wife received separate Nobel prizes.

Gunnar Myrdal (pronounced MEER-dawl) and his wife Alva Reimer Myrdal are the only couple to have received this distinction. Gunnar shared the Nobel Prize for Economics with Friedrich von Hayek in 1974, and Alva shared the 1982 Nobel Peace Prize with Alfonso Garcia Robles.

Mrs. Myrdal (1902-1986) grew up in a middle-class socially conscious family, the daughter of a building contractor and city councilman at Eskilstuna in eastern Sweden. She received her B.A. degree in 1924 and an M.A. in 1934 at the University of Stockholm. Her research was published in a book entitled *The Crisis in the Population Question.* In it she warned about the danger to Sweden because of its dwindling birth rate.

(Karl) Gunnar Myrdal (1898-1987) was born in central Sweden, the son of a railroad employee. He studied law and economics at Stockholm University and so impressed his professors that they named him to the faculty upon graduation. Gunnar and Alva Reimer were married in 1924, the year after he received his law degree. He received a Ph. D. in economics in 1927.

Alva's career began as a schoolteacher, but she is remembered as a sociologist, diplomat and writer. Those who knew her say that she was "engagingly self-confident with an infectious and tinkling laugh." They also said that she had "seemingly unquenchable energy." The book about Sweden's population crisis brought her national attention. She championed the cause of voluntary parenthood and sex education, a daring thing in those days.

In 1955, Mrs. Myrdal was appointed Ambassador to India. There were some who said that it would never work because her social convictions clashed with many conventional views. However, she made a good impression on Prime Minister Jawaharlal Nehru and she received his Award for International Understanding in 1981. Swedish business leaders were impressed with the carefully prepared reports she sent back to Stockholm about trade possibilities.

Alva Myrdal's greatest challenge came in 1961 when the government asked her to become "Special Assistant on Disarmament" to the Swedish Foreign Minister. After being notified of the appointment, she asked that it be kept secret for two weeks while she familiarized herself with the subject. It became her passion for life.

The following year Alva became a member of Parliament from the ruling Social Democratic party. She was also named head of the Swedish delegation to the United Nations Disarmament Conference in Geneva. In 1966 she was named to the Swedish Cabinet as minister in charge of disarmament and church affairs. Her book, *The Game of Disarmament: How the United States and Russia Run the Arms Race* (1976), chastised both governments for carrying on an "arms race that has brought costs that are ruinous to the world economy." In addition to the Nobel and Nehru awards, Mrs. Myrdal also received the West German Peace Prize (1970) and the Albert Einstein Peace Prize (1980).

When asked if the long separations from her husband didn't put stress on their marriage, Alva answered that they were deeply interested in each other's work and "we never found anybody else so interesting to talk to." When asked why she continued to be so active in social reform movements for the world, she replied: "If you have a chance to reform things, don't you think you should?"

Mrs. Myrdal kept an interest in youth, even when she was past eighty. After receiving the Albert Einstein award she said, "There is a climate of despair that is being forced on the youth of today by the ever-present threat of nuclear war." Concerning this despair, she wrote, "I have never, never allowed myself to give up."

Besides her political work, Alva liked to cook, walk, read poetry and novels, and was attentive to her children. They had a son in Sweden, a daughter in West Germany, and a daughter, Sissella, who is the wife of Harvard University president, Derek Bok.

Gunnar had a long and distinguished career as Professor of Economics at the University of Stockholm (1933-1950), General Secretary of the United Nations Economic Commission for Europe (1947-1957), and Director of the Institute for International Economic Studies at the University of Stockholm (1962-1967).

Myrdal was called "the leading economist and social scientist of his epoch" by a *New York Times* writer. He left his influence on America as well as Sweden. One of the charges made against Sweden's high standard of living was it was responsible for the nation's high suicide rate. Myrdal countered this by saying: "This is a fantastic lie. Why should the protection of your life from economic disasters and from bad health, the opening of education for your people, pensions for the old people, nursery care for children — why should that make you frustrated?"

In 1938 Myrdal accepted an invitation from the Carnegie Corporation to direct a two-year study of Negroes in the United States. He recruited forty-eight writer-scholars for the task. Some of his predictions proved to be wrong. He had been optimistic that Negro rights would be championed by the labor unions and in the North. In the end, he became disillusioned about the American constitution guaranteeing human rights. Still he had great confidence that America would right its wrongs.

Myrdal's major work based on the Carnegie research program was written up in the book, *An American Dilemma: The Negro Problem and Modern Democracy.* The study helped to destroy the "separate but equal" racial policy in the United States. When the Supreme Court gave out its ruling in 1954 that segregation was unconstitutional, the court stated that separate but equal implied enforced inferiority. They cited Myrdal's research as the primary evidence. The work appeared in two large volumes and has been compared with the writings of Toqueville "in its importance as a study of the United States."

Above his desk in Stockholm hung two framed documents: The Declaration of Independence and a citation from Lincoln: "To sin by silence when they should protest makes cowards of men."

He was an early advocate of Keynesian economics which urged governments to improve economic conditions by employing more people. He later abandoned this view since it ignored social justice and was used to support inflationary policies, bringing more problems to the poor.

The Third World's hunger became Myrdal's obsession. He urged that education and social structures were the key to changing this. In his book, *Asian Drama: An Inquiry into the Poverty of the Nations* (1968), he warned that the United States was heading for a disaster in Vietnam. Myrdal claimed that the United States had become a hostage of the Saigon government and urged that America open negotiations with the Communists (which we eventually did anyway). Nonetheless he was a target of Communist derision. They called him "bourgeois."

Despite his disappointments with America, he never lost his confidence in it. He stated: "A strong America is a wise America. You are not very good losers. Every time you are losing, an element of insanity enters your thinking that is very dangerous. What you really need is not more private consumption but help for the poor." Interviewed in New York, he said: "America is the one rich country with the biggest slums, the least democratic and least developed health system and the most niggardly attitude against its old people."

I remember Myrdal's comments on America and noted that he was rarely popular with our State Department. We Americans are sensitive about foreigners making judgments about us. However, the issue is this: Was Myrdal correct in his judgments? Agree or disagree about their solutions to social problems, there is no denying that the Myrdals were one of the world's most unusual husband and wife teams.

CHAPTER 43

The Norse Centennial Celebration In America

THE NORWEGIANS IN AMERICA had their "party of the century" at the Minnesota State Fair Grounds on June 6-9, 1925. Worship services in both English and Norwegian were held on Sunday in the Hippodrome. The grand finale came on Tuesday night in the centennial pageant, with music being furnished by the Luther College Band of Decorah, Iowa, directed by Carlo A. Sperati.

Even Calvin Coolidge, president of the United States, and Mrs. Coolidge were present, as well Lord Byng, Governor-General of Canada, and Lady Byng. The Bishop of Oslo, Johan Lunde, brought greetings from the church in Norway. Greetings were also brought from King Haakon VII, the Storting (parliament), and the University. A medal was struck with a Viking ship on one side and Leif Eriksen on the other to commemorate the event.

They had a lot to celebrate. It had been one hundred years since Cleng Peerson (1782-1865) had set out from the Stavanger harbor with his sloop, the "Restauration," to bring a load of Norwegian immigrants to the New World. It wasn't much of a ship, just fifty-four feet long and sixteen feet wide, registered to carry thirty-seven tons. On board were fifty-four passengers, including twenty children and 6,300 pounds of rod iron. To be sure, Norwegians had come to America before, but never a whole boatload. This marked the beginning of the immigration from Norway to America. Professor Theodore Blegen of the University of Minnesota gave an address about Peerson.

Music and speeches were a prominent part of the celebration. The Centennial Exhibition had twenty-two departments of exhibits. These included pioneer life, church, schools, agriculture, the press, literature, art, men in public service, charity and mutual aid, women's arts and crafts, societies and organizations, music, trade and commerce, Norwegian skiing, Sons of Norway, Daughters of Norway, the medical profession, industries, engineering and architecture, a Minnesota state exhibit and a Norse-Canadian exhibit. They took over the entire Fair Grounds in St. Paul for the celebration. Dr. Knut Gjerset, curator of the Luther College Museum (now Vesterheim), was chairman of the exhibits.

An athletic program of baseball, soccer, bicycle racing, plus a track and field meet provided extra entertainment. Baseball teams from Concordia, Luther and St. Olaf colleges held a tournament. The soccer games were played between the Norwegian-American Athletic Associaton of Chicago and the Norge Athletic Club of Minneapolis.

Prof. Olaf Norlie, famous for his published statistics on Norwegians in America, wrote an article entitled "Why We Celebrate" in the centennial book. He pointed out that George Washington traced his ancestry back to Norse ancestors in Yorkshire in 1030 and that he was a proud member of the Scandinavian Society in Philadelphia. He also cited William Jennings Bryan's claim that he had descended from Norwegian stock which had settled in Ireland.

Norlie noted that most of the English immigration to America came from Norwegian counties in England. He also claimed that the heaviest Irish immigration came from the Norwegian element in Ireland and that "most of the French stock in America has come from the Norwegian sections of France." The "Pilgrim Fathers" who came to America on the Mayflower were "mainly of Norwegian descent," according to Norlie, the same counties where "William the Conqueror met with most opposition from his kinsmen in the Norwegian counties of England." These are some interesting claims.

A lot of Norwegian pride was shared as the people at the Centennial were reminded that the first white child born in New York City was of Norwegian stock. Norwegians came over with the Dutch settlement in New York and others settled among the Swedes along the Delaware River in 1638. Norwegians were also early land owners in downtown Chicago, the area called the "Loop."

The Norwegians were proud of their patriotism in war. During the Civil War, 9% of the total Norwegian population in America enlisted to save the Union and to fight against slavery. In World War I, 6% of the Norwegians were in the military while only 4% of the country at large was drafted. All three of my uncles eligible to be in the Army fought in France — two returned.

More than anything, the Norwegian-Americans celebrated their heritage of freedom. It had begun in the local assemblies called the "Things," before the coming of Christianity. Norlie cited the claim of B. F. De Costa that our freedom of speech is derived from the Northmen.

There's no doubt about it, this was a time for the Norwegians to boast of their success in America. The centennial book states that over five thousand graduates of Norwegian technical schools had come to America where many of them achieved fame in engineering, shipping, finance, business, commerce, lumbering, fishing and the skilled trades. The list included famous musicians, journalists, writers, publishers, churchmen, educators and schools, painters and sculptors. He cited F. Melius Christiansen, director of the St. Olaf Choir; Ole Rølvaag, author of *Giants in the Earth;* and Col. Hans Heg, who led the 15th Wisconsin Regiment in the Civil War.

Norwegian-Americans in public service were given their due. By 1925, twelve of them had served as governors: Knute Nelson, J. A. O. Preus and Theodore Christianson in Minnesota; Andrew Lee, Charles Herreid, Peter Norbeck and Carl Gunderson in South Dakota; James Davidson and J. J. Blaine in Wisconsin; R. A. Nestos and A. G. Sorlie in North Dakota, and J. E. Erickson in Montana. Senators and congressmen were also recognized, including Asle J. Gronna, Martin Johnson, H. T. Helgeson and Olger Burtness from North Dakota. Considering that the Scandinavians didn't arrive in large numbers to America until after the Civil War, that was an impressive record. Why did they succeed so early in public life? Their high rate of literacy and passion for political freedom, are cited as the reasons.

Knute Nelson, born near Voss, Norway, and Rasmus B. Anderson, born at Albion, Wisconsin, were given special attention. Nelson was the first Scandinavian to become a governor in the New World (Minnesota). He later became both a congressman and a senator. Erling Rolfsrud has written a delightful book on Nelson. Governor Preus called him "one of the most illustrious of her sons that Norway has given to the New World." Anderson organized the first department of Scandinavian languages and literature in America at the University of Wisconsin

172

in 1875. He was also the first Norwegian to serve as an ambassador (Denmark) from 1885 to 1889. The Encyclopedia Britannica has called him "Father of Norse literature in America."

Norsemen are fond of statues. The Leif Eriksen statue in Boston and the statue of Ole Bull, the famous violinist, in Minneapolis' Loring Park are pictured in the book. When the two hundredth anniversary celebration will be held in 2025, I hope they'll include the statues in Minot's Scandinavian Heritage Park of two famous skiers, Sondre Norheim and Casper Oimoen, both born in Norway. There are only four statues of skiers in the whole world.

I have a feeling that there might have been just a little bit of bragging in all those speeches and perhaps even some interpretations of the tradition which had their heroes walk on water. My guess is that no one minded all the hyperbole about the Norse achievements. But there was also thanksgiving to God for his mercies.

Every ethnic group should celebrate its successes and hold up its values for their future generations and for their neighbors to see. A reason why Norwegian-Americans have had a good success rate is because they've been challenged by American pluralism. It takes people of many backgrounds to build good communities. We can learn a lot from each other.

CHAPTER 44

Stave Churches
And Dragon Heads

D RAGONS LIVE ONLY in storybooks today, but to many people of the past they were real. The dragon heads on the stave churches of Norway have fascinated me. I've wondered what is the relationship between that beast of mythology and the religion of the "White Christ" in the northlands of Europe.

I was surprised to discover the connection. Dan Lindholm has provided a scintillating study in his book *Stave Churches in Norway*, published by the Rudolf Steiner Press in London (1969). I discovered the book in a shop in Trondheim. Besides the story, there are over 110 pages of photographs which show the magnificent artistry, especially the wood carvings, of these elegant structures.

At one time there were over one thousand stave churches in Norway; today only thirty-three remain, few in their original design. Strangely, they're catching on in America. The Borgund church from the Sogn region of western Norway was replicated in the "Chapel in the Hills" near Rapid City, South Dakota. It was dedicated in 1969 in memory of Rev. and Mrs. Anton A. Dahl, a pioneer Lutheran pastor in the Upper Midwest. The other authentic stave church is at EPCOT Center at Disney World in Florida, which also claims to be an exact replica.

The stave churches, built out of wood, made their appearance before A.D. 1050 and continued to be built until the "Black Death" which struck Norway in 1349. This was an era of church building made possible through the introduction of the tithe by King Sigurd Jorsalfar (the Crusader). Every tenth calf born, every tenth fish caught, and every tenth sheaf of grain belonged to the Lord. The tithe was divided between support for the poor, the bishops, the clergy and a fourth was used for building churches. In this way, church construction flourished.

The wooden stave churches (stavkirker) were the center of worship for people in the hinterlands. Stone was used for building the cathedrals,

174

the places where a bishop was in residence, like Trondheim, Bergen, Stavanger and Oslo. These stone edifices are some of the finest buildings in Norway, but it is the stave churches that have touched the hearts of the common people and have come to characterize the Norwegian spirit. It was possible for every community to have one of these since wood was plentiful all over the land.

The interior architectural design resembles a Viking ship upside down. A similar pattern of wood supports is used. The churches were built of a fir tree called "malmfuru," a huge tree with a straight trunk with a hard texture. The malmfuru has become extinct in Norway. The Douglas fir of western United States is the closest tree to it today and is the material out of which the Black Hills stave church is constructed.

A sermon in a medical book written in Old Norse offers an explanation of the stave church. "The church is created out of many parts in the same way as the Christian faith unites many nations and languages. Part of Christendom is with God in heaven, part in this world, so part of the church means the divine glory and part Christianity on earth. The altar signifies Christ. All gifts offered to God must be hallowed on the altar and in the same way our deeds are only pleasing to God when they are hallowed by the love of Christ." The rest of the sermon goes into detail about the symbolism of each part of the church: The doors, floorboards, benches, walls, roof, corner-posts, beams, joists and rafters, and the bell. It concludes: "Everything in the design of the church and the preparation for the service must be understood in its spiritual meaning and refected in our inner life." The whole structure has an educational function.

What fascinates me most about these churches, however, are the dragon heads which stick out from the ends of the roof. Why did this symbol of ancient paganism adorn a Christian church? Some people suggest that their faith was a mixture of both the old and new religions. Admittedly, people do not make an instantaneous change from one faith to another. But Lindholm's research suggests something far more complicated and interesting.

The dragon is the symbol of evil and Christ is represented as the Conqueror. The stave church, according to Lindholm, "reminds one of the conquered dragon in a way that hardly any other building does." The

175

Volsunga Saga about Sigurd as dragon slayer is woven into the architecture of these churches. "Sigurd is the conqueror of the dragon which greets us at the doorways," according to Lindholm.

When people enter the stave church they must face their enemy, the dragon, also called the "great serpent." This reflects the Genesis story of the temptation of Adam and Eve. The people of the Middle Ages felt no conflict between the biblical story and their mythologies. They grew into the Christian faith not so much by teaching, but through ritual and symbols. At first it was seen as magic, Christ was more powerful than his enemies. The liturgy was done in Latin.

Both Sigurd, the conqueror of the dragon, and the Risen Christ had their places in the stave church. Lindholm points out that the "heathen" pictures appear only on the outside of the church. The people of the far North could not relate themselves to the story of Abraham and the prophets as they first experienced the new religion. But they knew the story of Sigurd. The downfall of the pagan gods and heroes was represented to them in the "Götterdammerung," as later described in Wagner's opera, *The Ring of the Nibelung*. (See Chapter 26.)

It was curses and guilt that brought the destruction of the pagan world in this story. This is eqivalent to the doctrine of "Original Sin" in Christian theology. That is why the Sigurd saga themes are carved only on the doorways to the stave church, to remind those who enter of the dangers of evil that threaten them outside of the church.

Art historians have been puzzled about the dragon image. C. S. Lewis and J. R. R. Tolkien also used the dragon reminiscent of the Norse mythologies. Usually the dragon looks like a reptile with wings. The Old Testament portrays Leviathan as a great sea monster which was overcome by the Lord. Germanic and Celtic artists also had a sea serpent. The classic battle was between St. George and the dragon depicted by a statue in the cathedral in Stockholm. (See *The Scandinavian Heritage*, Chapter 94.)

The dragon image was so powerful an image that it provided the design for the Viking ships. Here it was used for the good of people. However, when the English, Irish and French saw these serpent-like ships approaching their coasts, it was the sign of the worst kind of evil.

The dragon's warning as people entered the stave church was to remind them that "a man could become a dragon when he was overwhelmed by excessive passion or growing desire," according to Lindholm. This reinforced the "Original Sin" teaching as taught by St. Augustine (354-430). "Everyone," according to Lindholm, "entering a stave church doorway had to face for a moment the image of the animal qualities hidden deep in man's being." The sword replaced the gods for the Norsemen. By the time of their "breakout" (about A.D. 800) many confessed, "we no longer believe in the old gods, but in our own swords, and in the power and measure of our own strength." Lust and revenge were the motivating powers within the Viking breast. That was the beast within them.

Their new religion taught the Norsemen forgiveness and mercy. But it took centuries before the old dragons were eradicated. The sermon from the medieval medical book concludes, "It is essential for us, dear brothers, to cleanse our hearts before celebrating the festivals so that God does not find anything displeasing there."

A third authentic replica of a stave church in America is being planned — in Minot's Scandinavian Heritage Park. It will replicate the church in Oslo's Bygdøy Park which was moved from Gol, Hallingal, in 1886, by King Oscar II. It was partially remodelled into more classical form in its renovation. There are a number of near-replicas of stave churches too, including one near Spicer, Minnesota, built in the late 1930s. Maybe we'll see more of them.

CHAPTER 45

King Haakon's
'Vampires'

WHEN HITLER ORDERED the attack on Norway, code-named "Weseruebung," on April 9, 1940, the Norwegian government was following a strict policy of neutrality. After a harrowing experience of close brushes with death, King Haakon VII and his staff arrived in England where they directed Norway's participation in the war. There is much written about the role of the Norwegian Resistance Movement, which has an excellent museum at Akershus Castle in Oslo.

Less is known, however, about Norway's active participation as one of the Allies. In a surprisingly short time, Norwegians brought an army, navy and air force into the Allied effort to free their homeland and to destroy Hitler's war machine.

Norway's biggest contribution to the fight against the Nazis was its merchant marine of almost five million tons. Even though one of the world's smallest nations in population, Norway ranked fourth in the size of its fleet. Twenty percent of the world's tankers were Norwegian. One of Vikdun Quisling's first acts as the Nazi appointed head of civilian government in Norway was to order all Norwegian merchant ships to head for home, or to German or neutral ports and to await further command. None of the captains complied and 85% of the merchant fleet escaped enemy control.

The Norwegian government in exile was eager to have Norway be an active military ally in opposing Hitler. They also wanted to have a significant part in spearheading the invasion to liberate Norway. By mid-summer 1940, the Norwegian navy was operating in the Atlantic from Iceland to Great Britain. In June 1944, sixty Norwegian ships took part in the landings at Normandy, together with fighter squadrons and naval ships. About fifty Norwegian officers served with a division from Scotland in the invasion.

Norway had only a small air force when the war began, but Norwegian fliers moved quickly to England and then to "Little Norway" near Toronto, Canada, to begin training. The first squadron of the Royal Norwegian Air Force became operational on April 25, 1941, just a year after the invasion of its homeland. They were equipped with Northrop seaplanes ordered from America before the war. They operated under the British Royal Air Force Coastal Command which was doing anti-submarine patrols and convoy duty. In 1943 they were equipped with Sunderland flying boats stationed in the Shetland Islands. They patrolled from the north coast of Norway to the Azores and to Iceland.

The first fighter squadron, known as "331," was put into action by the Royal Norwegian Air Force in 1941. A second, known as the "332" Squadron joined them in 1942. They flew relentlessly in the defense of England and in establishing air superiority over the English Channel. In 1943, "331" Squadron led all the Allied air units in the destruction of enemy planes. The "333" Squadron was organized in 1943, using Catalina flying boats and Mosquito fighter-bombers. They were stationed in Scotland and flew operations over Norway. No occupied country had as many pilots in the British Royal Air Force as did Norway during the war. They were also in staff positions.

A problem for the Norwegian military force in exile was lack of recruits. Yet many Norwegians escaped to England in fishing boats, or into Sweden and were flown to England, where they volunteered for duty. The British navy offered as many ships as the Norwegians could staff. The forces were scattered from Scotland to Iceland and even in the Arctic and Antarctic regions. Many also trained in Sweden to be ready either for the invasion of Norway, or to take charge when the Nazis were defeated. That was a slim hope in 1940 as the German military were mopping up western Europe.

One of the fascinating and little known planes flown by the Norwegian fliers was a De Havilland built "Vampire" jet. In an article written in *Aerospace Historian,* General Bryce Poe II (retired Air Force) tells of his experience with this plane. General Poe's wife, Kari, is Norwegian-born. He has also been stationed in Norway.

Designing the Vampire began in May 1942. Production began in September 1943. Its prototype was the first plane built in either the United States or England which flew over five hundred miles per hour. This was attained in the spring of 1944. Contracts were let for three hundred Vampires. Besides combat missions, it became a test plane for more jet research.

Until new technologies were developed, the early military planes had to choose between speed and fire power, or protective armor. Limited fuel capacity was also a problem. So drop-off and bag fuel tanks were installed. The Vampire range, however, was just a little over an hour of flight time because of its appetite for fuel. It could carry two 1,000 pound bombs, but for only seventy miles. The original fuel tanks held about 240 gallons. In its early stages, the Vampire was designed as an air-defense fighter. Later it was tested for ground attack.

The Vampire had only a 40 foot wingspan and was barely over 30 feet long. It weighed only 7,000 pounds empty and a little over 12,000 pounds loaded and was powered by a 3,300 pound Goblin 3 engine. In 1948 the Vampire set an altitude record of 59,446 feet. The specifications claimed that it could fly 531 miles per hour at sea level. One feature that every flyer noted was that it did not have an ejection seat. Because of its twin fuselages, there were risks in bailing out.

Norway wasn't the only country to purchase the Vampires. Thirteen nations had them. It was being built in Australia, Switzerland, Italy and France, as well as in England after the war. When NATO was organized, many countries were using American built planes, but the Royal Norwegian Air Force was primarily equipped with Vampires and the Royal Danish Air Force with Meteors, both British built.

After logging 1,600 hours of flying in Korea and in South East Asia, General Poe got his first look at the Vampire Mk. 52 at Gardermoen AFB north of Oslo in 1952. He hadn't flown anything like it before. The first question he asked the Squadron Commander was "How do you start the engine?" It turned out to be quite simple: "Push the button on the dash." It started smoothly with a little rumble. The close fitting leather helmet kept out much of the engine noise. They warned him about one thing, however. "Keep your thumb off the bloody button, the guns are hot!" The plane had two weapon/tank hard points, one on each wing. It also had four 20mm cannons under the cockpit. The brake system drew no praise from General Poe, but he did write favorably about its quick take-off capability. No daily engine run-up was required.

General Poe seemed to have almost forgotten this plane when he ran across an advertisement for one in the "Trade-a-Plane" paper. That prompted his reminiscing and writing an article on it. He described the Vampire as "an airman's airplane" with combat potential in World War II. Its greatest contribution, however, may have been to advance jet aircraft. The Norwegian fliers enjoyed the plane. They used to sing about it: "She's not so very, very big, but she's just as big as the Russian MIG!"

There's a lot more than meets the eye in the winning of a war. Each part is crucial. King Haakon's Vampires, as they were called, played their part in the Allied victory, especially in the development of jet aircraft which are taken for granted today.

CHAPTER 46

An American At The
University Of Oslo Law School

I'VE KNOWN BRAD PETERSON since he was in third grade. In the meantime, Brad has graduated from Minot's Magic City High School and Minot State University.

In the summer of 1989, after completing two years in the University of North Dakota Law School, Brad spent seven weeks at the University of Oslo's Law School. The University has an exchange program with UND. Brad was part of a group of ten UND students attending a special program concentrating on International Law.

They arrived in Oslo on May 16, the day before "Syttende Mai," when Norwegians around the world celebrate their Constitution Day. Brad considered himself fortunate to have arrived in time for Norway's most colorful celebration on May 17. He said the parade down Karl Johans Gate (Street, pronounced "GAH-teh") from the palace to the Parliament (Storting) took four hours, beginning at 10 a.m. He noted that King Olav V appeared in a business suit and not in military uniform, while he stood to salute each group. Norwegians pointed out that the parade did not have a display of military equipment, only the honor guard was in uniform.

There were two parades. The first was the adults wearing their festive clothes (bunads). The second parade was made up of students. Technical school students were dressed in red and the business students in blue. The people lined up on the streets were all dressed up in their Sunday best.

The law students were feasted with a smorgasbord breakfast before the parade, complete with aquavit. Brad thought the aquavit tasted a little like kerosene. But they had a choice spot at the Palace to watch the parade. He was definitely impressed. Brad liked King Olav, having gotten to see him four times during his stay, including the closing of the Parliament with its elaborate pageantry.

Norway hosted a famous visitor while the Law School was in session. Pope John Paul II came to Oslo in early June. Brad noted that there was little local publicity about his arrival in Norway, though large crowds of tourists came especially to see him on the first-ever visit of a pope to the Scandinavian lands. The crowd, estimated at about 100,000, heard the pontiff speak on the Akershus Castle grounds. Security, Brad said, was tight. Copters hovered overhead, metal detectors were used for checking people at gates and sharpshooters were watching crowds from trees. King Olav V, as head of state, was dressed in his military uniform for the occasion.

The summer law students got an in-depth briefing on the Norwegian constitution as a part of their program. And they learned about King Olaf Haraldsson (St. Olaf - died 1030), Norway's "eternal king."

They were taught by a prestigious law faculty who were well informed about international law. After the constitution, they received a thorough briefing on Norwegian legal history. Brad pointed out one basic difference between how law is practiced in Norway and in America — Norwegian law is based on "code" rather than the study of "cases." They also have two laymen (non-judges) sitting on the bench with the presiding judge. They have the power to override the judge's decisions at the local level, but this hardly ever happens. They move a lot faster than in America. If a case is heard on Tuesday, there will be a decision by the end of the week, instead of weeks later as happens here in some places. The Supreme Court has seventeen judges.

The one thing that Brad liked about Norwegian law is that there is just one system for the whole country. The law student doesn't have to become knowledgeable in fifty-two systems as in America: federal, one for each state and the District of Columbia.

Apart from the classroom, Brad enjoyed getting to meet students from Norway and other countries. He found that the European students were more liberal in their political views than his. They thought he was too conservative. When asked if there were other students in America with such conservative views, he said, "Yes, I know of five or six more." He confirmed to me what I had learned from some friends in Norway that the Soviet Union is running a propaganda campaign to change its

183

image in Norway. Many of the younger generation feel quite comfortable having the Russian Bear for a neighbor.

Another difference noted by Brad was that Norwegians aren't so interested in the private lives of their public officials as we are in America. They're more concerned about performance than image. The scandals that often ruin public officials in America are more apt to be ignored in Norway, he noted. And while Norway prides itself on its openness and lack of ethnic prejudice, Brad observed that there was resentment against recent immigrants from Turkey and Afghanistan.

People read more newspapers in Norway, according to Brad. They don't have as much radio or television. Since radio and television are publicly operated, they don't have advertising.

One of the biggest differences in comparison to the American system is that students are not required to attend class lectures. Some of them obtain the reading lists and study the required bibliography, and then write their examinations. Brad didn't care much for that as he felt there's value in dialogging with a professor in class. The law school takes a minimum of five years in Norway, though a student may stay longer and take the tests whenever ready.

Competition is keen and the drop-out rate is high. Fifty percent of the students admitted to the Law School are not advanced at the end of the first year; thirty percent at the end of the second year; fifty percent the third year; twenty percent the fourth year; and ten to twenty percent at the end of the final year. The students, however, are not dropped from Law School. They may continue to attend until they graduate. The grade on the re-take wipes out an earlier lower grade. Examination papers are scored by professional readers rather than the professors. There were almost 3,700 students in the Law School in 1987.

I asked if drugs were a real serious matter in Norway. He indicated that they are not, but that a lot of alcohol is consumed by students.

There was some social life for Law School students. Having heard that not many professors attended the student's social events, the Americans went out of their way to invite them and twelve of the fifteen Summer School professors showed up. Their next strategy was to break up the faculty groups and get them to visit individually with small groups of students. It worked, and the faculty went on to have a jolly good time, unlike most of the parties to which they were invited on campus. This socializing was a surprise to the Norwegians.

The University was founded in 1811 by King Frederick VI, who ruled from Copenhagen. It began between Karl Johans Gate near where the Palace and the Continental Hotel stand today, but was moved away from the city center in the 1930s. Only the Law School has remained on its original site. The Nobel Peace Prize is awarded at the Law School. The permanent staff of the University totals about 3,300 persons. There are seven faculties: Theology, Law, Medicine, Arts, Mathematics and Natural Sciences, Dentistry and Social Science. The Department of Nursing, established in 1985, is an independent unit. Tuition at the University is free, but students pay a modest semester fee which is used for welfare purposes.

This was Brad's second trip to Norway. I asked if he'd like to return again. Without hesitation, he replied "definitely." I asked, "How soon?" He replied, "any time." There's no doubt that he was enthusiastic about his summer in Norway.

CHAPTER 47

The Earliest
Finns In Alaska

BACK IN 1840, the United States was struggling to pull itself together. The Louisiana Purchase from France had to be occupied with settlers. The "Underground Railroad" was providing passage for Negroes to freedom in Canada. Songs such as "Go Down, Moses," and "Steal Away to Jesus" were secretly sung among the oppressed slaves. The "Know-Nothing Party" was active in its opposition to any foreigners whom they regarded as a threat to the Anglo-Saxon establishment.

Alaska was not yet a part of America's "Manifest Destiny," though Americans had gotten the rights to fur trading in that far northwest land. American attention was more fixed on opening up trade with China for silk and tea, and illegal shipments of opium. In 1840, Alaska was the territory of the Russian Czars who were eager to expand their claims especially to lands where they could harvest the hides of sea otters. That was the year when Captain Adolph Etholin arrived in Sitka from Finland to assume governorship of the Russian colony in North America.

How did a Finn receive such an appointment? Just thirty-one years earlier, Finland became a Grand Duchy of Russia, a considerably higher status of self-government than they'd had under Sweden for hundreds of years previously. Many Finns became prominent in Russian government positions.

One of the requirements for Captain Etholin was that he must be married in order to exercise the appointment as governor. He courted a proud and pious Swedish woman named Margaretha Sundvall. But she refused to accompany him as his wife to Alaska unless there would be a Lutheran pastor to provide "spiritual leadership and worship." Lady Margaretha's determination prevailed.

On board ship were a number of Finnish carpenters who were going to build a Russian Orthodox Cathedral. The cargo also included the materials to build a Lutheran Church. They left Helsinki, the new capital of Finland, on August 23, 1839, and arrived in Sitka (originally called "New Archangel") on May 12, 1840.

Among the travellers was Pastor Uno Cygnaeus. On August 23, 1840, he held the first Protestant worship service in Alaska and dedicated the Sitka Lutheran Church building in November. The outside of the church was very plain, but the interior was richly decorated. Among the furnishings was a large oil painting of the "Ascension" by a famous artist of the time, B. Godenhjelm. A beautiful pipe organ was imported from Germany. Gilt chandeliers hung from the ceiling and the altar rail was covered with velvet and fringed in gold and silver. The building was complete with pews, communion ware and a baptismal font. It was even carpeted.

The altar painting was later lent to St. Michael's Orthodox Cathedral, one of the present-day landmarks of the city. It can still be seen there.

The church became the nucleus of the Finnish community. Services were conducted in Finnish and Swedish on alternating Sundays and if there was a fifth Sunday in the month the service was in German. Pastor Cygnaeus returned to Finland where he became the "founder of the Finnish common education" and the President of the Teacher's Training College. He died in 1888. On the centennial of his death there was a special celebration commemorating his life and work.

There is an interesting story connected with this church at the time that Russia sold Alaska to the United States in 1867. Preceding the transfer of Alaska, both the Russian Orthodox and Lutheran congregations were granted deeds to their property so that they were not included in the sale. The Finnish congregation has a status unlike any other Lutheran Church in America. It was also the first Lutheran congregation to be established west of the Mississippi River.

For the first ten years after Alaska became American, the church building was under military protection and was well cared for. From 1877 onwards the same cannot be said. There was no pastor for the congregation and things fell apart. Though the building was locked, it was plundered and many valuables were stolen. In 1888, U.S. Judge LaFayette ruled that the building was a "Public Menace" and ordered its removal. The lot was fenced in with materials taken from the building.

The congregation still remained, but was inactive for the next fifty years.

In August 1940, the congregation reclaimed its property and constructed a new building the following year. Starting anew with only forty-one people, the congregation had slow but healthy growth. Their building was destroyed by fire in 1966, but a new building currently in use was dedicated the following year. Some of the original furnishings are on display in the present church. Most of the original members are buried in unmarked graves in the Lutheran Cemetery in Sitka.

During these years, great changes were taking place in Finland. When the Russian Empire collapsed in 1917 and the Bolshevik Revolution took control of the land, the Finns, with the aid of the German army, gained their freedom. In search for a safer place to live, large numbers of Finns had migrated to the United States. In the winter of 1939-1940 Finland fought a fierce war with the Soviet Union over control of the Karelian Peninsula.

In Alaska, meanwhile, the little group that had come with Captain and Mrs. Etholin in 1840, had laid a good foundation. Their work was not in vain. In recognition of this early settlement, the First Annual Assembly of the Alaska Synod of the Evangelical Lutheran Church in America was held in Sitka in 1988. A cloissone pin (medallion) was designed to commemorate the occasion. The Finnish community in Alaska never became large, but it claims a bit of fame in that fabulous land at the time it became American. The present congregation has about four hundred members.

During World War II, the church was also a Servicemen's Center with over 80,000 persons signing the guest registration. After World War II, the facility was also used as a Fishermen's Center. It provided laundry, showers and lockers for 3,000 fishermen. There was also a recreation center with a piano, record players, three hundred records, a library, writing materials, magazines, a kitchen for meals, and free coffee and cake.

The use of the center by fishermen led to the establishment of a ceremony held at the opening of the fishing season called the "Blessing of the Fleet." This event is held annually by the seaside.

I'm indebted to Rev. C. Thomas Kangas, himself a proud Finn and the pastor of Holy Cross Lutheran Church in Powers Lake, North Dakota, for information about this early Finnish community in Alaska. He was a pastor in Anchorage before moving to Powers Lake in 1988.

Sitka is located in southern Alaska in the Alexander Archipelago, on the west coast of Baranof Island, about one hundred miles west of Petersburg and a little more than one hundred miles to the southwest of Juneau. It was the Territorial Capital until 1900 when the seat of goverment was moved to Juneau. About eight thousand people live there today. The name Sitka is probably derived from an Indian word meaning "by the sea," and is the name given to the city after the American purchase.

Ask anyone who has travelled in Alaska and they'll tell you it is one fabulous place for scenery and vast expanse. If you should take a cruise from Seattle up to the forty-ninth state, try to book one which stops at Sitka and take a good look around. Remember those adventurous Finns who settled there thirty years before European settlements were established in North Dakota.

CHAPTER 48

Early Norwegian Immigrant Views On America

ORGANIZED IMMIGRATION of Norwegians to the New World began with Cleng Peerson who brought the first group on the "Restauration" in 1825. This set in motion an exodus of about 800,000 people from Norway to America. The English, French and Spanish were the original European colonists who established kingdoms in North America. It wasn't long before large numbers of Germans arrived, particularly in Pennsylvania. But Germany had not yet become united and there never was an imperial German colony in America. But even so, German almost became the language of Pennsylvania alongside English in court cases.

Three well-educated Norwegians came to America in the 1840s and have left a written record of what they thought about this new land. They were Hans Brandt, a physician; J. W. C. Dietrichson, a pastor; and Ole Raeder, a lawyer.

Most Norwegians came directly from their homeland and entered by way of New York. Some, however, sailed from Gothenburg in Sweden, Hamburg in Germany, and Le Havre in France. Those sailing from France entered America in New Orleans and settled in Texas. Between 1850 and 1870 a large number of Norwegians also came to America through Quebec.

Brandt embarked May 18, 1840, from Hamburg to New York on a voyage of sixty-seven days, which he described as "difficult and unpleasant." He was not impressed with his fellow passengers whom he wrote "revealed a great deal of ignorance of the states to which they were going." Their goal was to pick the gold up off the streets in New York, then return home and live like kings. He noted that shortly after arriving, disillusionment set in because they couldn't find work to match their skills and didn't have money for return passage. There was no gold to be found on the streets.

After staying in New York where he concentrated on learning English, Brandt went in search of his fellow countrymen in Wisconsin and

190

Illinois to give them medical care, going first to Milwaukee, a city of just 1,800 inhabitants. Though trained as a physician, he served as lawyer, doctor, minister, mediator and police officer in some of these communities.

The first Norwegian colony in Wisconsin was at Muskego, about twenty miles southwest of Milwaukee in Racine County, the home of the Hegs from Lier near Drammen in Telemark. Hans Heg, a Colonel in the Union Army, was killed at Chickamauga in Georgia during the Civil War. His statue stands in front of the Wisconsin State Capitol in Madison.

Brandt walked 150 miles through uncleared forests and prairies from Wisconsin to visit the Norwegians in Illinois, located about 150 miles southwest of Chicago near Ottawa. He found conditions depressing, with more disease than in Wisconsin. It wasn't profitable to be a physician there, Brandt wrote, because the people wouldn't pay him even for medicine. He noted that there were a "couple of so-called holy men from Stavanger" who added to the confusion of the community by their interpretations of the Bible. He also mentioned that the drinking water in Wisconsin was better than in Illinois.

The only people in Norway that Brandt advised to come to America were farmers, and then only if they had enough money to pay for their passage and to buy forty acres of land. He thought that tanners, shoemakers, tailors and carpenters "might find it easier to make a living here than in Norway, especially in the Western states." He advised against the seaport towns and larger cities as they were overcrowded and had no decent jobs for immigrants. He warned of corrupt politics, materialism, lack of educational opportunities and medical quackery. Brandt settled in Missouri.

Dietrichson, one of the pioneer pastors of the Norwegian Synod, made two trips to America to "bring order and stability to the religious life of his countrymen." He visited the colony at Muskego in 1844 and conducted a service. He was deeply moved by the response of the people to hearing the liturgy and sermon in Norwegian, and seeing the Norwegian clerical robes again. It made them feel "at home."

One of Dietrichson's encounters in Chicago was with Gustaf Unonius who had led a colony of Swedes to the New World. Unonius left the

Swedish Lutheran ministry to become Episcopalian. Dietrichson regarded this as indifference to the Gospel. T. F. Gullixson, former pastor of First Lutheran in Minot, also made such comments about Unonius in some of his writings. The State Church of Sweden, however, often urged Swedes immigrating to America to join the Episcopalian Church rather than the Augustana Synod made up of Swedish immigrants. Dietrichson was instrumental in having Herman Amberg Preus, great-grandfather of Bishop David Preus, called to Wisconsin as a pastor. Dietrichson wrote of the hard times the immigrants were having in America.

Ole Raeder, a distingished lawyer, was sent over by the Norwegian government in 1847 to study the American jury system. His letters were published in Norwegian newspapers.

Raeder was more optimistic about America than Brandt. He wrote that America would undoubtedly some day become the leader of the world. So he urged Norwegian immigrants to become Americans "as is the duty of holders of American soil." But, he noted, "this need not prevent them from remaining Norwegian for a long time to come." Raeder would have loved Minot's Norsk Høstfest.

Politics has always been an important part of American life, because this is a nation in which the people have political self-determination. In the 1840s, Jefferson was still popular. The Whigs (precursers of the Lincoln's Republican Party) were battling a radical wing of the Democratic Party called "Locofocos." They attacked the American banking system and wanted to keep the government out of banking. They were afraid that it would encourage setting up an aristocracy. The Locofocos appear to have had some things in common with the Populist movement of the late nineteenth century.

Raeder credits the Norwegians with defeating a referendum that would have given Wisconsin a constitution. As a result, Wisconsin didn't become a state until 1848. One of the issues was whether married women could own property separately from their husbands. Raeder favored this. When the issue of a constitution came up in Illinois, copies were circulated in English, German and Norwegian.

A number of other splinter movements from Democratic Party were also making their appeals for support of the people, especially the

"Barnburners" and "Hunkers." The Barnburners were accused of wanting to burn down the barn to get rid of the rats (in the government). The Hunkers were accused of remaining loyal to the party because they were "hankering" for political jobs.

This was the America that met the early Norwegian immigrants. It was by no means a place for the innocent and naive. It was a tough world just to survive. Contrary to what is popularly thought, however, it was not just the impoverished that came to America. There were people that had money enough to buy land, construct buildings and make loans to their friends. With hard work, inventive minds and frugal living, they built up some excellent farms and businesses.

Recent immigrants are still doing this. I visited with a young Palestinian man some years ago. He told me, "Anyone can make it in America." He earned a Ph. D. in psychology and holds a responsible position in health care today. There are many others. Every generation would benefit if the people would think of themselves as "immigrants." Inherited wealth has some inherent dangers, even though it may be everybody's dream. America is still the land of opportunity to those who will risk the challenge.

CHAPTER 49

'Skis Against
The Atom'

THE WORLD HAS KNOWN many heroes, each of them important to their times. The twentieth century, however, has reason to regard Knut Haukelid of Norway as a hero to be singled out for our time. The story of his heroic efforts to keep Hitler from getting the atomic bomb has been told many times by writers and movie producers. The most fascinating of these accounts is his own book, *Skis Against the Atom*, published originally in 1954. A second revised edition was published in 1989 by the North American Heritage Press of Minot, North Dakota, in cooperation with the Norsk Høstfest.

Haukelid is no stranger in Minot. In 1985 he was inducted into the Høstfest's Scandinavian-American Hall of Fame. My wife and I had the privilege of being his hosts. Haukelid holds dual citizenship in both the United States and Norway, his parents having lived in America when he was a youth.

Skis Against the Atom is an "exciting, first-hand account of heroism and daring sabotage during the Nazi occupation of Norway." A movie, *Heroes of Telemark*, starring Kirk Douglas, has also been produced.

Haukelid discussed what motivates people to such heroism. Is it patriotism or a desire for adventure? He answered, "only in very few cases was it a desire for adventure that impelled them to take up arms against the foreign invaders. There is little that is adventurous about war, and the boys had small chance of satisfying a desire for adventure in a war in which toil and hunger, and the idea of death at the hands of a firing squad, were our companions. We lost many of our best comrades, not only in battle but also as helpless victims in the hands of the Gestapo."

When the invasion of Norway took place on April 9, 1940, Haukelid was in Trondheim. He woke up in the morning to discover that the city was already occupied. Collecting his ski equipment, he sneaked out into the countryside together with a friend and hoped to find a Norwegian military detachment. They travelled thirty miles south to Støren where they boarded a train. All went well until they got to Lillehammer where all traffic stopped. The German forces were only ten miles to the south. They witnessed the bombing of Elverum where King Haakon and Crown Prince Olav were seeking shelter under the trees. The Nazis intended to kill the Royal Family and then set up a puppet government.

Despite the fact that the Norwegians defeated the Germans at Narvik, they were forced to surrender when the British and French withdrew their armed forces for the defense of France in June 1940. Haukelid expressed deep disappointment to me that they took all their guns and ammunition along. After escaping from arrest and playing hide and seek with the Nazis, he fled to Stockholm, which he said was full of spies from every country in Europe.

Knut went to England to be trained for a return to Norway and fight behind the lines. His group's task was to destroy the "heavy water" operation at the Norsk Hydro plant at Vemork, a village about a mile west of Rjukan, about fifty miles west of Oslo. The town is situated so deeply into the valley that during the winter no sunshine reaches the streets. The first attempt to accomplish this mission by the British using gliders failed and all the soldiers were killed, most of them executed by the Nazis, in violation of international rules of war.

"Heavy water" (deuterium oxide), was produced in large quantities only at the hydro plant at Vemork. Before the war, the German government had tried to buy the heavy water from the Norwegians but were refused. One of the goals of their invasion appears to have been to confiscate the heavy water and bring it to Germany for building an atomic bomb.

A curious fortune of war which favored the Allies happened on June 2, 1942. Hitler asked his scientists how long it would take to develop the bomb. They told him two years. "By that time," he said, "we will have won the war," and so he cut the budget for its development. In early 1943, when the Russian front had come to a standstill and the Nazis had sustained heavy losses, he ordered its resumption, but by that time over a half a year had been lost.

Fortunately, the English were kept advised through Norwegian informants about everything happening at the hydro plant. They also were informed about the design of the plant so that the saboteurs might enter the building even if blindfolded and know where to find the heavy water.

It was a cold night in January 1943 when the Norwegians parachuted over the Hardanger Vidda, "the largest, loneliest and wildest mountain area in northern Europe." Haukelid wrote that "no human beings live on these desolate expanses, only the creatures of the wild," including large herds of reindeer. The drop was successful. Luckily they found a hut for shelter, because the next day one of the worst storms that Haukelid had ever experienced struck the mountains.

Each of the men was issued a cyanide pill to be bitten if captured. Death would follow in three seconds. The alternative was torture and execution, and possibly revealing the secret of their mission. The Nazis never found Haukelid. Five of his company, however, did bite the pill during the war.

The strike on the Norsk Hydro plant took place on February 28. Nine men entered the plant undetected by the Germans and destroyed the heavy water. Then they escaped to Sweden, though a massive search combed the area. The plant was back in operation in two months. Then Allied bombers struck the plant, still not putting it out of commission totally, but Norwegian lives were lost.

The Nazis decided to move all the heavy water to Germany. Haukelid was assigned the task of making certain that it would not leave Norway. On Sunday morning, February 20, 1944, the ferry carrying the cargo in steel drums sank in the deepest part of Lake Tinnsjø on the way to Notodden. Knut had gone on board disguised as a laborer and planted explosives. This was a very difficult task for Haukelid because there were Norwegians on board who also lost their lives. Because of Allied insistence, the Norwegian government in London gave its approval. That ended Hitler's hopes of building the bomb.

Informers were a constant threat to the Norwegian Resistance Movement. The Nazis paid well in money and supplied scarce goods to those who collaborated. According to Haukelid, sixty-two Norwegians paid with their lives for being traitors. There were undoubtedly many more.

John Steinbeck's book, *The Moon is Down* (1942), tells us more about the struggle for Norway's freedom.

After the destruction of the heavy water, Knut's job was to train Norwegians to take control of the country after Hitler's defeat. They were also to make certain that the Nazi forces in Norway did not return for the defense of Germany. Only 20,000 of the 380,000 Germans in Norway made it back for the defense of their homeland.

The Allies feared that the Germans might make a "last stand" in Norway or would destroy Norwegian industry before leaving. Restraint was exercised so the home guard did not have an open battle with the Germans. This would provoke reprisals and the executions of many innocent civilians. They all remembered Lidice, Czechoslovakia, from the early days of the war.

Fortunately, the German forces obeyed the command to lay down their arms and the war ended without further destruction. The home forces were joined by the "Viking Battalion" from America in taking charge of their nation.

The whole world owes a debt to those brave men who frustrated Hitler's plans for the bomb. They also paid a price. Forty of the 110 men in Haukelid's company died. Without the training on skis during their youth, this sabotage operation could not have been possible.

Haukelid returned to the Høstfest in 1989 to autograph the new edition of his book, *Skis Against the Atom*. It's one of the most exciting stories of World War II. Be sure to read it.

CHAPTER 50

'Under The Oaks' —
Norwegians At West Koshkonong

AMONG THE OAK TREES, about twenty miles to the southeast of Madison, Wisconsin, one of America's earliest Norwegian settlements was established in 1839. It was called West Koshkonong, named after a lake. The people had left their homeland despite the pleas and warnings of the clergy, who spoke in the name of the king. They warned of great sea-monsters in the Atlantic and of Indians lined up in New York harbor ready to scalp them. Leaders of the Norwegian government didn't want to lose people, but they left anyway. The old wanderlust of the ancient Vikings was coming alive as they looked for a better life. When the pastors saw that they could not keep the people from emigrating, they fervently admonished the confirmands on how to live in that land of "Barbarians."

It was not an easy life to which they journeyed. There were no roads or schools. According to Erling Ylvisaker, author of *Eminent Pioneers*, "every home was self-governed, self-educated, and self-provided — as far as their provisions reached." He cited the story of a farmer's wife who pulled a sledge loaded with cheese and butter for twenty miles to market in Madison.

Homesickness hit them hard. Some lost small children and other family on the boat en route to the New World. Fever and cholera epidemics made death a familiar visitor to every cabin in the woods. More than one young bride died of a broken heart or in childbirth, leaving a distraught young husband to build a coffin and lower her body into the earth. The stronger ones survived, and they were many. Through tears and brawn they eked out a life that has left a healthy heritage for their children's children. It was common to press a rose between the pages of a book after a funeral to save some remembrance of one who died. This was still being done when I was a child.

Back in Norway, the church was the center of social life. In America they had no houses of worship or pastors. The Norwegian State Church did not provide pastors for the departing emigrants. Religious quacks took advantage of the trusting immigrants. It was not until five years later, in 1844, that Rev. Claus Clausen of the Muskego community southwest of Milwaukee spent a few weeks among them to organize a congregation. Later that year, Rev. J. W. C. Dietrichson, trained for the ministry in the Church of Norway, arrived. He had been promised $150 a year. He gathered sixty people under the oaks for the first service. A new log church was dedicated on December 19. It was the first Norwegian Lutheran church to be dedicated in America.

The Consul-General from Norway was not very flattering about the building. He said it looked like a barn, but was "neat and tasteful inside." There was not much support from the old country for those who settled in the new land. They left Norway at their own risk.

The new pastor was used to having people tip their hats to him and salute with their hands. In Norway, he was the king's appointee. The story is told that when the pastor and his young wife came to spend a few days at a certain home that Mrs. Dietrichson "wanted to know if there was fresh bread in the house." Upon learning that the bread was two days old, she said, "My husband must have fresh bread." Dutifully, the hostess baked fresh bread for them. They had travelled first-class across the ocean so they wouldn't have to associate with "ordinary passengers."

When it came to baptisms, if the name chosen by the parents sounded too "Yankee," Dietrichson would give the child a Norwegian name. One mother wanted her daughter baptized "Thea Alice." Dietrichson named her "Torbjor Aslon." However, after Dietrichson returned to Norway in 1850, the mother enrolled her daughter in confirmation class as "Thea Alice."

There was no postal system to deliver mail in those days in Wisconsin, so when the pastors travelled from place to place to organize congregations and conduct services, they also carried the mail. Pastors had to be robust in those days as they were often the ones who shovelled the paths through the drifts after a snowstorm. Despite his arrogance, Dietrichson was no loafer. He worked hard to serve the people's spiritual needs, and they were many in a strange land.

The lay people took their religion seriously. It's told that one farmer never permitted his family or hired man to begin breakfast without first singing a hymn to give praise to the Giver.

In 1852, Rev. A. C. Preus and his wife walked more than twenty miles to Koshkonong to begin their new work. He organized the building of a new church which would seat one thousand. It was the Norwegian custom to build churches on a hill. It had eight walls. Bjørnstjerne Bjørnson wrote that this signified their high regard for the church.

The "Klokker" was a familiar person in the church service. He was a layman. We might call him a "deacon." He prayed the opening and closing prayers, led the singing and was often the catechism teacher, going from house to house to teach the children. The klokker was usually well educated and was the one who would write letters for the people back to Norway. They wouldn't ask the pastor as they thought he was "far removed from farm thoughts."

By 1860, the West Koshkonong church had eight hundred members. Central Church in nearby Edgerton has about two thousand members today.

Not everything was peaceful and quiet under the oaks of Koshkonong. There were some whose affection for liquor got them regularly into fist-fights. This did not end with the past century. (I remember seeing such a scuffle on the streets of Walcott as a young boy.) When the pastor preached about things they didn't like, they'd mock him in public by hitching up the horses and plowing on Sundays, or pulling a bottle from their coats when he was near. Such mockery was still going on when I was growing up.

There were those who had imaginative excuses for staying away from worship in those days too. One man said he didn't hear well. Another said he had to tend his traps as there were always more muskrats in them on Sunday than any other day.

There was also strife in the congregations. The doctrine of "predestination" became a hot topic in the 1880s. Most of the people knew practically nothing about the subject, but they'd bring in all kinds of Norwegian "heathens" to the church meetings to vote. They even went to court with their disputes. Civil judges had to warn them not "to make public fools of themselves."

But most of the people attended faithfully and they gave generously of their time and means to support the church. They hauled the water to mix mortar for the building, others hauled bricks and sand. There was no thought of being paid for these services. There were no trucks or pavements and they often lived in humble houses themselves, but they wanted the best for the church. Today the attitude is often that people want the best for themselves and that anything left over ought to be good enough for the church.

A later generation thought the octagonal church was too out of style. In 1892 they destroyed it with dynamite and built a new Gothic style building. There were many tears among the faithful that night.

Many of the original settlers at West Koshkonong moved to Iowa and Minnesota. As land became more scarce, many of their descendants moved still further west into the Dakotas, Montana and Canada. A large number continued moving west across the Rockies to the West Coast during the 1930s. But wherever they moved, many of those original Koshkonongers remained faithful to the values of their heritage, while struggling to survive and live useful lives in the New World.

First East Koshkonong Lutheran Church, Cambridge, Wisconsin. First Norwegian Lutheran Congregation in America. Present building erected in 1893.

CHAPTER 51

Concordia College — 'Fostering Mother'

REAT IDEAS AND PROJECTS usually begin in a small room with just a few people. Often the events take a different turn from what was envisioned by the original planners. The story of Concordia College in Moorhead, Minnesota, is a case in point. I was reminded of this in 1989 when I returned to my Alma Mater, Concordia College, to attend a Homecoming chapel service.

In the 1880s when Norwegian immigrants began pouring into the Red River Valley of North Dakota and Minnesota, there was concern about their children's education. The existing schools didn't meet the needs of these newcomers. Language, culture and religion all played a part in the planning that led to Concordia's founding.

Fortunately, good records were kept. One of these accounts, *Concordia College — Through Fifty Years* (1891-1941), was written by Rasmus Bogstad who was associated with the school for nearly all his professional life and was president from 1902 to 1909. The *Cobber Chronicle* by Erling N. Rolfsrud is also an excellent story of the school.

It all started at a meeting in Crookston, Minnesota, on January 6, 1891. The leading Lutherans of that city wanted a Norwegian college. Having heard about the meeting, some Grand Forks and Fargo people also attended. Crookston dropped its plans, but the Grand Forks Norwegians started a school in 1892 which lasted just two years.

There were already several schools in Fargo-Moorhead. The Congregationalists had established Fargo College. The Episcopalians started Bishop Whipple School in 1882 in Moorhead and the Swedish Lutherans opened up Hope Academy in 1888, also in Moorhead. North Dakota Agricultural College (now NDSU) started in rented quarters in the fall of 1891.

Even though relations were strained between Norway and Sweden over the independence issue, the Norwegians made overtures to the

Swedes to join their corporation. The Swedes agreed that the Norwegians could attend their school and have an instructor teaching Norwegian, but could not be on the board of directors.

About that time the Episcopalians were looking for a buyer, their school having closed after five years for lack of students. The Red River Valley had filled up with foreign immigrants, Norwegians being the most numerous. They offered to sell their $30,000 campus to the Norwegians for $10,000.

Moorhead wasn't a paradise. Organized in 1871, it was called the "wickedest city in the world." A newspaper reported that "almost every night there is a shooting." Crooks, gamblers and prostitutes had free run of the city. When North Dakota entered the Union in 1889 as a "dry" state, the saloons moved to Moorhead and provided free rides across the river. More than one unsuspecting farm worker walked into a tavern through the front door, but after being mugged and robbed was carried out the back and dumped into the river. Fargo was no place of innocence either, being called the "divorce capital of the world."

Raising the money to pay the $10,000 wasn't easy. The newly arrived Norwegians didn't have much money and hardly any to spare for a school. Yet they did.

Rasmus Bogstad was a young pastor from Norway who had been educated in America and had barely begun his pastorate at nearby Kindred. He was called by the newly formed "Northwestern Lutheran College Association" to teach religion and Norwegian. Upon arrival, he was told that instead of teaching he would have to raise money.

The school was named "Concordia," Latin for "hearts in harmony." But its founding was marked with derision from the "Yankees." With established schools struggling for existence, they scoffed at the idea that the foreigners from Norway could have any success. What they didn't know was that Norwegians were highly literate and that English would be the language of instruction.

Bogstad traveled with endless energy against all kinds of adversity to raise the $10,000. He succeeded. Tuition was $7.50 for the spring and fall terms, and $25 for the winter term. Board was $2.25 a week and room 50 cents a week. It cost an extra twenty-five cents a week for heat in winter. Concordia students were not allowed to leave the school after 7:00 p.m. because Moorhead wasn't a safe city.

Bogstad not only gathered money, but recruited students. Concordia opened with just 12 students on October 15, 1891. There were over 200 enrolled for the winter quarter. Bogstad began working for Concordia on November 1. At that time, St. Olaf and Luther colleges had enrollments of about 125. In 1893, the year that financial panic struck the nation, Concordia had 261 students.

The other private schools began to fold due to hard times, but Concordia raised more money for buildings. Professors were active in politics too. Hans Aaker, the principal (later called president) ran for mayor of Moorhead on the Prohibition ticket in 1900 and won. He kept his promise "to clean up the town." Saloons had to close at midnight.

By the time that I arrived on campus as a freshman in September 1944, Fargo-Moorhead was pretty civilized. It was hard to believe the stories which some of the old-timers told. Tuition was still a bargain, only about $100 per semester. When the World War II veterans began to arrive in the fall of 1945, enrollment began to grow and that called for more buildings.

"Alma Mater" is a term referring to the school where one has graduated. It means "fostering mother." That's a good description. I was a farm boy who knew how to pluck a rooster, harness horses, milk cows and operate a tractor. I loved every day of it.

Because of declaring my intention to be a pastor, I enrolled in college. Concordia, just 40 miles away, was the most natural place to become qualifed for seminary. In the spring of my senior year at Oak Grove Lutheran High School in Fargo, I walked the two and a half miles to Concordia and announced myself to the registrar. As soon as he learned that I would be pre-seminary, he took me into the office of Dr. J. N. Brown, the president. Brown told me that I'd be a student of theology for the rest of my life (I thought I'd be done after eight years) and that I should take a classical course of studies, concentrating on philosophy, Latin, Greek, Hebrew, plus basic sciences, history and psychology. I went back to the farm to cultivate corn and worried all summer, wondering how I'd ever survive.

But I made it and President Brown was right. I have been a student of theology ever since. What happened was a complete transformation of my world view. Singing in Paul J. Christiansen's concert choir, attending concerts of world renowned musicians, associating with serious students of great ability, even putting on a football uniform as a freshman, had a powerful effect on my life. In a very true sense, Concordia became a "fostering mother" to me and I'll ever be grateful. In my associations with friends from the big name and Ivy League colleges, I've never felt that I'd been academically deprived in that school started by Norwegian immigrants one hundred years ago.

Bogstad would not just turn over, but would spin in his grave if he were to learn about Concordia's Centennial Fund Campaign of $46.5 million. He would never have understood how $25 million could already be pledged before the drive was officially announced at Homecoming 1989. It would also have amazed him to see the excellently equipped campus of nearly forty buildings for the almost three thousand students. Back in the 1890s they couldn't even field a football team to play the Swedes who called them "corn cobs" because the campus was surrounded by corn fields. Today the "Cobbers" have gained national recognition in athletics even though the school offers no athletic scholarships. Over ninety-eight percent of those who lettered in four years of sports graduated in four years with a B.A. degree between 1981 and 1988. This compares to the national average of forty-five percent who graduate in five years. Over eighteen thousand degrees have been awarded in its first century.

And what's it for? The college catalog states: "The purpose of Concordia College is to influence the affairs of the world by sending into society thoughtful and informed men and women dedicated to the Christian life." This is expressed in the Hymn to Concordia — "On Firm Foundation Grounded." The motto of the school is "Soli Deo Gloria" — "To God Alone the Glory." May it ever be so.

CHAPTER 52

The Veblens —
An Eminent Immigrant Family

THE CREATIVE ACTIVITY of parents does not end with the birthing of children. That's where it really begins. What can parents give their children that will make them a blessing to the world? The story of Thomas and Kari Veblen makes our imaginations spin and think of greater horizons for human potential.

The name "Veblen" was not unknown to me as a young person, it was a town in northeastern South Dakota, not far from where I grew up in southeastern North Dakota. Only later did I learn that it originally referred to a Norwegian immigrant family.

The best known of this family was Thorstein Bunde Veblen (1857-1929), born in Manitowoc County, Wisconsin, who wrote *The Theory of the Leisure Class* in 1899. It was a critical discussion of the new industrial society. Historian T. K. Derry of Oslo wrote: "Thus Scandinavia was identified in American eyes as ranking very high among the European sources from which the new nation had been recruited." Thorstein won fame throughout the world for his writings.

Like many other young children growing up in an immigrant home, he did not learn English until he started school. Yet he was able to graduate from Carleton College in Northfield, Minnesota, in just three years, proving himself to be a brilliant scholar. From there he studied at Johns Hopkins and Yale universities, receiving a Ph. D. from the latter in 1884.

When Thorstein could not find employment, he returned to his father's farm at Nerstrand, Minnesota, where he spent the next seven years reading. Then he enrolled at Cornell University as a graduate student where he impressed his economics professor, J. Laurence Laughlin, so much that when Laughlin moved to the new University of Chicago as head of the economics department in 1892, Veblen went along. Though brilliant, he did not advance to the professorial level at Chicago.

206

Veblen was appointed to an associate professorship at Stanford University in 1906 Three years later he went to the University of Missouri. In 1923, he gave up teaching and moved to California where he died in 1929. Though brilliant in academic work, Veblen's personal life tended to be disorganized. Still the academic world highly respected him for his insights in economics and the effects of the economy on society, and he became even more famous after his death than when he was alive.

My interest in this famous economist was his parents. What kind of people were they? What influence did they have on his life? His mother, Kari Bunde, was the first woman to emigrate from Valdres to America. Thomas and Kari packed up for America in 1847. Just the day before leaving, a son died and they had to bury him immediately. The trip across to America was difficult. Every child under six died en route and had to be buried at sea.

Crossing the Atlantic in 1847 was not without incident. Leaving from Drammen, the ship went to Hamburg where the captain told the passengers that he had changed his plans and wasn't going to America. Fortunately, they met a captain of a whaling vessel who had just returned from the Arctic with a load of blubber. To show their appreciation for his offer of passage, the immigrants helped unload the cargo and cleaned up the boat for its trip to America. It was no simple task to rid the ship of the whale oil smell. They scrubbed furiously for days to get rid of the oil and its odor.

The captain turned out to be a very caring person. He conducted religious services, administered medical care and gave courage to the people as the ship heaved and tossed on the stormy seas. The ocean was unusually rough that summer. They arrived in Milwaukee, via Quebec, four and a half months later on September 16. They had only three dollars upon arrival. The day after getting to Milwaukee, Thomas walked twenty-five miles to Port Washington for a job with another Norwegian, even though he was very weak from the trip.

The struggle made the Veblens more determined not only to survive but to succeed in the New World. A son, Andrew (Anders), was born in 1849. He went on to become a professor of physics at Iowa State University and is known as the "Father of the Bygdelags," organizations which provided for the fellowship of the immigrants in the new land. A daughter, Betsy, was born in 1850.

Their encounters with Indians was a new challenge. They hadn't known "Redskins" in the Old World. The Indians often came to visit them, asking for food. On one bitterly cold morning, a young boy was along who was shivering without shoes and had only a blanket wrapped around him. Kari gave her own shoes to the grateful lad. This generosity left its mark on the children.

Christmas was a special celebration, regardless of how poor they happened to be. They scrubbed their house clean. The men chopped wood and everybody took a bath in wooden tubs that were so large children could splash in water up to their necks. At the dinner table, Kari led in hymn singing and Thomas read the Christmas Gospel with as much emphasis as if he had been the pastor. Then gifts were distributed and there was candy too. The calm and quiet of the evening turned into a a noisy party. (Having had seven children all together in our home for Christmas, I know how much noise those pent up energies can make.) The Veblen's Christmas celebration lasted for two weeks.

Sunday was a day of solemnity. They didn't do field work, only necessary chores. One Sunday, one of the boys found his father's carving knife and whittled on a piece of wood. When his sister saw it, she scolded him saying, "Oh, now what have you done? The preacher will surely come and cut out your tongue because you whittled on Sunday." During the thirteen-day Christmas holiday, Mrs. Veblen put her knitting aside and the spinning wheel didn't make a turn. Knitting was usually done during conversation. Talking made the knitting go faster. It was a scandal of some magnitude when it was learned that some newly arrived young women from Oslo knitted on a Sunday afternoon. Those "city girls" were not highly regarded for their irreverence to things held to be sacred.

Building barns and houses became a necessary skill. They built with rugged construction. Some of the buildings are still standing after more than one hundred years. They used hardwood which they cut and hewed, not even sparing the decorations expected on a barn.

These folks loved to read. Kari subscribed to the *Skandinaven*, a Norwegian newspaper from Chicago. They also worked hard at learning English, so well that Thomas could correct errors when they appeared in documents.

But most important of all was the education of their children. The pastor was usually the one who kept urging that this be done. No good mind must be wasted. Teachers, "huslaerers," came to the home and the living room was turned into a schoolroom. They were strict about learning. Yet the children developed deep affection as well as respect for them. An incentive to learn the catechism was that if a child could recite well on Monday morning, he would be excused from recitation for the rest of the week. In just a few months, Anders learned subtraction, multiplication and division. Their daughter, Emily, was said to be the first Norwegian girl to be graduated from a college in America.

It's true that their children studied under prestigious professors, but it was their mother who was remembered as their best teacher. She taught them the "A, B, C's" and about life, including instruction for their religious faith and hymns. But she also helped to shear sheep, spun yarn, wove cloth, and made clothes for both men and women. She made linen from the flax they grew and remembered the poor. During the Civil War, times were hard. Mrs. Veblen helped a destitute widow who lived alone. She also cared for the sick of the community, visiting them and bringing them food. The neighbors regarded her as highly as a trained physician. And she had a good success record. When she didn't have medicine, she gave advice which worked as well as medicine. Using poultices and massage, she cared for a little boy who had shot himself in the arm. He was well within a week.

The Veblens were successful. When they later moved to Minnesota, they had cleared their land, paid all their bills, and had a fine team of horses which had cost $600. But their greatest achievement was the family that they left behind. Can any of us do more?

CHAPTER 53

The Adventures Of A Norwegian 'Cheechako' In Alaska

THE STORY OF HAROLD EIDE is one of the most fascinating tales I've ever read. His book, *The Norwegian: A Rollicking Tale of Wild Trails and the Lure of Gold*, was given to me by my son, John. He discovered it while stationed with the Army at Ft. Wainwright in Fairbanks, Alaska.

Eide, born in 1896, three hundred miles north of the Arctic Circle in Norway, had spent a year with an Arctic expedition in Spitzbergen Island, the northernmost inhabited place in the world while only seventeen years old. In the spring of 1914 at age eighteen, Eide got off the boat in New York City without knowing a word of English. He was dazzled beyond imagination by what he saw in the New World.

The newcomer's thoughts had been to go to Minnesota or North Dakota, even though he had no relatives anywhere in America. But after one day in the Big Apple, he decided that it would be too boring to be a farmer. Having seen a picture of San Francisco in his hotel room, Eide bought a train ticket to the Golden Gate to seek his fortune. San Francisco was not too bad a place for a Norwegian in those days, as many of his fellow countrymen had settled there.

While switching trains in Chicago, Eide stopped into a clothing store to buy a new suit for $15. In a hurry to catch his train, he had the clerk wrap it rather than put it on. Imagine his surprise when opening the box in the men's room on board the train and discovering a rumpled up old tramp's suit. He'd learned his first lesson on survival in America. No one would ever make a sucker of him again.

San Francisco was a fun place for a young Norwegian and Eide thought seriously about staying there permanently. But then he met another Norwegian just back from Alaska who told him about the wonders of that vast land and all the gold to be had just for picking it out of the streams.

Eide was on the next train to Seattle and found the first boat to Alaska. When he arrived in Nome, he bought one hundred pounds of

210

equipment, incluing a Krager rifle and ammunition. He left for the wilds, having spent his last eight dollars on a supply of Union Leader tobacco. As he left Nome, the last words he heard were: "Good luck, kid, but I know you will never come back alive." The prediction nearly proved to be true.

Mosquitoes, bears, rivers, snow, frigid temperatures and lonesomeness tested his courage and physical strength. On September 15, Eide was caught in a snowstorm while crossing a plain. It took all his effort to reach the forest for which he was heading. Once in the shelter of the trees, he used his axe to cut logs and build a 10 X 16 cabin with a fireplace. He used wooden pegs in place of nails. Skins of a bear and several caribou covered the earthen floor, and mud filled the cracks in the walls. The hardest part of the construction was cutting shakes for the roof and making it waterproof. Moss was packed into the cracks.

When Christmas came, Eide cut a tree and decorated it with the tinsel formed from empty tobacco pouches. The winter was a long one. So he sang hymns which he'd learned in Norway and read large sections of the Bible to keep his sanity. This gave him consolation, for he'd not found a fleck of gold dust yet.

Spring finally came and the search for gold began in earnest. After many failures, he finally found the coveted metal. There was more gold in the streams than he'd ever imagined. Unfortunately, he threw away a lot of platinum because he didn't know what it was. It was worth even more than gold. So with his pockets and rucksack loaded with gold, Eide headed back to San Francisco looking like an impoverished hobo. He didn't dare to tell anyone about his gold and other passengers insisted on giving him charity. It had been over a year since he'd had a haircut, and a beard was beginning to show.

For three months Harald Eide lived like a rich king. But being inexperienced with money management, he was taken advantage of by "freeloaders," especially a troupe of twenty threatre actors who moved in on him. He rented a whole floor of the Palace Hotel for them. Then one day, after paying the hotel bill, he discovered that he had only twenty-five cents in his pocket. So he told the actors that the party was over. They'd have to move out. He'd also bought a Cadillac and had a hired chauffeur who was outfitted with the proper clothes for the job.

Eide gave these to his driver and set off on foot for Seattle to find more gold. Passing through Oregon, he worked in a lumber camp long enough to buy a steamship ticket and had enough money left over to get outfitted for another expedition.

While waiting in Seattle, Eide saw a drunk sailor being robbed by a couple of hoods. He jumped into the fray and with his fists knocked one of them flat, while the other fled. A fight promoter, watching his skills with fisticuffs, offered him $100, win, lose or draw, to get into a ring with a prize fighter. Eide accepted, even though he'd never seen boxing gloves before.

The unexpected boxing match meant a week's delay on returning to Alaska. So Eide got a job and trained at night in a nearby gym. When the night of the fight came, he had to borrow trunks and shoes before entering the ring. Having no experience in such matters, Eide decided he'd regard his opponent as if he were an Alaskan bear. He wouldn't get close unless he saw his chance to score. Even though he floored his opponent in the first round, Eide did not respond to the cries of the crowd which screamed, "Finish him off." After a few rounds the veteran became careless and came out swinging wildly for the kill. Quick as a flash, Eide caught him with a solid right to the jaw and then a flurry of body blows. The referee declared him a winner and he collected the $100, but declined a contract for more fights. He wanted more of Alaska's gold.

Returning to his former panning site, Eide found the sluice box which he'd left behind. This time he hit it bigger than before. He'd also learned how to be careful with his money.

Back in San Francisco, he was amazed to learn that his chauffeur had set up a taxi business and had banked his profits. This was an unexpected surprise. He was richer than he thought.

After spending several weeks in the Palace Hotel, Eide became restless and made plans to travel north again. On the way, however, he decided to visit with an acquaintance who lived in Oregon that he'd met in Alaska. Carlson was glad to see him again and invited him to stay as long as he liked. Mrs. Carlson was a "take-charge" person and decided to play the role of "matchmaker." She tried to fix him up with a local beauty who seemed quite cooperative. The Carlsons also pointed out that there were eighty acres for sale across the road from their farm.

Eide suddenly remembered that he had some business to attend to in Seattle the following morning. He took the next afternoon train. Two days later he was on a boat en route to Alaska — still a free man.

After finding his fortune in the streams of Alaska, Eide turned writer and lecturer and has since regaled thousands with his tales of the North-lands. He described himself as a "Cheechako" when arriving in America. That's an Eskimo word for "greenhorn." But one year in the wilds had changed all that. It did for many others too.

CHAPTER 54

Golf — An 'Exploding' Sport In Scandinavia

WHEN WE LED A TOUR to Scandinavia in 1984, Paul Kemper took his golf clubs along, but he never found use for them. It just wasn't that much of a sport over there.

While staying in a hotel in Racine, Wisconsin in October 1989, we discovered that a Scandinavian tour group was also staying there. That naturally got my curiosity. What brought them to this city made famous by its Danish culture?

Two large busses drove up and unloaded its passengers. I made a remark about the weather to one of them. He answered with a Danish accent. I changed over to speaking Danish and learned that he was one of ninety-two people from Scandinavia getting acquainted with managing golf courses in America. We were in for a surprise which led to an enjoyable visit.

They were on a two-week tour which took them first to Racine where they were the guests of the Jacobsen Corporation. The Jacobsen corporation was started by an immigrant from Denmark. It manufactures lawn mowers and equipment for maintaining golf courses. Jacobsen has a lot of trade with Scandinavia. From there they went to Minneapolis where they visited with Don White, Chairman of the Department of Horticulture at the University of Minnesota. They also visited a sod farm near Stillwater and National Turfco, a company which deals in products used in the maintenance of golf courses. Leaving the Midwest, they travelled to Charlotte, North Carolina; to Orlando, Florida, to visit Disney World and the EPCOT Center; and then on to Miami and New York, inspecting golf courses at each stop.

We visited with Svend Andreasen of Esbjerg, Denmark; Erik Sørenson of Hjørring, Denmark; and Gunnor Sundstol of Kristiansand, Norway. Gunnor was the only Norwegian in the group, though there were two Swedes along who were working on golf courses in Norway. Twenty eight of the group were from Denmark, nineteen from Finland and forty-two were from Sweden. All of the visitors were men except four women, two of whom were spouses of the golfing promoters. Their reason for coming to America was to get acquainted with American techniques in maintaining golf courses. The Scandinavian countries import all their golfing supplies.

We were wondering how popular golf is in Scandinavia. Gunnor told us that Norway's first golf course was built in 1925. During World War II, the Nazis ordered the golf course to be plowed up to grow vegetables. (I'm surprised that the Norwegians did not press this as one of the accusations at the War Crimes Trials in Nuremburg at the end of the war). Today there are about twelve golf courses in Norway, with many more being planned. They hope to have fifty by the year 2000.

Denmark was the first to have a golf course in Scandinavia, having built one in 1921. There are sixty-five golf courses today but plans have been made to build ten more. They told us that many Germans come to play golf in Denmark because it's cheaper than in their own country. Golf is a rich person's game in Germany, they said, but not in Scandinavia. They were convinced that golf should be available to everyone.

Sweden has the most golf courses in Scandinavia, about two hundred with another one hundred being planned. The Scandinavian visitors enthusiastically exclaimed that golf will be a major sport in their countries before 2000. Soccer is the major sport in Scandinavia today.

Because of its long winters, golfing in Norway is a summertime sport, but Denmark and Sweden, being further south, also have winter golf. They use the same fairways in the winter, but different greens. They told us that snow doesn't last long in southern Sweden and Denmark.

All golf courses in Scandinavia, according to those visitors, are operated as clubs. People who belong to golf clubs in any other part of the world can play in Scandinavia just for a daily green fee, about $20 for all day and not just 18 holes. They were surprised that we had open golfing for non-members in America. They asked, "How will people learn the rules if they are not taught?" We explained that people in America may take golf for credit in high school and college, or just learn from a friend. This seemed a bit strange to them.

Memberships in the Danish golf clubs cost about $300 a year, plus the initiation fee. They were were quite shocked to learn how expensive this can be in America. Hjørring has one course of nine holes, but it was being enlarged to eighteen. They expected to have 650 members by 1990. Esbjerg had 1100 members with 300 on the waiting list. This usually takes about two years to gain membership. Many people from Great Britain also come to play golf in Denmark.

We were surprised to learn that Erik Sørenson was acquainted with some of my wife's family in Denmark. My wife had an uncle and a cousin in Hjørring who had a large store which sold paint, carpeting, wall paper and other home decorating materials. Erik knew this store well. I showed him my new book, *The Scandinavian Spirit*, and he quickly recognized the sketch of the church in Bindslev, a small village in northern Denmark. His grandparents were buried in the churchyard. My wife's grandparents are also buried there. Erik had lived for a while in Vancouver, British Columbia, and in California when he was a young boy, so he spoke English fluently.

Gunnor Sundstol was well acquainted with Minot's Norsk Høstfest, so I gave him a program of the 1989 celebration. He is a personal friend of Bjøro Haaland, a country western singer who is a favorite of Høstfest goers. It was interesting to discover that he was acquainted with a number of people from Skien, Minot's sister city. We also talked about the Sondre Norheim statue in Morgedal. This visit turned into another instance of binding our ties more closely to Scandinavia through a serendipitous happening.

Just how popular is golf becoming in Scandinavia? They told us it was "exploding." So if you are a golfer, pack your clubs the next time you travel to Scandinavia.

CHAPTER 55

Immigrants —
The 'Other Side Of The Story'

MOST OF THE SCANDINAVIAN immigrant stories tell about people who became successful as the "rest of the story." But that isn't the "whole story." When I lived in St. Louis, I was asked to visit a man in the City Hospital who'd had a stroke. He didn't belong to any church, but since he had been born in Norway, the family at whose home he had roomed wanted a pastor who could speak Norwegian to visit him.

A few days later I called the hospital to ask how he was. He had died. I inquired about the funeral arrangements. They said that there were none since his body was donated to a medical school for teaching purposes. I wrote a letter to his family in Norway to tell them what happened to Lars, but received no reply.

A friend told me of riding in the Badlands of western North Dakaota while looking for a lost steer and found a human skeleton. No identification. Whoever he may have been, the family would never learn what happened to him.

Ole Rølvaag (1876-1931), the famous professor at St. Olaf College who wrote *Giants in the Earth*, wrote another book entitled *The Boat of Longing*, published after his death in 1933. Even though he never finished it, *The Boat of Longing* was his favorite book. In the Norwegian text, he had listed chapter titles of Volume 2 which were never written. So we'll never know the "rest of the story." The reason for not completing it was because he was diverted by his prairie trilogy: *Giants in the Earth*, *Peder Victorious*, and *Their Father's God*. Death intervened to prevent this series from being completed too. There was to have been another volume.

As much as I have appreciated the prairie trilogy, I agree with the author, there is a pathos in *The Boat of Longing* that haunts the reader long after the last paragraph is read. The book was re-published in 1985 by the Minnesota Historical Society with an Introduction by Einar Haugen.

Rølvaag wrote of this book, "I have put more of myself into that book than into any other." He added, "If I had not myself experienced the tortures which a father's heart can suffer at the extinction of the dreams he has built around his children, I could never have written this book." Two of Rølvaag's children died in their youth, his oldest son in 1915 and the youngest, Gunnar, from drowning in 1920.

Whereas most writers have glorified the immigrants and the successes in America, according to Haugen, Rølvaag was concerned with "the cost of immigration." The American "melting pot" threatened the "values of home, religion, and historical continuity." Rølvaag's writings reflected this concern. He wrote in the Preface, "It is a mistaken belief that the immigrant has no soul." Sub-titled, "Moving Pictures," he stated: "Through long association with the persons in these pictures I have learned to know and love them. It is, therefore, with a feeling of regret that I now part with them and send them out into the world. Take them in and be good to them. They need it." Rølvaag had deep feelings for the immigrants from his homeland. It was for them and about them that he wrote.

The story begins in northern Norway (Nordland), in the vicinity of the island of Donna, where Rølvaag was born. But the main part of the novel takes place around "Seven Corners" and Cedar Avenue in Minneapolis, close to Augsburg College and the University of Minnesota. At the turn of the century, this area was known for "missions, peepshows, saloons, working people's homes, and churches." Back in the 1870s and 1880s, it was a Scandinavian ghetto for recent immigrants. The book concludes in Norway where it began.

Overshadowing the background of the story was a tragic storm which struck the fishing boats off Norway's west coast on January 25, 1893. It left many heart-broken widows, orphans, parents and sweethearts. Rølvaag was one of the fortunate ones who survived the storm, but the fright of it never left him. He wrote in his novel, *The Third Life of Per Smevik*, "I've seen storms strike suddenly before this and later as well, but never with the suddenness of this one — it was as if it had been let out of a sack! Although three men — strong men all — sat at the oars keeping the boat steady, the first fierce gust of wind threw her sideways as if she had been a matchstick. And then came a blinding blizzard and darkness."

For years afterwards, people continued to imagine that they saw a lost ship calling them out into the ocean to meet their lost loved ones. More than one person was seized by this "mirage" never to return again. The book also portrays the fears and superstitions that were latent among the people in those days.

The central character of the story is a young man still in his teens, named Nils Vaag. He was the whole life of his parents, Jo and Anna. The day that he told them that he would go to America brought a dark cloud over their lives. Fear and dread entered their lives, but in fatalistic resignation, they did not resist his leaving. Instead they reasoned that it would be for the best and that he would return with wealth in a few years. It would be for their good.

Nils' travelling companion was a young neighbor named Peder (Per) Hansen, whose older brother Otto had immigrated to Minneapolis a few years earlier. Nils sat in awe as Peder regaled him with stories of how easy it was to become rich and famous in America. Peder claimed that he would become a medical doctor in the New World. "Anybody," he said, "could become what they liked in America."

Just before sailing, Peder's father took Nils aside and asked him to look after his son because he was not a dependable boy. Worst of all, Otto was too fond of the bottle. Nils promised to write home to his parents how things were going for the Hansen boys. The one treasure he took to America was his violin, which often gave him great comfort.

No sooner were they on the boat when Peder started on his drinking career. It never stopped because Otto got him a job as a bartender. The only job Nils could find was being a janitor doing clean-up work in the saloon after hours. He ended up rooming with an overbearing alcoholic poet. One Sunday morning while the others were sleeping off their hangovers, Nils left early with the intention of going to church.

He stopped by the Mississippi river bridge near the University to skip some stones across the water. There he felt at peace and started to whistle an old Nordland melody. Unbeknown to Nils, an elderly woman was watching and listening. When he was about to leave, she stopped him, saying, "Aren't you from Nordland?" They had the same dialects. She said, "I could tell by the tune you were whistling." Nils didn't get to church that Sunday, instead he visited with the "Nordlaending" woman who wanted to catch up on the news from home.

To get Peder away from Otto and the saloon, Nils talked him into going up to Northern Minnesota to work in a lumber camp for the winter. They did well. But upon returning to Minneapolis in the spring, Peder took up with a slick stranger and together they disappeared one morning by train for parts unknown. Up to this time he'd been faithful in writing to his parents, but with his disappearance, the letters stopped.

Back in Nordland, there was joy with each letter that arrived from Nils. Peder's father visited them every day to read the letters and talk about the boys. Nils censored his letters so that he'd only hint about how things were going for the Hansens, like "they've both got jobs." He didn't tell them where. But now there were no more letters.

That didn't stop the parents from fantasizing about the success of their sons. After several years went by, Jo decided that he would go to Minneapolis to see for himself how the boys were doing. He got as far as New York. Not having been advised about entrance requirements to America, Jo was turned back. He had no letter promising support. Gloom overtook his spirit. But one day on board ship, he visited with a woman whom I'm guessing was also returning with disappointment. She spun a story which seemed to tell Jo that she'd seen Nils and that he was living in a palace. There were no slums in Minneapolis, she said.

Upon returning home, Jo told Anna and Hansen that any day now the boys would be returning with great wealth. That same evening, Jo behaved as a possessed man and told Anna that he was going fishing. He rowed out from shore and disappeared from view. Night and morning came, and he didn't return, and "there was never so much as a sliver" seen of the boat again.

That's the "other side of the story." There were many immigrants who disappeared from their families forever. Rølvaag wrote of the high price of immigration to America, on both sides of the Atlantic. Of the successful ones we have heard much. But there were many whose last words were "Farvel Far, farvel Mor" ("Goodbye Father, goodbye Mother"). There were many parents who came to the New World asking people on the streets, "Har du set gutten min?" ("Have you seen my boy?"). Children may leave their parents, but the hearts of parents always travel with them, even if they never see them again.

CHAPTER 56

Margaret —
'Maid Of Norway'

GREAT IMPORTANCE OFTEN hangs on slender threads. Such was the case in Scotland as the fourteenth century began. In the days when royal families were the rule rather than the exception, succession to power was often marked by violence. Many times unexpected events occurred which changed the destiny of nations. The birth of Margaret — "Maid of Norway" — was carefully noted by the ruling houses of the North Atlantic. War and peace hung in the life of this little girl.

Margaret's grandfather, Alexander III (reigned 1249-1286), the king of Scotland, had three children, two sons and a daughter named Margaret. His wife, also named Margaret, was the daughter of England's King Henry III. This meant that there was peace on the border of those two countries. Alexander's two sons died childless. His daughter, Margaret, married King Erik II of Norway. Their only child, a daughter born in 1283 in Norway, was also named Margaret. She became the Queen of Scotland at age three when King Alexander died. This Margaret has been remembered as the "Maid of Norway."

Scotland and its surrounding islands were a favorite place of Norwegian adventurers in those days. Large numbers of Norsemen lived in Caithness, Sutherland, the Isle of Man, the Orkneys and Shetland Islands, as well as in the eastern part of Scotland. They came mainly as settlers and traders.

Events of history often do not work out as planned. About twenty years earlier, the king of Scotland wanted to buy the Hebrides from King Haakon the Old of Norway. Haakon refused and the Scots attacked the islands. Haakon responded by assembling a huge naval armada. Norway was the greatest sea power of the North at that time. No decisive battle was fought, but the winter storms came and the scattered fleet sailed home. Haakon died and the new king, Magnus, agreed to the sale. To seal the "Treaty of Perth" (1266), a royal marriage between Norway's Prince Erik and the Scottish Princess Margaret was arranged.

THE SCANDINAVIAN ADVENTURE

The year 1286 began with frightful storms. Waves up to sixty feet high have been known to have rolled across the North Sea in such times. It was so bad that March 18 was predicted to be the "Day of Judgment." In defiance of this prediction, King Alexander held a royal feast on that date about twenty miles away from his home. On the way home in the dark of night, his horse slipped over a cliff and the king was killed. He had just been married a second time to a French princess named Yolanda. Since there were no heirs from this second marriage, little Margaret of Norway became the prize that every royal marriage-maker in northern Europe would conspire to catch.

The struggle began. England's King Edward I, Margaret's great uncle, wanted to protect his interests and keep his border peaceful so he could wage war in France. He wanted to arrange a marriage of his youngest son to the young Queen who was then only three years old. His son, also named Edward, was only two. Scotland's ruling classes were assembled to swear allegiance to Margaret on pain of excommunication. But since no woman had ever been the ruler of Scotland, many were uncomfortable with the idea. The king of France, eager to undermine England's power, wanted to protect Yolanda's interests. This alarmed Edward.

It was agreed that Margaret was to sail to Scotland and take up residence as the Queen, although six guardians would run the country — two earls, two bishops and two barons. In May 1390, Edward's ship arrived in Bergen to bring the royal child to England. Erik refused to let her go.

To make certain that Erik would agree to the royal marriage between Prince Edward and child Queen Margaret, Edward lent Erik two thousand pounds of sterling silver. There was another problem. According to the rules of the church, this marriage was illegal because they were too closely related. Margaret's mother was Edward's niece. Pope Nicholas IV was persuaded to give his permission and everything seemed all set for Margaret to go to Scotland with the support of the English.

In September, the time came for Margaret's voyage to the royal marriage in Scotland. The ship stopped at the Orkney islands which were ruled by Norway. The autumn seas were stormy. Little Queen Margaret, perhaps being homesick, became ill and died in the arms of the Bishop of Bergen who had accompanied her. She was just seven years old.

When news of Margaret's death reached Scotland, the contending parties for power chose up sides. Bloodshed was inevitable. By this time, there were many pretenders to the throne, but it finalized in a contest between two people: John Balliol and Robert Bruce. Both claimed the right of power after Margaret's death.

Robert Bruce is one of the most famous names in Scottish history. He also had Norse blood, having been descended from Lodver, a Norwegian earl of the Orkneys. His ancestors had joined Duke William of Normandy in his conquest of England in 1066. As a result, the Bruces were among the Anglo-Norman elite with the inside track to power. Robert's father had accompanied Edward, while still a prince, on a crusade to Palestine. Robert was known as one of the three "most accomplished knights in Christendom."

After twenty years of destruction and bloodshed, Robert Bruce led the Scottish forces to victory over the English at the Battle of Bannockburn (June 1314). An equestrian statue of Robert stands on the site. An excellent book on the struggles of Scotland in that time is *Robert the Bruce: King of Scots* by Ronald McNair Scott (1989).

For a short time it appeared that the thrones of Norway and Scotland would have a common ruler. Except for the frailty of her health and the stormy sea voyage which struck her down, Margaret might have become the mighty Queen of the North.

The Norwegians and the Scots have a long and interesting history. Edvard Grieg's paternal ancestry goes back to Scotland. And there have been many others. The name Margaret, spelled in various ways and which means "pearl" in Greek, is common to European royalty. There was even a "St. Margaret" of Syria in the third and fourth centuries, but historians are not certain now that she ever existed. "Margaret" came into Scandinavian history from Scotland.

Margaret I (reigned 1388-1405) combined the thrones of Denmark, Norway and Sweden. The present Queen Margaret II of Denmark (since 1972) is highly regarded by her people and throughout the world.

223

The royal name Margaret also belongs to our family. My paternal great-grandmother proudly bore that name. I never knew her, but a Norwegian historian, Hans Hyldbak, who did know her has praised her in a published poem.

The present King of Norway, Olav V, was baptized "Alexander Edward Christian Frederick," combining the names of kings of Scotland, England and Denmark. Then he was given the name of Norway's "eternal king" upon arrival in Norway as a two-year-old boy.

Can you imagine so much history hanging in the balance through the life of a little girl. Just suppose that Margaret — "Maid of Norway" — had lived. The events of a nation would have been quite different and many lives and much property would have been spared destruction.

A young Queen Margaret ponders her future fate.

CHAPTER 57

Martti Talvela —
Finland's Singing Shepherd

WHERE DID MUSIC BEGIN? I have a theory that it began in the loneliness of shepherds watching their flocks and only later moved to the great concert halls of the world. It is said of King David that he played the flute while taking care of his father's flocks near Bethlehem. People sing at their natural best when they're alone, whether taking a shower, working or travelling. I've herded sheep and have a feeling for the loneliness of a shepherd. Singing came naturally as it also did while I was driving a tractor, cultivating corn and plowing fields.

The people of Finland are great lovers of music. There are over sixty music institutes in this land of about five million people. In his book, *Music in Finland*, Paavo Helisto of the Finnish Broadcasting Company tells about the little city of Kaustinen with only 3,500 people. It hosts an annual folk music festival that attracts 60,000 people during the summer. Up to 100,000 attended in the early 1970s, but that was too many for the community to accommodate. This interest in folk music is worldwide, however, not only in Finland.

When you think of music in Finland, it's natural to remember Jean Sibelius after whom a magnificent concert hall has been built in Helsinki. But today there is another great musical star in that land of lakes and forests. Martti Talvela (born 1935) is a sheep farmer who stands six feet seven inches tall. Since 1961 he's been able to stay with his flock only about four months a year. The rest of the time he's playing leading roles in opera throughout Europe and America.

The Talvelas lived for more than five hundred years near a little village called Hiitola on the shores of Lake Ladoga in the Karelian peninsula not far from Leningrad. This was one of Finland's choice areas which the Soviets forced the Finns to give up during World War II. Most of the Finns, including the Talvelas, left Karelia and moved to the Finnish mainland. The experience of living near Russia has never left this great musician whose heart is in farming. It has enabled him to put deep emotion into his performances of Russian operas such as *Boris Godunov* and *Khovanshchina*.

Talvela claims to have made his debut as a professional singer (that is, one who gets paid for his services) at age five. The family doctor paid him five silver marks if he would sing something. He was then, as little boys are supposed to be, a soprano. Today he's a deep bass. He also has a keen sense of humor and states that "I've always tried to keep my fees high after that."

Tavlela first came to my attention through an article by Howard Reich in the *Chicago Tribune* (Jan. 25, 1984), after making his Chicago recital debut. While he is compared to singers like Placido Domingo and Luciano Pavarotti, Talvela shuns commercial success and avoids talk shows in order to maintain a private life. He cuts down on the number of his appearances so he can return to his sheep farm in Finland. Unlike the other great stars, he does not record with the major companies, but rather with Bes, which he describes as a "little Stockholm company that makes my records with time and care." He also spends a lot of time giving recitals rather than concentrating on operatic performances. He explains, "It's easier to carry an artistic message when you don't have to deal with stage directors."

Though comparatively little known in America, Talvela has been a major success in Europe. Interviewed in Chicago, he explained that "in the United States, as in any other country, people like to have their own heroes. It's not easy for a foreign singer to make a career here because America has plenty of its own singers." He stated that "to succeed here takes all your life, all your blood. The American audiences do not seem all that interested in vocal recitals. The opera is a social event, but the recital often is considered obscure and difficult, what with its many foreign languages." He also noted the American preference for tenors over basses.

Talvela speaks English, Swedish, German and Russian. He has, according to Harlow Robinson in an article in *Opera News* (Feb. 1, 1986), an uncanny ability to learn quickly. Though he doesn't speak Italian at all, he once memorized an Italian opera in just three weeks. It was a flawless performance.

226

The Finnish musician is particularly at home in Russian operas. He's studied Russian history and culture. Having lived so close to the Soviet border during his childhood, he has a natural feeling and understanding of the Russian spirit. All the furniture in his farm home is Russian, having been purchased by the original owners who traded extensively with businesses in St. Petersburg (now Leningrad) in the nineteenth century. About Finland's giant neighbor to the east, Talvela said, "I think the complicated relationship between Finland and Russia has been somehow misunderstood. Our relations with the Soviet Union are not hostile." That was also my observation in visiting Finland.

Talvela was twenty-four years old before he saw his first opera — *Boris Godunov* — in Helsinki. The famous Russian bass Ivan Petrov sang the title role. Afterwards, Talvela decided "I thought this was something I could do." A schoolteacher at the time, he then entered into vocal competition and was soon under contract with the Royal Opera in Stockholm. It wasn't long before he sang a title role in *Berlin* (1962). Talvela pays special tribute to the conductors for transforming him from an inexperienced singer to becoming a professional on the stage.

The Russian opera, *Boris Godunov*, seems to be his favorite. He has sung the title role over two hundred times in three different versions — the original by Mussorgsky, plus Rimsky-Korsakov and Shostakovich. *Boris Godunov*, first performed in St. Petersburg in 1874, took place in Russia and Poland between 1598 and 1605. In the Prologue, Boris Godunov accepts the crown of Russia in Moscow at the Kremlin as the popular choice of the people. There is a great deal of Russian Orthodox piety in the opera, with the monasteries playing an important part in it.

Like so many people in high positions, the Czar's downfall was human frailty and self-doubt combined with palace conspiracies. He became mentally agitated and finally insane. In the final scene, Boris prays for mercy, collapses and dies. It's high drama from the Czarist period which profoundly portrays the Russian soul. Talvela was a natural to play the part of the Czar with his huge stature and dark, bushy beard.

Talvela was one of ten children whose father played the violin, but doubted that anyone could make a living in Finland as a musician. He got his start in music by singing folk songs at home and hymns in church. His first study of music was in a nearby city at a teacher's institute, but it was only one of his several subjects. He also taught carpentry. Later he directed the highly successful summer festival in Savonlinna. He gave this up in 1979 to devote his energy to singing. He has a very simple philosophy about being a stage performer. "You don't need to sell yourself — just give your heart, and learn how to open your soul," he said.

He's gotten high compliments for his performance as Dosifei (also called Dositheus) in the opera *Khovanshchina* at the Metropolitan Opera House in New York. There he played the part of a stubborn charismatic religious leader of the Old Believers in the Czarist period. This is a musical drama also by Mussorgsky and involves a plot against the Czar during the reign of Peter the Great. In the final act, the Old Believers, having been condemned and then pardoned, built a funeral pyre in a forest near Moscow and marched to their deaths into it while singing hymns.

Talvela also enjoys folk music. Regarded as one of the outstanding singers of the world, he still loves his sheep. Talvela said, "As you get older, life changes you. You no longer think about being a star or not being one. Life makes you more quiet and more selfish with your time in a positive way. For me, being a singer and a farmer is enough." Perhaps we could lure Talvela away from his flock to perform at the Norsk Høstfest, if some farmer would invite him to his ranch to inspect his sheep.

CHAPTER 58

Folktales
Of Scandinavia

"FOLKTALES" ARE AMONG the oldest of stories in the world. They are, however, often confused with fairy tales. Fairy tales, also called "wonder tales," are full of supernatural marvels and usually take place in make-believe places. Folktales are legends or sagas from the lives of real people and places. They are based on beliefs which were accepted by the social group in which they were told. They are also relevant to the concerns that people felt about the meaning of life. They belong to the realm of what really happens in this world rather than imaginary. The story teller believed that they happened and expected the listeners to accept them as true.

Some legends are "local" in character, relating to a specific geographical place. Others are "migratory." They could be told as happening in a variety of places. These stories are different in their world view from the scientifically oriented world in which we live. But it has not been so many years ago when the truths claimed by these stories were accepted as facts in the communities where they were told. And even when people no longer believed the legends, they still liked to tell them, especially to children. Folktales are usually overdone with moral lessons.

In a tale about St. Olav, it's told that trolls were chasing the king to kill him because he was a Christian. The only way of escape was to spur his horse over a cliff and across the fjord. When the horse landed on a rock at the other side, the hooves made imprints three inches deep. People believed that a nearby rock which resembled a tower was one of the trolls which Olav changed into a stone. Because it resembled a parson wearing a cloak, people called it "The Priest." In modern times the stone was dynamited to make way for a highway.

In Denmark, we are told, a church was being built in Hadderup. Trolls came every night and smashed what the workmen had built during the day. The only way to make peace with the trolls was to agree that the first woman that came to the church as a bride would belong to them. Sure enough, one day a bridal party came from another community past the Hadderup church. A thick, black fog arose. When it cleared, the bride was gone. It's claimed that bridal parties afterwards make a long detour to avoid the Hadderup church.

People create such folktales even today. About thirty years ago, when the New Rockford (North Dakota) High School football team lost a game to nearby Carrington, the students vented their frustration by honking their horns when driving past a lone tree by the highway. They kept doing it for years afterwards, even when not returning from football games. The highway department has since removed the tree and I suppose that they've also stopped honking their horns.

In the Swedish countryside, there was supposed to have been a great church bell which had many coins visibly imbedded into it while being cast. It happened that while the metal for the bell was in the smelter, a certain Lady Wallron was passing by. She dropped an apron full of silver coins into the molten metal, saying whenever the bell rang it would say her name, "Wallron." The craftsman had been drunk when the lady came by so he was not tending to his job. When he saw the bell and struck it, he became so angry at the unmelted coins and their loud sound that he killed his apprentice. Still the bell sang, "Wall-ron." It was not allowed that a country bell should ring louder than a city bell, so one day someone knocked a hole in it.

In a fierce battle of the Danevirke on the border of Denmark and Germany (Slesvig), it looked as if the Danes were going to be defeated. The young Danish king was inexperienced in battle and ignored the advice of his commanders. Then suddenly there appeared a tall, slim lady on a snow-white horse, dressed in black. Her face was veiled as she spoke: "Shame on him who will not follow me." The Danes took courage and the enemy fled. Then she vanished. The soldiers believed that it must have been the late Queen Thyra, the wife of old king Gorm. She is believed to have influenced her son Harald to "make Denmark Christian."

In medieval Iceland the story was told about a priest who was fond of merry-making in the church, especially on Christmas eve. He delayed the Mass and continued the dancing, drinking and gambling. His old mother, Una, came three times to the church to plead with him to stop the merriment and get on with the service. As she returned to her house, a voice warned her of catastrophe, saying "There'll be none left but Una." She saw a fearful looking man outside the church. Believing him to be the devil, she hurried to find a neighboring priest to save her son. But it was too late. When they returned, the church had sunk into the ground and she could hear the wailing of the people from deep underground. A new church was built some distance away, but there was no dancing in it on Christmas Eve.

Petter Dass was a well known priest in Norway and was famous for being an outstanding preacher. This was during the time when Denmark ruled over the land. One day Petter received a command from the king in Copenhagen to preach for him on Christmas Day. The text would be on the pulpit. But he had only a few hours to get there. This didn't stop Petter. He called for a "spirit of the air" to carry him to Denmark. The carrier, however, demanded as his price that he could claim the souls of all who fell asleep during the sermon. It was agreed. The church was already full when Petter arrived. The sheet of paper on the pulpit was blank — no text. So Petter said: "Out of nothing God created the world!" and preached a sermon so forceful that it held everyone's attention. No one fell asleep and the devil got no souls that day.

One of my favorite stories is how St. Olav got the cathedral built in Trondheim. It's one of the finest churches in the world. The problem was to get a spire put on it. That was beyond Olav's skill, so he offered the sun to whomever could complete the task. When no man was able, a troll who lived nearby offered to complete the church. The troll demanded that Olav would not say his name, assuming that he could not learn it. Olav didn't want the troll to get the sun, so he set about to learn his name. Sailing along a cliff one night, he heard an old woman singing, "Heaven's Gold (the sun) when Tvaester came home." Olav arrived just as the spire was put in place. He shouted: "Tvaester! You've set the vane too far to the west!" Immediately upon hearing his name, the troll fell dead on the ground. (The real truth is, however, that the church was not built until 1070, 40 years after Olav's death.)

These are the kinds of stories that Scandinavians told in the old days. Not only Scandinavia, but all countries have their favorites. This was their entertainment and these stories also contributed to their view of the world. They fostered fear in the listeners and prolonged the superstitious beliefs that had survived since days immemorial. It affirmed their fear that God's chief delight is to punish sinners.

There is something naturally appealing in these stories as there is a degree of residual guilt in almost everyone. The humor in the stories can be harsh and dark. But it reflected the mood of the people in that isolated part of the world. People today may not take ghosts and magic as seriously as those people did, but they are often in bondage to modern superstitions of their own making.

The late Queen Thyra encouraging the battling Danes.

232

You will also enjoy
reading these other
Scandinavian-interest
books
published by

**North
American
Heritage
Press**

These are available at
your local book store
or Scandinavian gift shop

The Scandinavian Heritage

By Arland O. Fiske

This hard-to-put-down book of 100 interestingly-told stories is about the people, places, traditions and history of Denmark, Finland, Iceland, Norway and of course Sweden. Well-known Scandinavian-American syndicated newspaper columnist Arland O. Fiske offers well-written and researched vignettes on topics which vary from Viking burial customs to the Scandinavian Royal Families.

Here's some excerpts from the book's foreword by Dr. Sidney A. Rand, former president of St. Olaf College and United States Ambassador to Norway:

"Arland Fiske is a good story teller. In these vignettes he has taken events in Scandinavian history and made them live and breathe. Some of them deal with well-known historical figures; others tell us of persons and places that do not dominate the pages of history. But there is a human warmth and interest in each one.

One virtue of this collection of articles is its breadth. So often we read about the Norwegians or the Swedes or the Danes or the Finns, they are presented almost as competitors for places in history. Here is an author who is attracted to and charmed by the exploits and accomplishments of all the Scandinavians. The reader may make comparisons or draw contrasts; the author does not.

Fiske's collection of "little stories" is easily read and can be taken a bit at a time if preferred. Each story has its own attraction."

NOW... The Scandinavian Heritage Book. Based on the popular syndicated column by well-known Scandinavian-American author Arland O. Fiske.

100 interestingly told stories about the people, places, traditions and history of Denmark, Finland, Iceland, Norway and Sweden.

A best seller, now in its fourth printing!

---

248 pages, 6"x9", softbound   No. HP-120 $9.95

The Scandinavian World

By Arland O. Fiske

CONTENTS

Well-known Scandinavian-American author and syndicated columnist Arland O. Fiske delights us, in his unique story-telling way, with stories and tales of the Scandinavian World.

100 interestingly told stories about the people, places, traditions and history of Sweden, Norway, Iceland, Finland and Denmark.

The Scandinavian World

Arland O. Fiske

Foreword by Alvin N. Rogness

---

248 pages, 6"x9", softbound   **No. HP-121 $9.95**

The Scandinavian Spirit

By Arland O. Fiske

ARLAND O. FISKE

*Well-known Scandinavian-American author
and syndicated columnist Arland O. Fiske delights us,
in his unique story-telling way, with stories and tales of
Scandinavian people, places, history and traditions.*

"The Scandinavian Spirit is a charming potpourri of anecdotes and observations about Scandinavians of every stripe — saints and scoundrels, kings and country folks, pirates and preachers. Fiske's subject is anything and everything that anyone with Danish, Swedish, Finnish, Norwegian or Icelandic blood has done or said that he thinks might be of interest to people today. He has an uncanny ability to ferret out interesting stories and little-known facts that most of us would never discover for ourselves, and his folksy, down-home style makes you feel as if you are listening to the tales grandpa used to tell. So fix yourself a cup of rich Scandinavian coffee, settle down in your favorite chair, and prepare to enjoy a smorgasbord of stories that will brighten your day and warm your heart."

Dr. William H. Halverson
Professor at Ohio State University (retired)

"For Scandophiles — and there are acres of this growing specie — good things come in groups of three and Arland Fiske's third book on our Scandinavian heritage is full of interest. In pleasant, painless prose, the info is nicely sectioned off, the amount of each being not too much, not too little, just right. 'Know ye the rock from which thou wert hewn,' exhorts the prophet Isaiah. The Fiske trilogy fulfills that obligation."

Dr. Art Lee
Author of *The Lutefisk Ghetto*
Professor of History, Bemidji State University

*Well-known Scandinavian-American author
and syndicated columnist Arland O. Fiske delights us,
in his unique story-telling way, with stories and tales of
Scandinavian people, places, history and traditions.*

---

256 pages, 6"x9", softbound   No. HP-124 $9.95

Prairie Wind, Blow Me Back

By Evelyn Dale Iverson

Those who know the wind on the prairie know how capricious and powerful it can be. Yet men, lured by open land with rich black soil, bet against such odds that they could make a life for their families on this challenging frontier.

Evelyn Dale Iverson

Rakel: *"How can Renhild be so devious? I think she is the most evil person I have ever met!"*

"Nils thought of the prairie wind as a sparring partner. How could he beat this fellow?"

PRAIRIE WIND, BLOW ME BACK.

But where? It depends who and where you are.

For Nils, when he was homesick and struggling, it was his childhood home. But later it was other things.

For most of us, it is a glimpse of a different world a hundred years ago, and what life was like "in those days."

And like Nils, before we leave it, a look at desires, priorities, and values.

—*Evelyn Dale Iverson*

About The Author...

Evelyn Dale Iverson is a granddaughter of Nils A. Dale in this story, and a daughter of Hans M. Dale, the infant who came in a covered wagon to Dakota Territory over a hundred years ago.

The author is a native of Canton, SD, where her father was a professor and later the president of Augustana Academy. She graduated from Concordia College, Moorhead, MN, when her father was treasurer of that college. He also owned a part of the homestead in Miner County, which he felt close to, and his family visited often.

Almost all the names in this book are real places and real people, with the exception of Arne and Renhild, who are composites of others who lived "in those days."

---

158 pages, 6"x9", softbound   No. HP-122 $7.95

Skis Against The Atom

By Lt. Colonel Knut Haukelid

The outcome of World War II could very possibly have been much different if Knut Haukelid and his small, but courageous band of Norwegian soldiers had not been successful in sabotaging the Nazi's supply of "heavy water." The "heavy water" produced at a facility in occupied Norway was vital to Hitler's race with the United States to develop the atomic bomb. Knut Haukelid's "Skis Against The Atom" gives the reader an intimate account of the valiant and self-sacrificing service that the not-to-be-subdued Norwegians performed for the whole free world.

The exciting, first-hand account of heroism and daring sabotage during the Nazi occupation of Norway.

KNUT HAUKELID

Excerpted from the Introduction of Skis Against The Atom by General Major Sir Collin Gubbins, CO of Special Operation Executive

I am glad to write for my friend Knut Haukelid an introduction to this enthralling story of high adventure on military duty so as to give the background to the operations which this book so vividly describes, and to show how they fitted into the wider picture of "Resistance." I hope, too, it will enable the reader to have a fuller appreciation and understanding of the remarkable exploits of a small and devoted group of Norwegian soldiers.

---

252 pages, 6"x9", softbound   No. HP-123 $9.95

The Beckoning
By Nora Stangeland McNab

New York was still a raw and untamed land when sandy-haired young Andreas Stangeland piled sod to make his first shelter beside Bald Eagle Creek. The handsome young Norwegian, along with the legendary leader, Cleng Peerson, had been on hand to welcome the first shipload of Norwegians ever to drop anchor in an American harbor.

The tiny sloop *Restauration*, one-fourth the size of the *Mayflower* and carrying twice as many passengers, reached New York on October 9, 1825, after a voyage lasting 98 days. With Cleng, Andreas escorted the band of 46 men, women and children to their holdings in the woods, the "Black North" near Kendall, New York. Still buoyed by the adventure of his first year in America, Andreas was jubilant in the knowledge that his own 48 acres was paid for and ready to clear.

But he hadn't counted on the conflict that would tear him apart in those first dark months. Did he really want to be American or simply part of a close-knit Norwegian colony in a land of strangers?

Nor had the young baker from Stavanger counted on falling in love — with an American! A merry, brown-eyed schoolteacher. And, to Andreas' great despair, too young for him.

A Story of Love

by Nora Stangeland McNab

Nora Stangeland McNab has recreated the story of her great-grandfather, Andreas Stangeland, with insight and compassion. Part fact, part fiction, the story opens another window on those "sloopers" who came seeking freedom to worship in their Quaker ways. It is the story of every immigrant who is caught between the old and the new, the "then" and the "now." But more than anything else it is an engaging story of love, friendship, tragedy and triumph.

Nora McNab, a graduate of Purdue University, has been a freelance writer for several years.

---

262 pages, 6" x 9", softbound   **No. HP-125 $11.95**